PROBLEM SOLVING
AND COMPUTER
PROGRAMMING

RTC Limerick

3 9002 00002666 7

PROBLEM SOLVING AND COMPUTER PROGRAMMING

LIBRARY
LIMERICK COLLEGE
OF ART, COMMERCE
& TECHNOLOGY
class no:
acc. no:

PETER GROGONO
Department of Computer Science, Concordia University, Montreal

SHARON H. NELSON
Metonymy Productions, Montreal

ADDISON-WESLEY PUBLISHING COMPANY

Reading, Massachusetts • Menlo Park, California
London • Amsterdam
Don Mills, Ontario • Sydney

LIBRARY

LIMERICK COLLEGE
OF ART, COMMERCE
& TECHNOLOGY

class no: 519.4 GRO

acc.no: 7638

Library of Congress Cataloging in Publication Data

Grogono, Peter.
    Problem solving and computer programming.

    Bibliography: p.
    Includes index.
    1. Electronic digital computers—Programming.
2. Mathematics—Problems, exercises, etc.—Data process-
ing. 3. Problem solving—Data processing. I. Nelson,
Sharon H., 1948–   II. Title.
QA76.6.G758   519.4   81-7942
ISBN 0-201-02460-8   AACR2

Copyright © 1982 by Addison-Wesley Publishing Company, Inc. Philippines copyright 1982 by Addison-Wesley Publishing Company, Inc.

All rights reserved. No part of this publication may be reproduced, stored in a
retrieval system, or transmitted, in any form or by any means, electronic, mechanical, photocopying, recording, or otherwise, without the prior written permission
of the publisher. Printed in the United States of America. Published simultaneously
in Canada.

ISBN 0-201-02460-8
ABCDEFGHIJ-AL-898765432

PREFACE

This book has grown out of our perception of a problem. It has become common practice to combine the subject of problem-solving with a tutorial for a particular programming language in a single text. We believe that this practice is misleading; problem solving and computer programming are distinct activities. If we are taught to associate problem-solving methods with a particular language, our thinking is likely to become dominated by that language. This is as true of programming languages as it is of natural languages. If we learn to "think in Pascal" we may fail to find solutions that are expressed easily in LISP or SNOBOL, or we may get stuck with unwieldy solutions, or our ability to find insights into problems may be severely limited.

The structure of this book, from the separation into two major parts to the placement of chapters and examples within chapters, is intended to present a thematic rather than a linear approach. Programming problems, like many other problems, are amenable to solution by general problem-solving techniques and strategies. Like other problems, programming problems can be divided into subproblems, and the subproblems can be further subdivided, until we reach a level at which solutions are known or can easily be found. In programming, the first subproblem is to discover an appropriate algorithm and the secon~~~~~ problem is to implement the algorithm by writing a program. (problem-solving methods, of the kind that are developed in Pa this book, can be applied to both of these subproblems. Part 1 presents techniques and strategies which are not only aids to general problem solving but are also aids to good programming. Foundations for the programming sections of Part 2 are developed in Part 1, and the programming methodology of Part 2 is based on the tactics and strategies of Part 1.

There are many approaches to programming. For example, software engineers consider that writing a program is like building a bridge and mathematical programmers consider that writing a program is like proving a theorem. The problem-solving approach is not an alternative but is rather a complement to these approaches. It emphasizes the conceptual nature of programming, the numerous ways of obtaining insight into programming problems, and the distinction between a high-level algorithmic solution and a low-level implementation of that solution.

The discipline that has contributed most to problem solving is mathematics. This is not surprising; successful problem solving requires a high level of abstraction, the elimination of superfluous details, and appropriate notations. Mathematics is the language of abstraction and the source of many notations. Consequently, topics in discrete mathematics, such as induction, propositional calculus, and graph theory, are introduced in Part 1. These topics are not discussed in depth and supplementary reading in discrete mathematics is strongly recommended. Although technical skill in formal mathematics is not a prerequisite for programming, it is undoubtedly very useful, and for advanced programming the mathematician's concern with abstraction and precision is essential.

In Part 2 of this book we discuss the particular problem of writing a computer program. Although a large part of the work of designing a program can and should be done independently of a particular programming language, and is done in this way in this book, a language is needed if complete solutions are to be presented. The language in which examples are written is Pascal and the notation used for algorithms is based on Pascal. Pascal has been chosen because it has a simple and useful set of structuring techniques for control and data and it therefore provides an appropriate basis for an algorithmic notation. This notation, or something close to it, would be useful for writing programs in a procedural language other than Pascal. The development of each program in this book is largely independent of any particular programming language and would have been almost the same if another language had been used. (Although we have attempted to avoid using Pascal idioms, we have used the **with** statement to achieve compactness and we have not been able to avoid using the Pascal dereferencing operator.)

This book is intended for readers who already have some programming experience and who are familiar with Pascal or with another language with comparable features, such as PL/I or Algol-68. Programs are developed only as far as is consistent with a problem-solving approach. Complete versions of the programs would validate and echo their input data, would issue comprehensive error reports when necessary, and would solve a more general class of problems. They would also occupy a large amount of space and would contain much material irrelevant to the text. The programs contain few comments because the surrounding text provides adequate commentary. The same programs would be written differently and would contain more comments in a different environment. We must admit that we are not entirely happy with this situation, but we have yet to see a program suitable both for inclusion in a text book and for actual use.

Sometimes a discussion of a problem is separated from a related example or a program appears several chapters after the discussion it illustrates. This unconventional ordering is intended to expose underlying concepts rather than to quickly provide solutions for given problems. The point of a problem-solving approach is that it reveals strategies, techniques, and insights that, once discovered, may be applied in many different situations. Example programs are not meant to stand as particular solutions but are intended to illustrate concepts. Chapters are built around topics and sections are built around discussions so that the development of concepts rather than the evolution of particular solutions becomes the focus for study.

Most of the problems used to illustrate Part 1 are traditional. They are described in numerous anthologies, notably the excellent and enjoyable collections of Martin Gardner. These problems are not presented as a challenge to the reader, who has probably encountered them before, but rather for the light they shed on problem-solving techniques. Some of these problems are very old; one of them appeared in an Indian instructional text some 3000 years ago. There must be some reason for this longevity, and it may be the insight these problems provide into our ability to think and to solve problems. A further motivation for the inclusion of traditional problems is that they demonstrate the continuity of thought. We ought not to jettison thousands of years of intellectual work and achievement merely because modern technology has created a few new problems. We can often benefit by reexamining old problems and their solutions; such examination provides an understanding of how we reach solutions. From this understanding we can build not only new solutions for new problems but new solutions for old problems. Working through example problems will help us to develop insight into the techniques that each of us finds most natural and comfortable as well as insight into the examples themselves.

As we examined and worked through traditional problems, we realized that the traditional expression of many of these problems reflects embedded values and prejudices with which many of us are not comfortable. This discomfort accounts for the rewriting or recasting of some of the problems.

This book touches on many subjects. At the end of each chapter there are suggestions for further reading. In these sections, books and papers are referred to by author and title; full citations are given in the bibliography at the end of the book.

Many people have helped us during the preparation of this book. We are grateful to John Gannon, Henry Ledgard, Gary Boyd, and a number of others who reviewed various versions of the manuscript. Joel Hillel kindly invited one of us (P.G.) to attend his problem-solving seminars, and these seminars provided valuable background material for Part 1.

Montreal   P.G.
March 1981   S.H.N.

CONTENTS

INTRODUCTION

Life began, as far as we can tell, when a complex mixture of chemical compounds was so arranged that the most fundamental problems of living were solved. These problems were, and are, obtaining food, reproducing, and defending the organism against predators. All species must solve these problems or become extinct.

We do not know if there ever existed an organism that could only reproduce itself exactly; we do know that the reproductive mechanisms of all existing species allow small changes to occur between one generation and the next. Thus at any given time the individuals of a species will be slightly different from one another. If the environment changes slightly, the new conditions will favor some individuals and these individuals will tend to live longer and to produce more offspring than others. In this way, the population as a whole solves the problem of adaptation to a changing environment. This is the mechanism of evolution expressed in its barest form.

Evolution is a slow process which works best for a simple organism that has a short life cycle and lives in a slowly changing environment. Complex organisms, which have longer life cycles and live in more complex environments, require the ability to solve problems as they arise and the ability to do so as individuals rather than as a species over many generations.

The first organisms only acted on their immediate physical environment. As organisms became more complex, they attained the ability to react to their environment as well: they developed nervous systems and brains. The nervous systems of simple organisms, such as moths, enable them to absorb some information about the environment, process it, and respond to it in a particular way. The organism can recognize prey, pursue it, and eat it; conversely, it can recognize predators and attempt to escape from them. Although this appears to be problem-solving behavior, it is not true problem solving because the solutions to the problems are built into the nervous system of the organism. Confronted by a situation that does not arise in its natural habitat, such an organism will react in an inappropriate way, as, for instance, when a moth is confused by the flame of a candle. The "wired-in" solutions are only general enough to allow an individual to solve problems previously encountered by the species.

More complex organisms have more highly developed nervous systems, or brains, and can solve problems that do not arise in their natural habitats. A rat, for example, can be taught to obtain food by pressing a lever or running through a maze. This is true problem solving.

All species have evolved mechanisms by which to survive. Teeth, claws, horns, camouflage, the ability to run, climb, hide, and fly are all characteristics that allow members of a species to survive and perpetuate the species. Some species have also evolved the ability to think, and for a few species this ability has become the dominant survival mechanism. We are members of the genus *homo*, species *sapiens*: we have weak teeth, feeble claws, no horns, and we can neither run fast nor fly, but, for better or for worse, we are able to think and to solve some problems.

The English word "problem" is derived from a classical Greek word, *proballein*, which meant "something thrown forward." The root of this word, *ballein*, with a different prefix, *syn*, gave us the word *symbol* which, if it were true to its etymology would mean "thrown together with." Yet another prefix, *dia*, yielded the Greek word *diaballein*, which became *diabolos* and eventually the English word "devil." We are indeed "bedeviled" by something "thrown across" our paths from time to time. A problem is *that which is forced into our awareness, a challenge*, something to be overcome or crossed over. The overcoming or crossing over are often, however, physical activities only in a metaphorical sense; we solve problems first of all not by climbing or jumping over obstacles but by the mental effort of envisioning solutions. Although we may be haunted or tormented or kept awake at night by some devilishly difficult problem, our solutions are arrived at not so much by mysterious rites or the preparation of potions but by methodical and often logical thought processes.

As thinking beings we are constantly involved in solving problems. How do I get to the other side of the street? How can I finish my assignment by Friday? Shall I have supper for less than $5 or can I get to the bank by four o'clock? Whom shall I marry?

These are problems of the kind that the evolution of our species and our own upbringing have taught us to solve, and although they are interesting problems, they are not discussed further in this book. They are too complicated, too diverse in their ramifications, and too vaguely defined to be amenable to solution by direct application of the methods we will discuss. Nevertheless, this book may help you to solve some problems of this kind, or at least give you some insight into how rational thinking might contribute to their solution.

The problems we encounter during the course of our work are usually related to the work we do; the problems a doctor is expected to solve concern sick people and the problems a plumber is expected to deal with concern malfunctioning pipes. Although people outside these two disciplines may detect a humorous relationship between them, the tools and knowledge that each practitioner brings to the work are quite different.

In a study of general problem-solving techniques we do not want to introduce specialized knowledge of medicine, plumbing, or other fields. Accordingly, the problems discussed in Part 1 of this book are puzzles and brain teasers. Most of these problems will probably be familiar to you and you will perhaps know the solutions to many of them. This will not detract from their function, which is to illustrate problem-solving methods.

The concept of mechanical computation is not new. The slide rule was invented in the seventeenth century by Delamain and Oughtred, both of whom taught mathematics in London. Pascal built the first mechanical calculating machine in 1642; the principles of this machine were used until electronic calculators replaced mechanical calculators a few years ago. Carillons, music boxes, and automatic looms all have a long history. What *is* new is the existence of a technology that enables extremely complex programs to be executed rapidly and precisely. This technology, in the form of electronic computers, has given rise to a craft called *programming* and to an assortment of craftspersons called *programmers*.

In Part 2 of this book we adopt the point of view that in writing a computer program we are solving a problem. The problem is always of the form, "make the machine do so-and-so" and the solution is a program that causes "so-and-so" to happen. This problem is amenable to solution by any or all of the techniques discussed in Part 1.

There are many approaches to programming other than through problem solving. Most of these approaches stress the importance of quality in the final product. At a time when computer systems are used to implement financial transactions, control civilian aircraft, design buildings and bridges, and guide satellites to distant planets, we cannot afford to underestimate the importance of software quality. The emphasis on the quality of the final product may, however, lead to the neglect of the early phases of program construction. Early attention to program specification and design can aid us greatly in the production of high quality software. How do we choose appropriate algorithms, or if there are no appropriate algorithms, how do we invent the algorithms we need? It is at this stage that problem-solving techniques are most useful. We need means of obtaining insight, of decomposing complex problems into simpler subproblems, and notations in which to express our solutions.

PART 1

PROBLEM SOLVING

CHAPTER 1
FOUNDATIONS

The methods that people use to solve problems are not understood in any detail and there is no complete, coherent theory of problem solving. Nevertheless, problem-solving activity has been extensively studied and consistent patterns of behavior have been observed. From these observations we can construct a simple model of the human being as a problem-solving machine; this model can give us insight into our abilities and limitations as problem solvers.

Although a simple model can help us to understand our own problem-solving methods, we must also be aware of its limitations. The model does not aid our understanding of flashes of inspiration, nor of deep insights, nor does it explain why some individuals have more flashes of inspiration or achieve deeper insights than others. It does, however, provide us with some simple rules that will help us to solve problems by more mundane methods when the flash of inspiration does not arrive.

1.1 MEMORY

Memory is indispensable for problem solving. When we are trying to solve a problem we must remember the problem statement, recall similar problems that we have seen before, and keep track of both our progress and our setbacks. We use different forms of memory, and it is useful to distinguish between them. Before we discuss different forms of memory, however, we will investigate what it is that is stored in memory.

Chunks

The memory of a computer has a very simple organization. It is divided into units of equal size and each item of data occupies either one whole unit of memory or a small number of units. Human memory has a more complex organization. First, there is no fixed size for a unit of storage. Second, the size of a unit seems to change with experience. The term *chunk*, which has no particular connotation of size, is sometimes used to denote one unit of information stored in a human memory. Some examples of the use of this term will make its meaning clearer.

In order to learn to read, we must first learn to recognize letters. Initially we see only the components of the letters as chunks and we perform a recognition procedure to recognize each letter. For example, three straight lines may denote A, F, H, K, or Z, according to their orientation and connection. After some practice we see each letter as a chunk. This does not mean that the recognition procedure is no longer performed; it means simply that we are no longer *aware* of performing it: we have trained ourselves to perform it unconsciously. After more practice, we can see short words as chunks, and eventually we are able to see long words and even short phrases as chunks. When we have learned to read fluently, the entire process of absorbing meaning from a string of printed symbols has become unconscious and automatic.

Later in life, when we develop other specialized skills, we learn appropriate chunks for them. In chess, for example, we learn first to distinguish the pieces and then the moves we are allowed to make. Later we recognize simple combinations of pieces, so that we may note without conscious study that a knight or a pawn is correctly placed to capture a rook, for example. A chess master recognizes more elaborate combinations involving several pieces not necessarily close to one another on the board. As the chess chunks grow larger the ability to remember sequences of moves also grows. It is hard for a novice player to reconstruct a game that has just been played because the novice can only recall the game in small chunks of one or two moves each. An experienced chess player can reconstruct an entire game without difficulty by recalling a smaller number of larger chunks.

Chunking helps us to learn physical skills as well. We do not worry about where to put our feet when we are crossing a room although each step involves a complex sequence of movements and balancing acts. Most of us learned to walk at such an early age that we can no longer remember the difficulties involved, but we may be able to remember the difficulties we encountered later in acquiring skills such as riding a bicycle, roller skating, or playing a musical instrument. In each case we must practice complicated sequences of muscular activities until they become automatic—'muscular chunks'.

Although chunks are highly personal units of information, people who share a field of specialization usually have many chunks in common. In order to discuss their specialty with one another, specialists give names to chunks; this is how and why technical jargon develops. Most people would have difficulty following a conversation in which terms such as emitter coupled logic, complementary metal-oxide semiconductor, and monostable vibrator were used because these phrases are composed of apparently unrelated and even meaningless words. An electronic engineer would understand the conversation quite easily because to an engineer each phrase is a simple, meaningful chunk; in fact, engineers go further and use abbreviations such as ECL, CMOS, and mono, demonstrating that these phrases are in fact familiar concepts to them.

We do not understand the means by which the brain assembles information into chunks. The most plausible hypothesis is that much of memory consists of associations between pieces of information and that a relatively small amount of hard data is stored. A chunk, according to this model, is a link (or a pointer, in computer jargon) to a set of associations.

Long-Term Memory

Long-term memory is the technical term for what most of us call memory. It is the accumulation of the memories of all we have experienced and learned. The capacity of long-term memory is for practical purposes unlimited: although learning seems to become more difficult as we get older, there is no evidence that a human brain can be filled up with long-term memories during the course of a lifetime.

We can retrieve information from long-term memory rapidly—usually in half a second or less. Sometimes, of course, we forget something and we are temporarily or permanently unable to retrieve it. The information does not seem to be lost altogether, however, because when we are reminded of what we have forgotten, we are able to remember that we once knew it; this suggests that it is the link, or pointer, to the information that has been lost, not the information itself. We assume in this discussion of problem solving that information relevant to the problem being solved has not been forgotten and can be recalled promptly.

It takes much longer, apparently between 2 and 10 seconds, to store a chunk of information in long-term memory than it does to retrieve it. This has an important effect on our problem-solving ability; although we can make effective use of previously stored information when we are solving problems, we cannot expect to add much new information to our long-term memory. For example, during a 5-minute thinking period we might retrieve 300 chunks from memory but we could only store about 15 new chunks. This may explain why people repeat unsuccessful behavior when they are trying to solve problems: they repeat unsuccessful operations because they do not have sufficient time to commit previous failures to long-term memory. Thus they have not "learned" that an operation or technique is not useful; the link between the knowledge of a problem-solving technique and the particulars of a specific problem has not been formed.

Short-Term Memory

In addition to long-term memory, we possess a secondary memory called *short-term memory* which is of much smaller capacity but of greater speed. The capacity of short-term memory seems to be between five and nine chunks. (This may have prompted Arthur S. Eddington's remark that "a science with more than seven variables is an art.") The storage and retrieval mechanisms of short-term memory operate so fast that we are unaware of any delay and the information in short-term memory is simply *there* for immediate use.

Unlike information in long-term memory, information in short-term memory decays quite rapidly unless it is constantly updated. This is not a serious problem because while we are actively thinking about a problem we are constantly examining the seven or so chunks in short-term memory; a particular chunk is recalled sufficiently often to ensure that it does not decay or it is replaced by another chunk that seems to be more immediately useful. The decay does explain, however, why we can so easily lose the 'thread' of our thoughts when we are distracted.

The small size of short-term memory is of critical importance in problem solving. It essentially limits the amount of data that we can analyze rapidly to at most nine chunks. This is one of the reasons why chunking ability is so important for problem solving.

External Memory

It is well known that pencil and paper are important aids to problem solving and we can now understand why this is so: paper is an extension of short-term memory. We can record information on paper at the rate of several symbols per second, which is much faster than we can store information in long-term memory. There is a difficulty associated with the use of paper, however: if we want to record chunks on paper, we need a notation for them. It is the existence or lack of a suitable notation that determines the usefulness of paper as a problem-solving aid.

Notation is an important aspect of problem solving and one we return to many times in this book. The application or discovery of a suitable notation is often a crucial step in solving a problem. Many numerical problems, for example, are solved more easily with the aid of algebra than without it. Diagrams are a form of notation in which relationships between objects are expressed in terms of spatial relationships in two dimensions. A computer programming language is a notation for expressing a solution, with the additional property that a program can be translated into instructions for a machine.

Paper is not the only form of external memory. A chess set is more useful than a pencil for solving chess problems. Chemists use three-dimensional models of molecules to help them visualize molecular structure. Although there are several ways of notating music on paper, some musicians prefer to use a tape recorder to store their musical ideas. People who are fortunate enough to have access to an advanced interactive computer system can use the computer as an external memory. Nevertheless, paper is the most commonly used form of external memory and it is indispensable to the problem solver.

1.2 PROCESSING

While we are solving problems we perform simple operations using operands in short-term memory. These operations take place quite rapidly, usually at the rate of about 15 per second, occasionally as frequently as 50 per second. This high processing rate is sustained for only short periods of time because it is frequently necessary to obtain more information from either long-term memory or external memory. Although the brain as a whole performs many operations—perhaps millions—concurrently, conscious operations on data in short-term memory appear to be carried out one at a time.

We cannot significantly influence the rate at which we process information; however, if we are to solve problems efficiently, we must avoid unnecessary processing. This in turn means that we must be able to distinguish useless activity from useful activity. We do not yet know enough to teach this ability to other people. There is evidence, for example, that highly creative people often persist in an apparently fruitless search where others would give up, and this may be the secret of their success.

Insight

The model that we have developed so far gives the impression that the problem solver calmly and steadily moves data from long-term memory into short-term memory, perhaps using external memory to make notes, and processes the information in short-term memory, all the while progressing steadily towards a particular goal until the problem is solved. Unfortunately, as we all know too well, solutions are not obtained so easily. We go round in circles, explore blind alleys, and eventually either solve the problem with a flash of insight or give it up.

The flash of insight that leads to a solution is picturesquely called the "aha! reaction." Most problems of the puzzle or brain-teaser type, including some of the problems discussed in the early chapters of this book, are easily solved once we have had the appropriate insight but are curiously opaque until then.

Insight is a notoriously difficult mechanism to analyze, but there are few things we can say about it. Insights do not occur spontaneously. We are much more likely to achieve an insight into a problem if we attempt to solve the problem than if we think about something else or go to sleep. Although there are many accounts of scientists and thinkers solving problems in their dreams or discovering that they know the solution when they wake up, without exception these people were deeply involved with their problems, and had been for some time, when the insight occurred.

Insight often seems to be the result of an association of ideas that are not usually associated. We tend to think of ideas not in isolation but in *frames*. Frames are useful because they tend to limit our thoughts to topics relevant to the object of study and help us to exclude irrelevant thoughts. A frame is a mental model of a familiar object or situation; the basic model is general but the frame can easily accommodate additional detail. The word *house* creates a frame; details such as *old, rambling, wooden,* and *balconied* fit naturally into this frame and allow us to construct an accurate mental model of the house. Sometimes, however, we can only solve a problem by introducing a concept from another frame or even by considering two or more frames simultaneously. It is interesting that the success of most humor and much poetry depends on similar associations between previously unrelated frames. Human creativity may be founded on the ability to make and to recognize connections where none existed before.

There are many accounts of deep insight in the history of science. Archimedes was given the problem of determining the volume of a gold crown. At the time, the only known way of determining the volume of an irregular solid was to melt it down and pour the liquid into a calibrated container. As Archimedes stepped into his bath one day, it occurred to him that it was possible to measure the volume of water displaced by an object without distorting the object itself. Archimedes achieved this insight by making an unlikely association between a gold crown and his own body. His actions subsequent to this discovery are too well known to bear repeating here; suffice it to say that scientists who run naked in the streets in these enlightened times are likely to get arrested.

Popular accounts claim that the insight of universal gravitation came to Newton when an apple fell from a tree in his garden.* There was of course more to it than that; Newton was already familiar with both Kepler's laws of planetary motion and Galileo's discoveries in mechanics. Nonetheless, it was a considerable achievement to unite the frame of terrestrial motion and the seemingly remote frame of celestial motion, the fall of the apple and the orbit of the moon. Newton constructed such a strong frame with his theory of universal gravitation that more than two centuries elapsed before Einstein was able to break out of it. Even when, during the nineteenth century, astronomers realized that the planet Mercury did not travel in a precise Newtonian orbit, they preferred the hypothesis of an unseen planet to a violation of the law of universal gravitation.

Some people are gifted with more retentive memories and greater powers of insight than others, but this does not mean that we cannot develop our ability to solve problems. Two components are involved in acquiring a new ability. One is knowledge, acquired by study, and the other is skill, acquired by practice. The knowledge we require for problem solving is not primary knowledge, which consists of facts, but a kind of secondary knowledge which consists of tactics, strategies, and

---

*The story of the falling apple is probably a myth created by Newton himself. For a fuller account, read Cohen's article, "Newton's Discovery of Gravity."

plans, and the knowledge of when to use them. Every discipline, including computer programming, has its own methods for solving particular problems and we use these whenever possible; when they fail, we bring in the general problem-solving machinery. You will encounter some of the rudiments of both specific and general problem-solving methods in this book. This knowledge alone, however, is not enough; to improve your problem-solving ability, you will also have to practice solving problems.

SUMMARY

In order to solve problems we need knowledge, skill, and experience. A systematic approach does not necessarily lead to a solution but it ensures that we make some progress and that we can at least discover the nub of the problem.

We go through the preliminary steps of solving a problem unconsciously and automatically if the problem is simple enough. It is usually when the problem is harder and leaves us initially confused that we need to take a systematic approach. If the problem is really complex, good groundwork is essential; subtle nuances that seem almost irrelevant as we venture forth may become critically important later on.

Some problems are easy to solve, or perhaps their solutions can be found in a book. Other problems are harder; we may need hours or days of thought and experiment to solve them. Yet other problems are extremely difficult to solve and even great thinkers may need years of effort to solve them. Although we may occasionally be fortunate enough to solve a simple problem with a flash of insight, we cannot rely on this as a method. We need to have systematic problem-solving methods at our disposal in order that we may deal with complex problems. These methods must not become a straitjacket, however, for creative insight and vision play an important role in problem solving.

FURTHER READING

How to Solve It, by Polya, and *How to Solve Problems*, by Wickelgren, are both good general introductions to problem-solving techniques.

Newell and Simon discuss the consequences of viewing the human brain as an information processing system in their monumental study, *Human Problem Solving*. Miller noted both the capacity of short-term memory and its significance for our problem-solving ability in his famous paper, "The Magical Number Seven, Plus or Minus Two." Kent does an excellent job of describing the brain as a computer in his stimulating book, *The Brains of Men and Machines*.

The human brain has been considered, at various times, to be like a steam engine, a gear box, a factory, and a telephone exchange. Our tendency to see our brains as organic manifestations of the latest technological gadget can be counteracted by acquainting ourselves with the history of thought. Bronowski's *The Ascent of Man* is exciting reading, and some of the same material is covered in greater depth in Koestler's popular accounts, *The Sleepwalkers* and *The Act of Creation*. Weizenbaum is also strongly critical of mechanistic models of mind and he discusses some of the implications of an oversimplified approach in *Computer Power and Human Reason*.

The concept of frames is borrowed from the field of artificial intelligence. Frames were introduced by Minsky in "A Framework for Representing Knowledge."

EXERCISE

1.1 Read the following list of letters once from left to right, and then close your eyes and recite the list from memory.

T X A P Y J F K E Q Z N

Now read the following list, in which the letters have been grouped into blocks of three, and then close your eyes and recite the list from memory.

S L B   U L G   D M O   R H C

Is it easier to memorize 12 letters or four chunks?

CHAPTER 2
STRATEGIES

Problem-solving methods can be divided into special methods, or *tactics*, which can be used only with a restricted class of problems, and general methods, or *strategies*, which apply to many classes of problems. Tactics are more likely to succeed but strategies are more widely applicable. Anything that applies to a very wide range of problems is unlikely to be a recipe for a solution. It is more likely to be an aid to understanding problems or a way of achieving a solution by mechanical means when inspiration fails. Whatever kind of problem we are trying to solve, we will need a clear statement of what we are supposed to do, what constitutes a valid solution, and what constraints there are.

In this chapter we discuss strategies. We consider the statements, rules, and goals of problems, and the use of abstraction to eliminate detail. We discuss the role of inference in problem solving, the technique of dividing a complex problem into simpler subproblems, and the concept of working backwards from the goal.

2.1 STATEMENTS, GOALS, AND RULES

A problem is presented to us in the form of a *problem statement*. The problem statement defines the problem, states the *goal* that is to be achieved, and provides the specific information that we need to solve the problem. The following is a problem statement.

Problem 2.1:   ANNABELLE'S UNCLE CLARENCE

Clarence is now three times as old as his niece Annabelle was ten years ago and Annabelle is now half the age that her Uncle Clarence will be in five years. How much older than Annabelle is Clarence?

The goal of this problem is to find a difference of ages. In order to solve the problem, we need some general knowledge about what age means in addition to the specific information concerning the ages contained in the problem statement. Thus a problem statement does not in general contain all of the information we need to solve the problem. Although the general knowledge we require to solve *Annabelle's Uncle Clarence* is elementary, other problems may require knowledge in specialized areas such as algebra, geometry, history, law, programming, or chess. It is pointless to attempt to solve a problem if it requires knowledge we do not possess. We cannot, for example, solve chess problems if we do not know the rules of chess.

A problem statement may contain information that is not relevant to the solution of the problem. For example, in *Annabelle's Uncle Clarence* we do not need to know the names of the people or the family relationships in order to solve the problem. In recreational problems irrelevant data may be thrown in to put us off the scent and real problems also are often cluttered with unnecessary information that we must clear away before we attempt solutions.

Problems may also contain *rules* specifying how the goal is to be reached. Rules, like data, may be either explicitly stated or implied by the problem statement. In the following problem the rules are explicitly stated.

Problem 2.2:   CHANGING THE GUARD

Four chess knights, two black and two white, are placed at the corners of a 3 X 3 board, as in Fig. 2.1(a). Each knight moves as a knight does in chess, two steps in one direction and one step in an orthogonal direction. A knight cannot be moved to a square that is already occupied. Find a sequence of 16 moves that leaves the black and white knights interchanged, as in Fig. 2.1(b).

Since this is not a chess problem, the knights' moves are explicitly defined. In standard chess problems the moves that the pieces can make are not defined because the rules of chess are implied by the problem statement. The rules of many problems are highly arbitrary but we are given no credit for solutions that ignore them. We can interchange the positions of the black and white knights in *Changing the Guard* by merely turning the board around, but clearly this does not solve the stated problem.

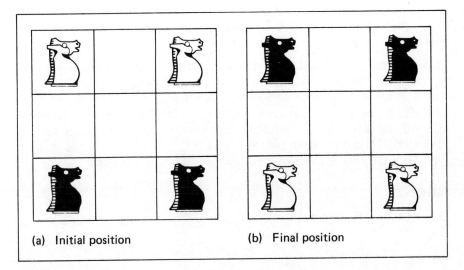

(a) Initial position   (b) Final position

Fig. 2.1
Changing the Guard.

The statements, goals, and rules of problems in the real world are often much more obscure than those of recreational problems such as *Annabelle's Uncle Clarence* and *Changing the Guard.* The strategy, however, is much the same: understand the problem statement, clarify any implicit information or rules, and identify the goal.

2.2 ABSTRACTION

Annabelle's Uncle Clarence describes a situation involving two people, Annabelle and Clarence, and the relationship between their ages. It is difficult but by no means impossible to solve the problem in the terms in which it is given. Here is an attempt.

Solution 1

From the fact that Clarence is three times the age that Annabelle was ten years ago, we can deduce that Clarence is three times Annabelle's age, less thirty (three times ten) years. We also know that Annabelle is half the age that Clarence will be in five years, and so twice Annabelle's age is Clarence's age plus five years, from which we can see that Clarence's age is twice Annabelle's age less five years. Therefore, three times Annabelle's age less thirty years, which is Clarence's age, must be the same as twice Annabelle's age less five years, because this also is Clarence's age. Three times Annabelle's age, less twice Annabelle's age, which is Annabelle's age, is therefore thirty less five, or twenty-five. Thus Annabelle is twenty-five, and Clarence is twice twenty-five, less five, or forty-five years old. The difference between their ages is therefore twenty years.

This solution is tedious and confusing because we have made no attempt to transform the problem before solving it. Although the problem was stated in terms of people and ages, it is actually a problem about numbers. There are two unknown quantities, Annabelle's age and Clarence's age; we are given certain relationships between these numbers and we have to find the difference between them.

Here is another solution to *Annabelle's Uncle Clarence*.

Solution 2

Let Annabelle's age be A. Let Clarence's age be C. Then we have:

$$C = 3(A - 10) \tag{2.2.1}$$

and

$$A = \frac{C + 5}{2} \tag{2.2.2}$$

From (2.2.1), we can obtain

$$C = 3A - 30 \tag{2.2.3}$$

and from (2.2.2) we can deduce:

$$C = 2A - 5 \tag{2.2.4}$$

Combining (2.2.3) and (2.2.4), we obtain

$$3A - 30 = 2A - 5 \tag{2.2.5}$$

and so

$$3A - 2 = 30 - 5 \tag{2.2.6}$$

or

$$A = 25$$

Whence, from (2.2.4),

$$C = 2 \times 25 - 5 = 45$$

and the difference between the ages A and C is given by

$$C - A = 45 - 25 = 20$$

The second solution is easier both to obtain and to understand than the first solution. This is because it is the solution of a different problem; it is, in fact, a solution to the following problem.

Problem 2.3: AUC

Given that

$$C = 3(A - 10) \tag{2.2.7}$$

and

$$A = \frac{C + 5}{2} \tag{2.2.8}$$

find the value of $C - A$.

Although *Annabelle's Uncle Clarence* and *AUC* are superficially quite different, we see at once that they are related, indeed in some sense equivalent, problems. Problem *AUC* is obtained by removing irrelevant information from *Annabelle's Uncle Clarence* and introducing a concise notation in which the relevant factors can be expressed. The problem is about the ages of two people, and these ages can be represented by two symbols, A and C. The problem statement can be translated into algebraic relationships between A and C; these relationships are called (2.2.7) and (2.2.8) in the statement of Problem 2.3.

The technique of removing superfluous information and introducing a more concise notation is a component of *abstraction*. Abstraction of this kind is performed in three steps. The first step is to *identify* the important objects or aspects of the situation; the second step is to *name* them; and the third step is to *define* the operations that may be applied to the objects and that are consistent with the rules of the problem.

In the case of *Annabelle's Uncle Clarence*, we first identify Annabelle's age and Clarence's age as the important components of the problem and then we name them A and C. Since ages are numbers, the operations we may apply to them are those of ordinary arithmetic and algebra. The most difficult part of the abstraction, the invention of algebra, has already been done for us.

The goal of abstraction is to construct an imaginary world which contains just enough structure to solve the problem and no more. In the world of A and C there are only ages and algebra; that Annabelle and Clarence are of different sex, have funny names, and are related to one another are facts that do not help us to solve the problem and so they have been filtered out by abstraction.

Changing the Guard can also be simplified by abstraction but the abstraction is of a somewhat different kind. One way to approach the problem is the direct one: draw a board of nine cells on a piece of paper and move pieces around on it. If you do this, you will probably find a solution, because the problem is not hard, but you will not gain insight into the problem. The difficulty is that it is not easy to imagine the effect of a sequence of knights' moves on a small board. The form in which the problem is stated gives it a visual opaqueness which resembles the verbal opaqueness of *Annabelle's Uncle Clarence*. How can we abstract visually?

A knight's move on a 3 × 3 board is limited in scope. The center square cannot be reached and so we need to consider only the eight border cells. From any border square a knight can make two moves. A move takes the knight either from a corner cell to the middle of a side or from the middle of a side to a corner. These observations can be made immediately from Fig. 2.2(a), in which the squares have been numbered and the knights' moves have been drawn as straight lines. The path in Fig. 2.2(a) can be regarded as a single continuous line that passes through each square in turn. It is a folded octagon and it can be unfolded as shown in Fig. 2.2(b). Fig. 2.2(b) is a visual abstraction of Fig. 2.2(a). The important relationship between the cells on the board is not the spatial relationship but the knights' moves connecting them. Fig. 2.2(b) is a knight's eye view of the 3 times 3 board.

We can now consider the problem on the abstract board. The initial position is shown in Fig. 2.2(c). Note that the knights have been placed according to the numbers on the board of Fig. 2.2(a). The black and white knights are interchanged by moving each knight four steps around the octagon, arranging the moves so that two knights never arrive on the same cell. The direction of movement (clockwise or counterclockwise) does not matter provided that all the knights move in the same direction. This is one possible sequence of moves:

$$1 \to 5 \qquad 6 \to 2 \qquad 8 \to 4 \qquad 3 \to 7$$
$$5 \to 6 \qquad 2 \to 8 \qquad 4 \to 3 \qquad 7 \to 1$$
$$6 \to 2 \qquad 8 \to 4 \qquad 3 \to 7 \qquad 1 \to 5$$
$$2 \to 8 \qquad 4 \to 3 \qquad 7 \to 1 \qquad 5 \to 6$$

This is a solution of the abstract problem. To solve the original problem, we must map the moves back onto the 3 times 3 board using the numbering system of Fig. 2.2(a).

In this problem, the first abstraction step is to identify that the moves are an important part of the problem. Naming the moves is accomplished in Fig. 2.2(a) and enables us to represent the abstract relationships between the positions in Fig. 2.2(b).

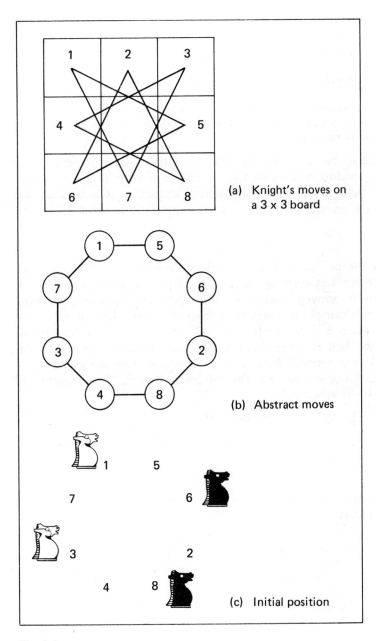

(a) Knight's moves on
     a 3 x 3 board

(b) Abstract moves

(c) Initial position

Fig. 2.2
Abstraction of
Changing the Guard.

Abstraction must always be performed carefully, and in particular we must always be aware that the abstract problem may not be equivalent to the given problem. The following problem illustrates this point.

Problem 2.4: THE THROW

Jim throws a ball vertically upwards at 80 feet per second. He is in a gymnasium, and at the instant he releases the ball, his hand is 36 feet from the ceiling. How long does the ball take to reach the ceiling?

The conventional abstraction in problems of this kind is to ignore the resistance to motion caused by the air and to assume that the earth's gravitational field is uniform. Elementary dynamics tells us that the motion of a particle in a uniform gravitational field is governed by the equation

$$s = p + ut + \tfrac{1}{2}gt^2$$

in which s is the position of the particle at time t; p and u are the position and velocity respectively at time $t = 0$; and g is the acceleration downward due to gravity. Before we can apply the equation, we must establish an appropriate coordinate system. If we use Jim's hand as the origin, then when $t = 0$, we have $s = 0$ and hence $p = 0$. The initial velocity of the ball is 80 feet per second upward and we assume that $g = -32$ feet   per second. Note that g is negative because gravity acts downward, but our coordinate system goes upward. The equation of motion of the ball is then:

$$s = 80t - 16t^2$$

When the ball strikes the ceiling, it is 36 feet from Jim's hand and therefore

$$36 = 80t - 16t^2$$

This is a quadratic equation for the time t; rearranging it and removing a factor of 4 gives:

$$4t^2 - 20t + 9 = 0$$

which factors to

$$(2t - 1)(2t - 9) = 0$$

giving the two solutions

$$t = 0.5 \text{ seconds}$$
$$t = 4.5 \text{ seconds}$$

It is clear at this point that something has gone wrong. When Jim throws the ball, it strikes the ceiling once and rebounds towards the floor. Why then do we obtain two values for the time of motion? Is either of them correct, and if so, which one?

When we first encounter problems of this kind in high school physics or algebra, we are usually told to say that one of the two solutions does not apply and that the other is the correct solution. The choice is often more clear-cut than in the preceding example; for instance, one of the solutions may be negative and therefore obviously inapplicable. This is unfortunate because it leaves us with the belief that formulas are unreliable and cannot always be trusted. A deeper analysis is needed, particularly for computer programmers who must be able to write programs that obtain the correct solution and automatically reject inapplicable solutions.

The difficulty in this example stems from the fact that the equation of motion

$$s = 80t - 16t^2$$

describes an abstract motion, not the specific motion of a ball in a gymnasium. It is a correct abstraction of the motion of the ball only from the time the ball leaves Jim's hand until the time it strikes the ceiling. We know that the ball leaves Jim's hand at time $t = 0$ but we do not know when it strikes the ceiling; that is what we are trying to find.

It is not hard to see why the abstract version of the problem has two solutions; the ceiling is an obstacle in the real world but it is only a number in the abstract model. In the abstract model, the ball goes straight through the ceiling, continues upwards to the apex of its trajectory, falls back through the ceiling, and continues downward with ever increasing velocity. The two values we obtained by solving the quadratic equation correspond to the two passages through the ceiling. In the real-world situation, only the first of these two times is applicable because it is the time at which the ball rebounds; after this time the equation is no longer an accurate model of the situation. The solution of the problem is therefore the smaller of the two results, 0.5 seconds.

Abstraction is a very powerful tool. The elementary examples of this section serve only to introduce it. Abstraction will be mentioned frequently in this book because it is a cornerstone of both problem solving and computer programming.

2.3 PROBLEM SPACES

We can generalize the method of abstraction introduced in the preceding section and show how it can be applied to an entire class of problems. For reasons that will become apparent later, this generalized form of abstraction is rarely of practical use in problem-solving situations, but it does provide useful insight into a variety of problems.

The class of problems that we consider in this section includes those problems in which *states* and *actions* are defined. The problem defines a *problem space* that consists of a set of states, including an initial state and a goal state, and a set of actions. An action causes a transition from one state to another; the solution of the problem is a sequence of actions that leads from the initial state to the goal state. Before we discuss problem spaces in detail, we introduce a new problem.

Problem 2.5:   TOWER OF HANOI

Three pegs are mounted on a board. The left peg holds a pile of eight disks of graded size with the smallest disk at the top of the pile. Fig. 2.3(a) shows the initial configuration. A move consists of removing the topmost disk from the pile on one of the pegs and putting it onto the top of the (possibly empty) pile on another peg. A disk may never be placed on top of a disk that is smaller than itself. Give a sequence of moves by which the pile on the left peg may be transferred to the right peg.

The problem is illustrated in Fig. 2.3. Fig. 2.3(a) shows the initial state and Fig. 2.3(b) shows the goal state. The problem space for *Tower of Hanoi* has the following components.

States:

In each valid state there is a pile of disks on each peg. (A pile may contain no disks, in which case it is called an *empty pile*.) No disk rests on a disk smaller than itself.

Actions:

A *move* consists of removing a single disk from the top of one of the piles and placing it on top of one of the other piles. A move must leave the system in a valid state.

In some states there will be one or more pegs with no disks on them. There are two ways of handling this situation: we could say that a peg has either no disks or a pile of disks on it, or we could say that a pile of disks contains zero or more disks. Although the second alternative may seem less natural, it has certain advantages; for example, a peg with no disks on it is no longer a special case. This is a simple application of a rule that is often useful: try to arrange things so that there are no awkward exceptions.

The problem space for the problem with eight disks is rather large and so we will consider a system with only three disks. Each of the three disks can be on any of the three pegs and therefore there are $3 \times 3 \times 3 = 27$ states. (There would be more states if the disks could be stacked in any order because we would have to calculate the number

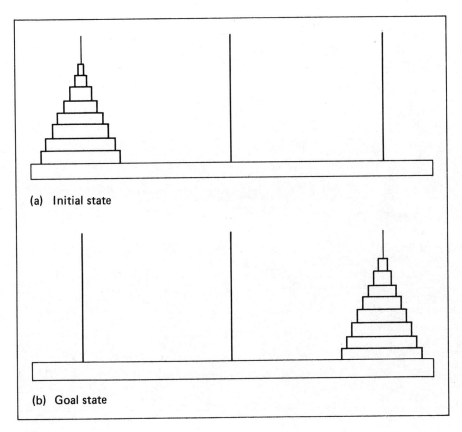

(a) Initial state

(b) Goal state

Fig. 2.3
Tower of Hanoi.

of possible configurations for each of the 27 basic states. In this case, however, there is only one possible configuration because the disks are stacked in order of decreasing size.) We can now draw a diagram of the problem space in the following way: on a piece of paper make 27 marks corresponding to the 27 states; then for each state, find the states that can be reached in a single move and draw a line between each of these states and the chosen state.

Fig. 2.4 is a diagram of the problem space for *Tower of Hanoi* with three disks. It was obtained by the method just described but it has been elaborated in several ways. Each state is represented by a numbered circle which encloses a picture of the corresponding position. The lines representing the action are labeled *s*, *m*, or *l*, standing for *small*,

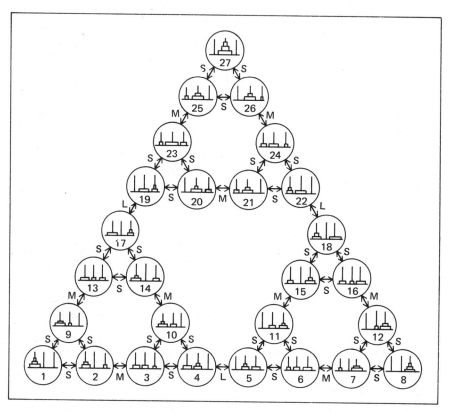

Fig. 2.4
The problem space for *Tower of Hanoi*.

medium, or *large* respectively, indicating which disk is moved. Every line has an arrowhead at each end, indicating that each move can be made in either direction.

This diagram represents a *graph*. A graph is a mathematical structure consisting of a set of nodes and a set of edges; the nodes are labeled, and each edge is identified by the labels of the two nodes it joins. In this case, the nodes of the graph correspond to the states of the problem and the edges of the graph correspond to the actions of the problem. We will refer to this form of diagram of the problem space as the *state-action graph* of the problem. Do not confuse this usage of the word *graph* with the Cartesian graph of a function.

There are many applications of graphs in problem solving and computer science. In particular, the state-action graph sometimes provides a useful model for representing a problem in a computer program. We digress briefly at this point to discuss graphs in more detail because they are an important topic in this book.

Graphs

Formally a graph consists of a set of *nodes* and a set of *edges*. The nodes may also be called *vertices*, but we will use the former term in this book. Each edge *joins* two nodes. If we label the nodes, we can identify the edges as pairs of labels. For example, using positive integers as labels, we might define a graph in the following way:

Graph G_1:

Nodes: 1, 2, 3, 4, 5, 6

Edges: (1, 2), (1, 6), (2, 3), (2, 5), (3, 4), (3, 5), (5, 6)

This information completely describes the graph to a mathematician or a computer. For humbler beings, a picture is helpful. In the diagram, Fig. 2.5(a), each node of G_1 is represented by a circle with the label inside it and each edge is represented by a line joining two nodes. Fig. 2.5(a) is one of several possible representations of G_1. In our imaginations we may think of graphs as parks with statues and gazebos at the nodes, paved paths along the edges, and signs saying "keep off the grass." Thus we might say, for example, that we can walk from node 1 to node 3 of graph G_1 by traveling along the edges (1, 2) and (2, 3) and that we can reach node 4 only by passing through node 3.

The graph G_1 is *connected*. This means that from any node of G_1 we can reach all the other nodes by traveling along edges. This is not a necessary property of a graph, as we can see from Fig. 2.5(b) which is an *unconnected graph* G_2 obtained by removing four edges from G_1.

We have not yet said anything about the directions in which we are allowed to travel along the edges. If the graph is *undirected*, we can travel in either direction along an edge. The existence of an edge (1, 2) implies that we can move from node 1 to node 2 and also that we can move back from node 2 to node 1; the pairs (1, 2) and (2, 1) describe the same edge. In a *directed graph*, or *digraph*, the direction is important; a directed graph is like a park with a one-way system. The existence of an edge (1, 2) tells us that we can walk from node 1 to node 2 but it does not allow us to walk back again. To go from node 1 to node 2 and back again in a directed graph, we need two edges: (1, 2) and (2, 1). Both of these edges exist in Fig. 2.5(c) which represents a directed

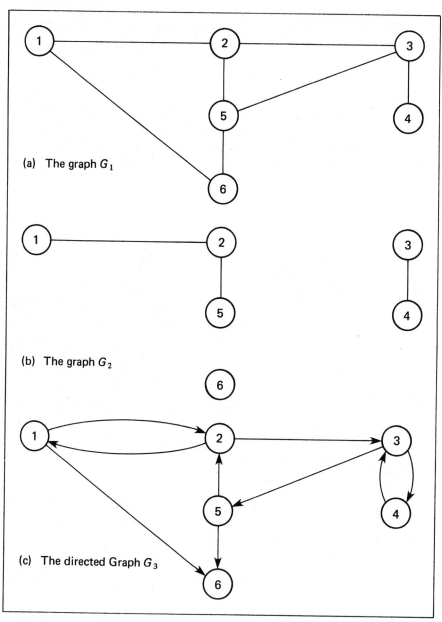

(a) The graph G_1

(b) The graph G_2

(c) The directed Graph G_3

Fig. 2.5
Graphs.

graph G_3. A directed graph is conventionally drawn with an arrowhead on each edge indicating the direction of the edge. G_3 contains the edge $(1, 6)$ but not the edge $(6, 1)$. Its complete description is:

Graph G_3:

Nodes: $1, 2, 3, 4, 5, 6$

Edges: $(1, 2), (1, 6), (2, 1), (2, 3), (3, 4), (3, 5), (4, 3), (5, 2), (5, 6)$

This is the end of the digression, and we return to *Tower of Hanoi*. Fig. 2.4, the state-action graph for *Tower of Hanoi*, contains a solution to the problem. State 1, at the lower left, is the initial state, and state 8, at the lower right, is the goal state. The solution is the sequence of seven moves connecting the states lying between the initial state and the goal state in the diagram.

Fig. 2.4 contains additional information that we do not need for the solution. Although the solution requires only eight states, the state-action graph has 27 states. If we increase the number of disks, the proportion of relevant states decreases still further. With eight disks, there are 6561 states altogether, of which only 256 are needed for a solution. The difficulty with problem spaces in general is that they are usually much too large for our purposes. We need methods for seeking the goal state in the state-action graph without having to construct the entire graph. Nevertheless, the state-action graph is a useful concept and may lead to a solution, as the following example demonstrates.

Problem 2.6: JUGS

You have two uncalibrated jugs, one holding 5 pints and the other holding 8 pints, and an unlimited supply of water. Describe a sequence of operations that leaves 4 pints of water in one of the jugs.

First, we consider the set of actions. Call the water supply the *source* and the drain into which excess water is poured the *sink*, then consider the following set of actions.

Actions:

Water may be poured into a jug from the source, from one jug into another, or from a jug into the sink.

Before we proceed to the set of states, we reduce the set of actions to a set that will be useful for solving the problem. Although we can partially fill a jug or pour part of the contents of one jug into the other, these operations are pointless because they leave an indeterminate quantity of water in the jugs. The useful actions are the following.

Actions (revised):

Empty a jug into the sink; fill a jug to the brim from the source; pour the entire contents of one jug into the other; pour water from one jug into the other until the receiving jug is full to the brim.

We assume that in the initial state both jugs are empty. In the final state, one jug must contain 4 pints of water. Since it is not immediately obvious what the intermediate states are, we commence by constructing the most general set of states, assuming that each jug may contain any quantity of water up to its maximum capacity. The problem space may be represented on ruled paper. In Fig. 2.6(a) the horizontal (x) axis represents the amount of water in the larger jug ($0 \leq x \leq 8$) and the vertical (y) axis represents the amount of water in the smaller jug ($0 \leq y \leq 5$). A point within this rectangle or on its boundary represents a state in which each jug holds a certain quantity of water.

The rectangle contains an infinite number of points which represent an infinite number of states. We are interested, however, only in those states that can be reached by a sequence of the useful actions we have defined. An action is represented by a straight line in the state graph. A line representing the filling or emptying of the larger jug is horizontal (parallel to the x-axis); a line representing the filling or emptying of the smaller jug is vertical (parallel to the y-axis); and a line representing the transfer of water from one jug to the other runs diagonally at an angle of $45°$ to the axes because the total amount of water in the jugs remains constant throughout this operation. Since each action starts and finishes with at least one of the jugs empty or full, the corresponding line starts and ends on a boundary of the rectangle. In other words, it is impossible to reach a point in the interior of the rectangle using the actions we have defined. If we start at the origin, or initial state, in which x and y are both zero, and draw all possible lines on the state-action graph, we arrive at Fig. 2.6(b).

The problem now is to find a path in Fig. 2.6(b) from the initial state to a goal state. The goal states, in which one jug contains 4 pints of water, are marked with rings in Fig. 2.6(b). Table 2.1 shows the sequence of actions leading to the goal state labeled A in Fig. 2.6(b). The jugs are called S (small) and L (large). $S \to L$ means pour the contents of S (or as much as will go) into L. The contents of each jug after an operation has been completed are shown on the right. This solution and another which leads to the goal state, labeled B in Fig. 2.6(b), are shown in Fig. 2.7.

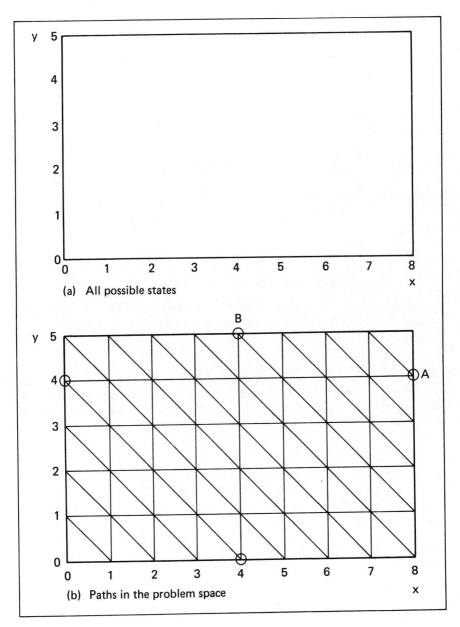

Fig. 2.6
The problem space for *Jugs*.

Table 2.1 Solution of *Jugs*

Action	Contents	
	S	L
Fill S	5	0
S → L	0	5
Fill S	5	5
S → L	2	8
Empty L	2	0
S → L	0	2
Fill S	5	2
S → L	0	7
Fill S	5	7
S → L	4	8

Students and Professors is another problem that can be solved systematically by considering its state-action graph. Here is a statement of the problem.

Problem 2.7: STUDENTS AND PROFESSORS

Three students and three professors want to cross a river in a boat that holds two people. Show how the crossing can be effected subject to the constraint that at no stage may the students be outnumbered by the professors on either bank of the river. (If students are outnumbered by professors they will become confused and will no longer be able to solve problems.)

In this problem a state is a situation in which there is one group of people on each bank of the river and one of these groups of people has the boat. An action consists of moving one or two people across the river in the boat.

First we need to know how many states there are. There are four ways of dividing the students because there may be 0, 1, 2, or 3 students on one bank, in which case there are respectively 3, 2, 1, or 0 students on the other bank. Similarly there are four ways of dividing the professors. The boat may be on either side of the river. If we choose all these things independently of each other, there are 4 X 4 X 2 = 32 states. Some of these states are not relevant to the solution, however. There are 12 states in which the professors outnumber the students on one bank or the other and two states in which the boat is on one bank

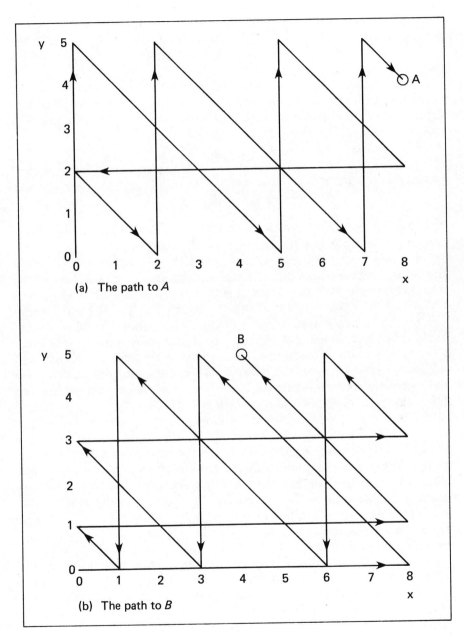

Fig. 2.7
Two solutions of *Jugs*.

and all the people are on the other bank. There are two further states in which the three students are on one bank with the boat and the three professors are on the other bank; these states can only be reached if the professors outnumbered the students in the preceding state, and so we can ignore them.

We need a convenient notation for representing states. Let S denote one student, SS denote two students, and SSS denote three students; use P in the same way to denote professors; let B denote the boat and | the river. The initial state is written

$$SSSPPPB|$$

and a typical intermediate state is written

$$PP|BSSSP$$

This means that there are two professors on the left bank, and three students, one professor, and the boat on the right bank.

There are five possible actions and each may take the boat across the river in either direction. The five actions are as follows: take in the boat (1) one student, (2) two students, (3) one professor, (4) two professors, or (5) one student and one professor. Some of the actions cannot be applied to certain states. For example, given the intermediate state, $PP|BSSSP$, we cannot send two professors across the river because there is only one professor on the same side of the river as the boat, and we cannot send one student because this would leave the student outnumbered by the professors on the left bank. In fact, at most three of the actions can be applied to any state.

Fig. 2.8 shows the state-action graph for this problem. It does not show the 16 illegal or unreachable states previously mentioned. The states on the left side are those in which the boat is on the left bank. A river crossing is denoted by a line labeled with the contents of the boat. Since all crossings may take place in either direction, no arrowheads are marked on these lines. The initial state is the first in the left column, and the final state is the last in the right column. There are four solutions, each requiring 11 crossings. Twelve of the 32 possible states are required for each solution.

The importance of the state-action graph is that it provides us with a firm concept on which to base a solution. We are often able to simplify a problem by considering all possible states and then eliminating illegal and unreachable states. We may also be able to reduce the number of actions by eliminating those that lead to an illegal state or take us further from the goal state. In many cases it does not matter that we cannot construct the entire state-action graph: we can gain insight into the problem merely by considering it.

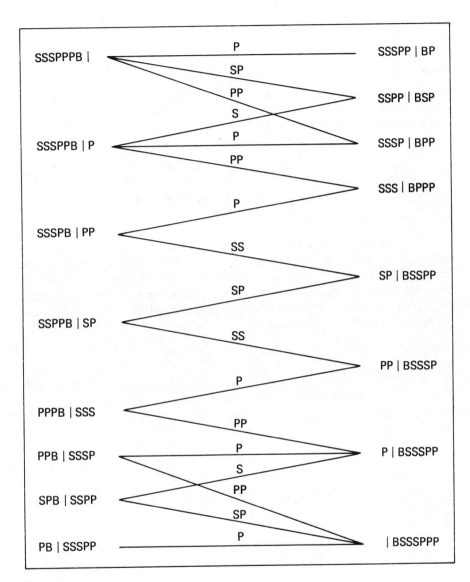

Fig. 2.8
The state-action graph for *Students and Professors*.

2.4 INFERENCE

Most problem statements contain or imply facts and from these facts
we can deduce or *infer* other facts. The number of facts we can infer is

usually large and the trick is to select from the available facts those that are relevant to the solution.

Problem 2.8: DONALD AND GERALD

In the following addition sum, each letter represents a single decimal digit and two letters cannot represent the same digit. Assign numerical values to each letter in such a way that the addition is correct.

$$
\begin{array}{ccccccc}
  & D & O & N & A & L & D \\
+ & G & E & R & A & L & D \\
\hline
  & R & O & B & E & R & T \\
\end{array}
$$

Hint: start by assuming that $D = 5$.

   Donald and Gerald can be solved by inference. The inferences are not hard to make; at each stage we look for the part of the problem that is most likely to yield new information. We start by writing down the sum with the given value of $D = 5$ incorporated, the carry digits c_1, c_2, c_3, c_4, and c_5 written in as unknown quantities, and the columns numbered for ease of reference.

	Column					
	1	2	3	4	5	6
Carry digit	c_1	c_2	c_3	c_4	c_5	
	5	O	N	A	L	5
+	G	E	R	A	L	5
	R	O	B	E	R	T

We can now attempt to solve the problem by making inferences from known facts.

1. Examining the sum column by column, we see that column 6 contains the most information. Since $5 + 5 = 10$, we can infer that $T = 0$ and $c_5 = 1$.

2. It now seems reasonable to attack column 5 because we know that $c_5 = 1$. Moreover, L occurs twice, which should help us. We have $2L + 1 = R + 10c_4$. (It is important not to forget the carry digits in problems of this kind.) Rewriting this in the form

$$R = 2L - 10c_4 + 1 = 2(L - 5c_4) + 1$$

we infer that R *must be odd*.

3. We can obtain more information about R from column 1, which tells us that $R \geq G + 5$. Since R is odd and $D = 5$, the only possible values for R are 7 and 9.

4. Column 2 now looks the most helpful because O occurs twice in it. We have $c_2 + O + E = 10c_1 + O$ and O cancels, giving $c_2 + E = 10c_1$. Suppose that $c_1 = 0$; then $c_2 + E = 0$ and therefore (everything is positive) $E = 0$. We know that $E \neq 0$, however, because $T = 0$ and every letter has a different value. Thus the hypothesis that $c_1 = 0$ is invalid and therefore $c_1 = 1$. Since we already know that $c_2 + E = 10c_1$, we now have $c_2 + E = 10$, which can only be true if $c_2 = 1$ and $E = 9$.

5. Now we know that $E = 9$, we can infer that $R = 7$.

6. From column 1, $1 + 5 + G = 7$ and therefore $G = 1$.

7. From column 4, we have $c_4 + A + A = 9 + 10c_3$, which we may write in the form $2A = 9 + 10c_3 - c_4$. The right-hand side must be even and therefore $c_4 = 1$. It follows that $2A = 10c_3 + 8$ and either $A = 4$ or $A = 9$. Since we have already discovered that $E = 9$, we can infer that $A = 4$ and $c_3 = 0$.

8. Now that we know $c_4 = 1$, we can complete column 5: $1 + L + L = 7 + 10$, whence $L = 8$.

9. From column 3, $N + 7 = B + 10$, or $N = B + 3$. The only digits we have not used so far are 2, 3, and 6, and so we have: $N = 6$, $B = 3$, and $O = 2$. The completed sum looks like this:

$$
\begin{array}{rcccccc}
   & 5 & 2 & 6 & 4 & 8 & 5 \\
 + & 1 & 9 & 7 & 4 & 8 & 5 \\
 \hline
   & 7 & 2 & 3 & 9 & 7 & 0
\end{array}
$$

This solution provides a pleasing example of a chain of inferences culminating in a tidy result. In many cases inference is not so helpful. There may be no obvious facts to infer or we may make inferences that do not get us any closer to the goal. If you try to solve *Donald and Gerald* without the initial assumption that D is 5, you will find that inference alone does not suffice and some trial and error must be used.

We can make inferences from information that is absent as well as from information that is present. The following problem illustrates this.

Problem 2.9: THE ANNULUS

The line AB in Fig. 2.9 is 2 inches long. What is the area of the shaded annulus?

The area of the annulus is the area of the larger circle less the area of the smaller circle. If we knew the radii of the circles, we could easily calculate their areas. We are not told what the radii are, but if we as-sume that the problem is fairly stated we can infer that we do not need to know them. From this we can deduce that the actual values of the radii do not matter and that we can choose them arbitrarily. If the radius of the larger circle is 1 inch and the radius of the smaller circle is zero, then AB is a diameter of the larger circle; the annulus becomes a disk, and its area is π square inches.

You may be sceptical of the foregoing argument, and if so here is an alternative version of it. Let the radius of the larger circle be R and the radius of the smaller circle be r. We can now calculate the area of the annulus as a function of R and r. In fact, it is easily seen to be $\pi(R^2 - r^2)$. We cannot calculate R and r and therefore the area cannot depend on their actual values but only on some relationship between their values. Provided that we maintain this relationship, we may choose any values of R and r. The only relationship we know is that a chord of the larger circle, 2 inches long, just touches the inner circle. This re-lationship is satisfied if r is zero and R is 1 inch. Thus the area of the annulus is $\pi(1^2 - 0^2) = \pi$ square inches.

In this case it is not particularly difficult to derive the solution without resorting to this stratagem because we can show that $R^2 - r^2 = 1$ by Pythagoras' theorem. (The dotted lines in Fig. 2.9 provide the necessary hints.) The saving achieved by the method of inference from the absence of information is more significant in the following problem.

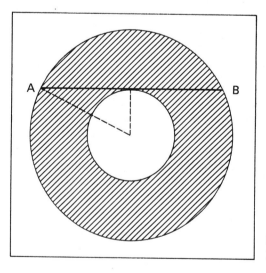

Fig. 2.9
The Annulus.

Problem 2.10: THE BORED SPHERE

A cylindrical vertical hole is bored through the center of a sphere. The height of the remaining solid, a sphere with a hole in it, is *h*. What is the volume of this solid?

There is a certain artificiality about problems such as the Annulus and the Bored Sphere. It is clear that they have been contrived in such a way that the given information seems to be insufficient for solving the problem. Although in actuality we rarely need to solve problems such as these, they serve to remind us that we are often provided with redundant information. There is no obligation to use redundant information, except possibly for validating an answer, and a solution that uses no more information than is strictly necessary is more general than a solution that makes use of unnecessary information.

2.5 SUBPROBLEMS AND SUBGOALS

It is often unrealistic to attempt to solve an entire problem all at once. Sometimes we can divide a problem into subproblems in such a way that by solving the subproblems independently we can obtain a solution to the original problem. Alternatively, if we think of solving the problem as traveling towards a goal, we can establish subgoals on the route and reach the goal by attaining each subgoal in turn.

The following problem involves lengths. The length we are required to find cannot be obtained directly and we have to establish subgoals that enable us to find it in easy stages.

Problem 2.11: THE LADDERS

Two parallel and vertical walls are *d* feet apart, and ladders of lengths *x* and *y* lean, one against each wall. How far above the ground is their point of intersection?

Fig. 2.10 is a diagram of the situation. We are given that $AC = d$, $AB = x$, and $CD = y$, and we are asked to find PQ.

Since it is not immediately obvious how to calculate PQ from the given lengths, we start by writing down relationships involving PQ and other lengths. The diagram has two pairs of similar triangles: triangle APQ is similar to triangle ABC and triangle CPQ is similar to triangle CDA. Thus we can immediately write down:

$$\frac{PQ}{BC} = \frac{AQ}{AC} \qquad (2.5.1)$$

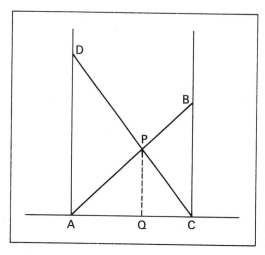

Fig. 2.10
The Ladders.

and

$$\frac{PQ}{DA} = \frac{CQ}{CA} \qquad (2.5.2)$$

The length AC is given, and the lengths BC and DA can easily be calculated by Pythagoras' theorem when we need them. From these equations, we learn that we can find PQ if we know either AQ or CQ. Thus we establish *find AQ or CQ* as a subgoal.

We have no way of finding these two lengths directly, but there is a simple relationship involving them:

$$AQ + CQ = AC \qquad (2.5.3)$$

One good reason for choosing this relationship, apart from its simplicity, is its symmetry. The problem as it is presented is symmetric in the sense that it contains the same information about each ladder and wall, and we should not favor one of the ladders more than the other in our solution. We should also, incidentally, expect the symmetry to appear in the final solution.

We now have an equation (2.5.3) containing two unknown quantities. We know that two equations containing two unknown quantities can be solved, and this suggests that we should look for another relationship between AQ and CQ. Thus our next subgoal is: *find another relationship between AQ and CQ.* We do not have to look far because if we eliminate PQ from (2.5.1) and (2.5.2) we obtain just such a relationship. We have

$$PQ = \frac{BC \times AQ}{AC}$$

from (2.5.1) and

$$PQ = \frac{DA \times CQ}{CA}$$

from (2.5.2). Therefore

$$\frac{BC \times AQ}{AC} = \frac{DA \times CQ}{CA}$$

and so

$$BC \times AQ = DA \times CQ \qquad\qquad (2.5.4)$$

Our second subgoal, finding another relationship between AQ and CQ, has now been achieved because BC and DA are readily computed. We can now eliminate CQ from (2.5.3) and (2.5.4) as follows:

$$CQ = \frac{BC \times AQ}{DA}$$

from (2.5.4) and

$$CQ = AC - AQ$$

from (2.5.3), whence

$$\frac{BC \times AQ}{DA} = AC - AQ$$

This equation can be rearranged to yield the length of AQ in terms of known lengths and thus we have achieved our first subgoal:

$$AQ = \frac{DA \times AC}{BC + DA} \qquad\qquad (2.5.5)$$

We now have

$$PQ = \frac{BC \times AQ}{AC} \qquad\qquad \text{from (2.5.1)}$$

$$= \frac{BC}{AC} \times \frac{DA \times AC}{BC + DA} \qquad\qquad \text{from (2.5.5)}$$

$$= \frac{BC \times DA}{BC + DA} \qquad\qquad (2.5.6)$$

From the given data and Pythagoras' theorem:

$$BC^2 = AB^2 - AC^2$$
$$= x^2 - d^2$$

and

$$DA^2 = CD^2 - CA^2$$
$$= y^2 - d^2$$

and therefore

$$PQ = \frac{\sqrt{(x^2 - d^2)(y^2 - d^2)}}{\sqrt{x^2 - d^2} + \sqrt{y^2 - d^2}}$$

The solution is symmetrical with respect to x and y, as we expected it to be.

The structure of the solution is typical of a solution that employs subgoals. Here is a summary of the technique we used:

Goal: Find PQ.

Progress: *PQ* can be found if either AQ or CQ is known.

  Subgoal: Find AQ or CQ.

  Progress: There is a relationship (2.5.3) between AQ and CQ.

    Subgoal: Find another relationship between AQ and CQ.

    Progress: There is another relationship (2.5.4).

  Progress: Find AQ by eliminating CQ between these two relationships, obtaining (2.5.5).

Progress: Obtain PQ from AQ (2.5.6).

When we have established a subgoal, we suspend work on the current problem and attempt to attain the subgoal. When the subgoal has been obtained, we can resume work on the original problem. The subgoal is a solution of a subproblem. Subproblems may themselves contain further subproblems, as the preceding example demonstrated.

It is important, but not always easy, to choose the correct subgoals. In attempting to solve *The Ladders*, many people start out by using Pythagoras' theorem and end up with a number of equations but no solution. There are no fixed rules for finding appropriate subproblems; intuition and experience must guide us.

The following problem provides another example of the need to establish suitable subgoals.

Problem 2.12: THE BIRD AND THE TRAINS

Two freight trains, one traveling at 20 miles per hour and the other at 40 miles per hour, are approaching one another. When the trains are 60 miles apart, a bird which was sitting on the front of the slower train starts to fly between the trains. It flies at 100 miles per hour and whenever it meets one of the trains, it immediately turns round and flies back towards the other. How far has the bird flown when the trains collide?

In this problem the goal is the total distance flown by the bird. The flight can be split into two parts: the part spent flying from the slower train to the faster, and the part spent flying the other way. This gives us two subproblems. Each subproblem can be further subdivided into yet smaller subproblems, each consisting of a single flight from one train to the other.

This method does lead to a solution. After some tedious algebra, we find that when the bird is flying from the slower train towards the faster, it travels $300S/7$ miles, and its trips in the other direction amount to $200S/7$ miles, where S denotes the infinite sum

$$1 + \frac{2}{7} + \left(\frac{2}{7}\right)^2 + \left(\frac{2}{7}\right)^3 + \cdots$$

The sum of this series is $\dfrac{1}{1 - \frac{2}{7}} = 7/5$, and the total distance the bird flies is

$$\frac{300}{7} \times \frac{7}{5} + \frac{200}{7} \times \frac{7}{5} = 100 \text{ miles}$$

The Bird and the Trains is more easily solved by a more appropriate choice of subgoals, however. The distance, time, and speed of a journey performed with constant speed are related; when we know two of these quantities, we can easily calculate the third. The bird always flies at 100 miles per hour; its changes of direction are irrelevant and may be ignored and we may consider its flight to be a single journey performed with constant speed. We know the speed and we want to find the distance flown. If we knew the time spent in flight, we could easily calculate the distance. Once we have identified the *time* as a subgoal, the problem is easy. The trains are 60 miles apart and they are approaching one another at 20 + 40 = 60 miles per hour; they collide after one hour has elapsed and during this time the bird has flown 100 miles.

It is important to ensure that the subgoals that we establish are not only appropriate but also that they are sufficient. If we define subgoals that are too weak, we may solve the subproblems only to find that the subgoals do not combine to solve the problem.

Problem 2.13:   THE ODD BALL

You are given 24 balls, one of which is known to be heavier than the others, and a balance. Identify the odd ball using the balance no more than three times.

The goal in this problem is to distinguish one ball from 23 others. We are allowed to use the balance three times, and each use of it must add to our knowledge. We can increase our knowledge by reducing the size of the set known to contain the heavy ball. This, then, is our subgoal: use the balance to eliminate balls of equal weight.

A natural first step is to put 12 balls on each side of the balance. One side must go down, and that side must contain the heavy ball. This method will halve the size of the set known to contain the heavy ball each time we use the balance. After one balancing operation, the set contains 12 balls; after two operations, it contains six balls; and after three operations, it contains three balls. We have failed: after three balancing operations, we still have three balls, one of which must be the heavy ball, but we have not identified it uniquely.

It is not sufficient to halve the size of the set containing the heavy ball at each balancing operation, but if we can divide it by three, we can solve the problem. The first use of the balance would reduce the size of the set containing the heavy ball from 24 to 24/3, or 8 balls; the second operation reduces it to 8/3, or, rounding up, three balls; and the third operation reduces it to 3/3, or one ball. Thus we establish a stronger subgoal: *divide the size of the set containing the heavy ball by three at each use of the balance.* This implies that after one weighing we must have a set of eight balls known to contain the heavy ball, and this in turn suggests that we use the balance to compare two sets of eight balls. There are three possible outcomes of this operation: the left pan may go down, or the right pan may go down, or neither pan goes down. In each case we have achieved our subgoal.

Similar reasoning may be applied to the reduced set of eight balls. We divide it into two sets of three and one set of two balls. Balance the two sets of three balls and again the result uniquely determines the set containing the odd ball. This leaves either a set of two balls or a set of three balls, and in either case the heavy ball can be identified in one more weighing. Here is the complete solution of the problem.

Solution:

Number the balls 1, 2, 3, . . ., 24. We denote the set containing the balls 1, 2, 3, . . ., 8 by [1 . . 8] ; other sets are represented in a similar fashion.

1. *First balance*: Put [1 .. 8] on the left pan and [9 .. 16] on the right pan. Choose a set as follows: if the left pan goes down, choose [1 .. 8] ; if the right pan goes down, choose [9 .. 16] ; if the scale balances, choose [17 .. 24]. The set chosen contains the heavy ball.

2. *Second balance*: Renumber the balls of the chosen set 1, 2, 3, . . ., 8. Put [1 .. 3] in the left pan and [4 .. 6] in the right pan. Choose one of the sets [1 .. 3], [4 .. 6], or [7 .. 8] as before. The chosen set contains the heavy ball.

3. *Third balance*: Balance any two balls of the chosen set. If one pan goes down, it contains the heavy ball. If the scale balances, the third ball of the set is the odd ball.

There are two important steps in the development of this solution. First, we established an adequate subgoal; the first subgoal, halving the size of the set containing the heavy ball, was not sufficient. Second, we realized that a balancing operation has three possible outcomes, not two.

The problem is in fact stated in a deliberately misleading way. It is possible to find the heavy ball if there are 27 balls altogether. If the problem specified 27 balls, however, most people would immediately think of dividing the set by three rather than by two. The number 24 suggests dividing by two first because it seems easier.

2.6 WORKING BACKWARDS

We should not always work from the initial state towards the goal state: it is sometimes more productive to work *backwards* from the goal state towards the initial state. This technique is applicable to several of the problems discussed in this chapter.

One way to solve *Jugs*, for example, is to assume that we have reached a goal state and that we have four pints of water in the larger jug. If we ignore the uninteresting possibility that in the preceding state the smaller jug contained 4 pints of water, we must have poured 4 pints from the larger jug to the smaller and this action must have filled the smaller jug. The capacity of the smaller jug is 5 pints and therefore it must have contained 1 pint prior to this action. Thus we have established a subproblem, the goal of which is to reach a state in which the smaller jug contains 1 pint of water. By considering the predecessor of this state, we can establish another subgoal and so on until we reach a subgoal that is easily achieved.

In this case, the advantage of working backwards is that we can construct a unique subproblem because we have a strong criterion: the goal state determines the preceding state uniquely if we ignore uninteresting operations. If we start from the initial state, in which both jugs are empty, several sequences of actions are possible but there is no criterion for deciding which of them will lead most rapidly to a solution.

The solution of *Ladders* provides another example of the use of working backwards. We could start by calculating all the lengths we are able to find, but it is more helpful to decide first which lengths we need in order to determine PQ.

Working backwards is also helpful for *The Odd Ball* although it does not lead directly to a solution. We can think about the *last* weighing rather than the first weighing. The final weighing operation must reveal the odd ball and it is therefore reasonable to assume that we will put two balls in the balance. If one side goes down, we have identified the heavy ball. But suppose that there are two balls of equal weight on the balance; then there must be a *third* ball which is heavier. Recognizing that we can select the odd ball from three balls in one weighing is the crucial insight that may enable us to solve the complete problem.

Working backwards means using the goal of the problem to obtain insight into the problem as a whole. It is an application of the more general rule that we should make use of all the information we have. It is useful when the specified goal reveals properties of the required solution.

SUMMARY

The strategies that we have discussed in this chapter can be applied to problems of many different kinds. The following notes constitute a summary of the chapter in the form of annotated slogans.

■ *State the problem clearly and understand it completely.* Problems are often stated in a confusing or misleading way. In a book of puzzles the deception may be intentional because a confusing problem is harder to solve than a problem that is clearly stated. Confusing problems are not confined to books, however; in most areas of life the problems we encounter are ambiguous, misleading, and full of irrelevant detail. It is often difficult to discover what the problems is, let alone to state it clearly. Even people whose job it is to formulate problems for others to solve are frequently unable to construct a clear and precise statement of what they want done.

It is futile to attempt to solve a vague or ambiguous problem. Never attempt to solve a problem until you are sure that you know exactly what it is that constitutes a solution.

■ *Make implicit rules and data explicit.* Problems are seldom stated completely. In many cases the unstated rules are conventional and are based on standard arithmetic, algebra, or a system that has special relevance to the problem. Sometimes, however, the "natural" rules do not apply for some reason: the coordinate system may not be Cartesian; a decision may have three possible outcomes instead of two; or a method that usually terminates may fail to terminate.

Sometimes it seems that the data supplied are insufficient. This could be because more data are in fact required or because the data supplied are sufficient provided that a particular method of solution is used. If you supply additional data, they must be appropriate and correct.

Do not embark upon a solution until you are sure that you have all the rules and data that you need to solve the problem.

■ *Eliminate superfluous detail.*   For the reasons outlined in Chapter 1, the amount of complexity that we are able to cope with while we are solving problems is quite limited. There is a certain amount of complexity that is inherent in any problem and that cannot be eliminated. Any additional complexity is not required for a solution and is an additional burden. Most problem statements contain superfluous information and it is important to eliminate it at an early stage. Removing detail is the first step in abstraction.

■ *Obtain insight into the problem.*   When we have solved a problem the solution often seems obvious. Indeed, it may be difficult to believe that others will not perceive the solution as soon as they see the problem. This is because while solving the problem we are obtaining insight into its mechanism. Turning this argument around, we see that insight may help us to see the way to a solution and therefore any means of obtaining insight should be exploited.

There are many ways of obtaining insight into a problem, some of them determined by the nature of the problem, and some by personal preference. Selecting symbols, choosing a notation, solving the problem for special cases, drawing diagrams, and varying the problem are all means of obtaining insight. The function of theory is to provide insight, and so it is important to find out if there is any theoretical knowledge that applies to the problem you are trying to solve or to related problems. Theoretical results are usually abstract and it may be necessary to discover the relationship between the general theoretical model and the particular problem before the theory can be applied.

■ *Use all the available information.*   This rule is not always easy to apply. The value of some of the information provided may not become apparent until we have attempted to solve the problem. We must be careful to distinguish available information from superfluous detail.

■ *Divide and conquer.* Dividing a problem into subproblems and solving each subproblem separately is a powerful and widely applicable method of solving complex problems. Be careful to ensure that the subproblems are independent in the sense that each can be solved without reference to the others. One useful method of dividing a problem into subproblems is to choose subgoals. It is often possible to find a subgoal that is attainable and that leads quickly to a complete solution.

■ *Work backwards.* If the goal is more precisely specified than the initial state, it may help to start with the goal state and work backwards towards an initial state. Look for situations in which a subgoal can be chosen more easily from the final conditions than from the initial conditions. Make sure that the actions of the problem are reversible.

FURTHER READING

There are many solutions of problems of the kind described in this chapter. Martin Gardner, in addition to his well-known column in *Scientific American*, has published a series of entertaining puzzle anthologies. He discusses the *Tower of Hanoi* in *More Mathematical Puzzles and Diversions*. Some of his other books are listed in the bibliography.

Newell and Simon discuss *Donald and Gerald* in their book, *Human Problem Solving*, and they also analyze the behavior of people attempting to solve this problem.

Combinatorial Algorithms, by Reingold, Nievergelt, and Deo, contains a detailed analysis of weighing problems similar to *The Odd Ball*.

EXERCISES

2.1   Draw a knight's eye view of

a) 3 $\times$ 4 board;

b) 4 $\times$ 4 board.

2.2   Suppose that we know the lengths of the sides a and b and the size of the angle A of a triangle ABC. We can find the length of the side c by using the *cosine formula*

$$a^2 = b^2 + c^2 - 2bc \cos A$$

If $\sin A < a/b$, this quadratic equation has two positive roots, giving us two values of c. Why is this?

2.3   Fig. 2.4 has an obvious kind of symmetry. Explain this symmetry, and use it to sketch state-action graphs for *Tower of Hanoi* with two disks and four disks.

2.4   The *Tower of Hanoi* may be generalized in several ways. We can, for example, provide more pegs. Investigate the problem of moving N disks from the left peg to the right peg when there are four pegs altogether. Draw state-action graphs for two and three disks, and attempt to find a formula for the number of actions required to move N disks.

2.5   State-action graphs can be drawn for games as well as for problems. Actions are not reversible in most games and so the graphs are directed. Draw part of the state-action graph for Tictactoe. How many states does the entire graph contain? How many can be reached in legal play?

2.6   Two solutions for *Jugs* are given in Fig. 2.7. Which solution uses the most water? In the first solution the diagonal lines run downward and in the second they run upward. What is the physical significance of this?

2.7   Verify that there are at most three legal states of *Students and Professors* that can be reached from a given legal state, although there are a total of five distinct actions.

2.8   Draw a state-action graph for *Students and Professors* that includes all 32 states. Identify illegal and unreachable states in your diagram.

2.9   Solve *The Bored Sphere*, first by inference, and then by algebra.

2.10   Suppose that in *Ladders* you are given the lengths of the ladders and the length of the line PQ. Can you find the distance AC between the walls?

CHAPTER 3

AFFINITIES

Problem solving would be an extremely time-consuming activity if we had to solve each problem in isolation. Fortunately we do not have to do this because most problems are related in some way to other problems. One of the cardinal rules of problem solving is: *look for a similar problem*. If we find a similar problem for which we already know the solution, we may be able to apply the solution to the original problem. Even if we find a problem that is similar but unsolved, we may discover that it is easier to solve than the original problem.

There are a number of ways of creating problems that are related to a given problem but that are easier to solve. For example, we can consider *special cases* of a problem. Conversely, we may recognize that the problem we are trying to solve is itself a special case of a more general problem.

In this chapter we examine various relationships that may exist between problems. We introduce two important mathematical concepts, isomorphism and induction, which define precise relationships between certain kinds of problems, and also the less precise concepts, similarity and specialization.

3.1 ISOMORPHIC PROBLEMS

The closest relationship that can exist between two problems that are not identical is isomorphism. Two problems are *isomorphic* if the states and actions of one can be put into a one-to-one correspondence with the states and actions of the other. *One-to-one* means that to each state or action of one problem there corresponds a *unique* state or action of the other. We might be tempted to think that isomorphic problems would be of equivalent difficulty, but this is not necessarily the case, as the following example demonstrates. We start by defining three games; each game is played by two players who make alternate moves.

Game: TICTACTOE

Tictactoe is played on a board of nine cells, as in Fig. 3.1. Players move by marking an unmarked cell with a mark that identifies the player. The marks conventionally used are O and X, and in England the game is known as naughts and crosses. The first player to mark three cells in a straight line (row, column, or diagonal) is the winner.

Game: NUMBER SCRABBLE

Nine playing cards, with values Ace (scored as 1), 2, 3, 4, 5, 6, 7, 8, and 9, are dealt face up. Players alternately take cards. The first player to possess three cards whose values add up to 15 is the winner.

Game: HOT

Hot is also played with nine cards which are dealt face up. Each card has one word printed on it; the words are *HOT, HEAR, TIED, FORM, WASP, BRIM, TANK,*

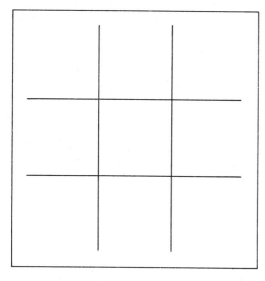

Fig. 3.1
A Tictactoe board.

SHIP, and *WOES*. Players alternately take cards. The first player to possess three cards containing the same letter wins the game. For example, *HEAR*, *TIED*, and *WOES* is a winning combination because each word contains the letter '*E*'.

The isomorphism between Number Scrabble and Tictactoe is easily seen if the cards are arranged in the form shown in Fig. 3.2(a). This diagram shows a magic square in which the total of any row, column, or diagonal is 15; no other grouping of three cells, other than those which can be obtained by rotation or reflection of this arrangement, has this property. The problem of choosing three numbers from the set {1, 2, 3, 4, 5, 6, 7, 8, 9} is therefore equivalent to the problem of choosing three cells in a straight line. Similarly, if we arrange the nine cards of Hot in a square, as shown in Fig. 3.2(b), we can see that the problem of choosing three cards with a common letter is equivalent to the problem of choosing three cells in a straight line.

This correspondence between the three games demonstrates that each is isomorphic to the other two. Although they are equivalent in a mathematical sense, they are not equally easy to play. Each game involves collecting and the goal is to collect three objects which share a certain property. We can easily see that three cells are in a straight line; it is harder to see that three numbers total 15 and harder still to see that three words contain a common letter. Moreover, the strategy of the game is easy to understand from the Tictactoe board but much

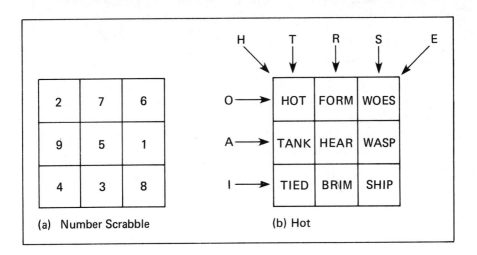

(a) Number Scrabble   (b) Hot

Fig. 3.2
Variants of Tictactoe.

harder to understand from a study of the nine words of Hot until we have been shown the trick of arranging these words into a square.

In every family of isomorphic problems, there is an abstract problem that captures the essence of the problem with a minimum of supporting structure. This abstract problem is not necessarily unique. In the case of Tictactoe, Number Scrabble, and Hot, the underlying concept is that of a *set*. Here is another game, Sets, isomorphic to the games already described, which uses the concept of sets only.

Game: SETS

From the numbers 1, 2, . . ., 8 we construct nine sets, as follows: {1, 5}, {2, 4}, {2, 6}, {3, 5}, {1, 4, 7}, {1, 6, 8}, {3, 4, 8}, {3, 6, 7}, {2, 5, 7, 8}. Players alternately remove a set from this collection. The first player to obtain three sets whose intersection is not the empty set wins the game. For example, {2, 4}, {1, 4, 7}, and {3, 4, 8} is a winning combination because the intersection of these three sets is {4}.

This is another example of the importance of abstraction. In theoretical work problems are usually presented in abstract form because this is the least "prejudiced" way of presenting them. This form may not be the form in which they should be solved, however; to solve them it may be necessary to construct a representation in which the structure of the problem is more apparent. The smart way to play Sets would be to represent each of the nine sets as a cell on a Tictactoe board and to collect sets from collinear cells, as if playing Tictactoe.

3.2 SIMILAR PROBLEMS

If we discover that the problem that we are required to solve is isomorphic to a problem that we have already solved, we are indeed fortunate. More often, however, we find that the problems are not isomorphic but are merely similar. Nevertheless, the solution of one may be a guide to solving the other. The following problem illustrates this.

Problem 3.1: MARGARET AND THE FOX

Margaret has to take a fox, a rabbit, and a lettuce across a river. Her boat will hold only herself and one other object, either the fox, the rabbit, or the lettuce. The fox cannot be left alone with the rabbit and the rabbit cannot be left alone with the lettuce. How does Margaret cross the river with her possessions?

It is natural, at least for readers of this book, to associate this problem with *Students and Professors* (Problem 2.7). The first similarity that strikes us is that both problems involve crossing a river. This is not a particularly significant similarity and we would not find it noteworthy if there were not other, deeper similarities. First, the boat is small: it can hold only two of the four objects at a time. Second, and this is probably the most significant similarity, some of the objects cannot be left alone together. The *reasons* they cannot be left alone together (the fox will eat the rabbit; the rabbit will eat the lettuce; and the professors will confuse the students) are quite different, but this is irrelevant as far as similarity is concerned.

These similarities actually do help us to solve *Margaret and the Fox*. The difficult element of both problems is that one object has to cross the river three times. *Margaret and the Fox* is a simpler problem than *Students and Professors*: it has only ten legal states as opposed to 16. It is easy to see, however, that we could construct a class of problems, each involving a boat, a river, and some objects that have to be taken across the river, and constraints on the permissible arrangements of the objects. It is even conceivable that we could construct general solutions, or at least strategies, that would solve all problems of this class. We can use abstraction to construct classes of similar problems just as we used it to construct classes of isomorphic problems.

Some caution must be exercised, however. If we decide that two problems are similar when in fact they are not, we may waste time looking for a solution that does not exist.

3.3 SPECIAL CASES

Two problems may be related by the fact that one of them is a special case of the other. Although a solution of a special case is not a solution of the general problem, solving the special case may provide us with enough insight into the general problem to contribute to its solution. A special case is obtained by restricting the problem in some way, thereby reducing the number of variables or parameters that it contains. Consider, for example, the following problem.

Problem 3.2: COLLISION COURSE

When a ship is at sea, there is always an officer on watch. Whenever this officer sees a ship for the first time, he takes a bearing on it. (In other words, he records the direction of the ship relative to his own ship.) A few minutes later he takes another bearing and if the bearings are the same he warns the bridge that the ships will collide unless one of them takes evasive action. Explain the reasoning underlying this policy.

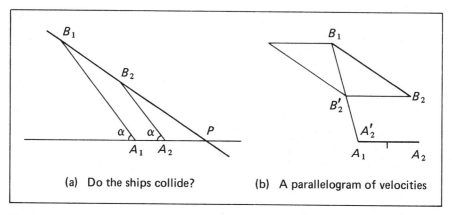

(a) Do the ships collide?   (b) A parallelogram of velocities

Fig. 3.3
Collision Course.

The officer on watch assumes that both ships are moving with constant speed and that they are not changing course; that is, he assumes
that their velocities are constant. Call our ship A and the other ship B,
and suppose that when the first bearing is taken, the ships are at A_1 and
B_1, and that when the second bearing is taken, the ships are at A_2 and
B_2, as shown in Fig. 3.3(a). If the ships continue on their present courses,
they will both pass through the point P. We have to prove that if they
do not change speed or direction, they will arrive at P simultaneously.

It is not easy to think clearly about this problem because there are
two objects moving in different directions. Consider the special case in
which our ship A is stationary. It is obvious that if our ship is stationary
and we take two bearings on another ship and they are the same, either
the other ship is moving directly away from us or it is coming directly
towards us. Since it has just come into view, it must be moving directly
towards us. Thus we have solved the problem rather easily for a special
case. Does this give us any insight into the general case? Is it possible
that by some transformation of the problem we can reduce the velocity
of our ship to zero? Since motion is relative, we can subtract the change
of position of our ship from the change of position of both ships. Then
our ship remains stationary, and the change of position of the other
ship is found by vector addition, as in Fig. 3.3(b). The ships start at
A_1 and B_1, as before, but now they move to A_2' (which is coincident
with A_1 because ship A is stationary) and B_2'. It is now obvious that if
B_1 and B_2' have the same bearings from A_1 and A_2', ship B is sailing directly towards ship A and the ships will collide unless evasive action
is taken.

Here is a problem that cannot be completely solved by considera-
tion of special cases, but we can at least make an educated guess at the
correct solution.

Problem 3.3: VOLUME OF A FRUSTRUM

Fig. 3.4 shows a cone with the top cut off; the correct name for this object is a frustrum of a right circular cone. The radius of the upper circular face is a and the
radius of the lower circular face is b. The perpendicular distance between the faces
is h. What is the volume of the frustrum?

The volume must be a function of the three distances that we are
given, a, b, and h. Call this function $V(a,b,h)$. It must give the correct
volume for all values of its parameters. In particular, it must be correct
in the following three special cases.

1. If $a = 0$, the object is a cone and its volume is $V(0,b,h) = \frac{1}{3}\pi h b^2$.

2. If $b = 0$, the object is an inverted cone and its volume $V(a,0,h) = \frac{1}{3}\pi h a^2$.

3. If $a = b$, the object is a cylinder and its volume is $V(a,a,h) = \pi h a^2$.

Of course, we can only get this far if we happen to know the formulas
for the volume of a cylinder and a cone. These special cases strongly

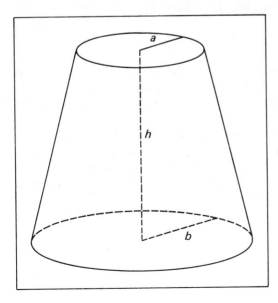

Fig. 3.4
A frustrum.

suggest a formula involving π, h, a^2, and b^2, and this also seems intuitively reasonable. The simplest such formula is

$$\frac{1}{3}\,\pi h(a^2 + b^2)$$

which gives the correct answer for the special cases $a = 0$ and $b = 0$, but when $a = b$ it gives $2\pi ha^2/3$, which is too small. The only term that we can add to this formula while retaining the symmetry of a and b is a term of the form kab. Thus we try

$$V(a,b,h) = \frac{1}{3}\,\pi h(a^2 + kab + b^2)$$

Adding the term kab does not change the value of $V(a,b,h)$ if $a = 0$ or $b = 0$, but when $a = b$, we have

$$V(a,a,h) = \frac{1}{3}\,\pi ha^2(k + 2)$$

We know, however, that this value must be πha^2, whence

$$\frac{k + 2}{3} = 1$$

and

$$k = 1$$

Therefore the complete formula for the volume of the frustrum is

$$V(a,b,h) = \frac{1}{3}\,\pi h(a^2 + ab + b^2)$$

This formula is in fact correct, although the reasoning we have used does not constitute a proof of this. It is easier, however, to prove a result that we suspect to be true than it is to formally derive an unknown result.

Special cases can be constructed in many ways. If a problem mentions variables, such as a and b in the preceding problem, we can try substituting numerical values for these variables. Special values such as 0 and 1 are particularly useful in many cases. If a problem mentions an integer variable, such as n, we try solving it for $n = 1, 2, 3, \ldots$. Even if the specialized problems are very simple, we are likely to gain insight into the general problem by solving them.

In some ways this approach is similar to working backwards. It demonstrates that we should define the terms, conditions, and goals of the problem carefully and that we will have difficulty in attaining the goal if we do not know what it is. In terms of abstraction, this implies that we should remove details and try to envision an appropriate solution. Then we try to find a path to the solution, working either from the solution back towards the initial states or by inference from the states to the goal.

3.4 INDUCTION AND MATHEMATICAL INDUCTION

It is important in problem solving, science, and mathematics to search for patterns. A pattern is a manifestation of a rule, and we study patterns in order to discover the rules which underlie them.

The phases of the moon form a pattern that has been studied and recorded by every culture on earth. The rules which underlie this pattern are the daily rotation of the earth, the monthly rotation of the moon about the earth, and the illumination of the moon by the sun. Seafarers know that the pattern of the tides is linked to the phases of the moon and that the deeper rule underlying this phenomenon is universal gravitation, which explains both the moon's orbit around the earth and the effect of the moon on the terrestrial oceans.

Philosphers used to say that progress in science was made by observing patterns and then formulating hypotheses to explain them, a process they called *inductive reasoning*. The modern view, however, is that observation is meaningless without theory and that therefore the hypothesis must come before the observation; that is, having formulated hypotheses, we test them by observation.

Mathematicians have an advantage over scientists in that they can indeed test their hypotheses and if they are lucky, they can also prove them. We will consider a simple example. One day, with nothing particular to do, we start adding cubes of integers:

$$1^3 + 2^3 = 9$$
$$1^3 + 2^3 + 3^3 = 36$$

Being familiar with numbers, we cannot fail to notice that the sums are both perfect squares: $9 = 3^2$ and $36 = 6^2$. This observation leads to a tentative hypothesis: perhaps all sums of the form $1^3 + 2^3 + 3^3 + \cdots$ are perfect squares. First we try to find a natural starting point. $1^3 = 1 = 1^2$ will do. Next we try a few more special cases:

$$1^3 + 2^3 + 3^3 + 4^3 = 100 = 10^2$$
$$1^3 + 2^3 + 3^3 + 4^3 + 5^3 = 225 = 15^2$$

Deterred by the massive computations involved in going any further, we now look at the numbers on the right-hand side and their square roots: 1, 3, 6, 10, and 15. Are these just arbitrary numbers, or is there a pattern? There is indeed a pattern:

$$1 = 1$$
$$3 = 1 + 2$$
$$6 = 1 + 2 + 3$$
$$10 = 1 + 2 + 3 + 4$$
$$15 = 1 + 2 + 3 + 4 + 5$$

An interesting phenomenon is beginning to emerge:

$$1^3 = 1^2$$
$$1^3 + 2^3 = (1 + 2)^2$$
$$1^3 + 2^3 + 3^3 = (1 + 2 + 3)^2$$
$$1^3 + 2^3 + 3^3 + 4^3 = (1 + 2 + 3 + 4)^2$$
$$1^3 + 2^3 + 3^3 + 4^3 + 5^3 = (1 + 2 + 3 + 4 + 5)^2$$

We can formulate a hypothesis, H:

$$H: \quad 1^3 + 2^3 + \cdots + n^3 = (1 + 2 + \cdots + n)^2 \quad \text{for } n \geq 1$$

This is a remarkable claim: we are asserting the existence of an infinite number of identities involving numbers. Only one value of n for which H is not true is required to disprove H, but to prove H, we must prove it for an arbitrary value of n so that our proof is valid for all values of n. It is here that *mathematical induction* enters the arena.

Principle: MATHEMATICAL INDUCTION

Let $P(n)$ be a statement about an integer n. To prove that $P(n)$ is true, it suffices to prove that:

1. $P(1)$ is true.

2. If $n \geq 1$ and $P(n)$ is true, then $P(n + 1)$ is true.

The principle of mathematical induction is not a theorem that we can prove; it is an *axiom**** which we assume to be true. Although there is a superficial resemblance and a similarity of name between inductive reasoning and mathematical induction, the two are quite different. Inductive reasoning involves guessing a rule from a pattern; mathematical induction, if we accept the principle, is a powerful proof method. Never-

---

*One of Peano's axioms of the natural numbers.

theless, the choice of names is not a coincidence: inductive reasoning can often be made rigorous by inductive proof.

We can in fact prove our hypothesis H by induction. Let $P(n)$ denote the statement

$$1^3 + 2^3 + \cdots + n^3 = (1 + 2 + \cdots + n)^2$$

The proof is in two parts. First we prove $P(1)$. This is accomplished by substituting $n = 1$ in $P(n)$ and obtaining the true statement $1^3 = 1^2$. For the second part of the proof we *assume* that $P(n)$ is true and we consider the statement $P(n + 1)$, namely

$$1^3 + 2^3 + \cdots + n^3 + (n + 1)^3 = [1 + 2 + \cdots + n + (n + 1)]^2$$

Since we are assuming that $P(n)$ is true, we can subtract it from this equation. On the left-hand side all the terms except $(n + 1)^3$ cancel and we are left with this equation:

$$(n + 1)^3 = [1 + 2 + \cdots + n + (n + 1)]^2 - (1 + 2 + \cdots + n)^2$$

The right-hand side is the difference of two squares, an important pattern to recognize because $a^2 - b^2$ simplifies to $(a + b)(a - b)$. If we are lucky enough to remember that $1 + 2 + \cdots + n = n(n + 1)/2$, we can rewrite the right-hand side as follows:

$$
\begin{aligned}
(1 + 2 + \cdots + n + (n + 1))^2 &- (1 + 2 + \cdots + n)^2 \\
= \left[\frac{n(n + 1)}{2} + (n + 1) \right]^2 &- \left[\frac{n(n + 1)}{2} \right]^2 \\
= [n(n + 1) + (n + 1)](n + 1) \\
= (n + 1)^3
\end{aligned}
$$

which is identically equal to the left-hand side. This completes the proof that if $P(n)$ is true, then $P(n + 1)$ is true and, by the principle of mathematical induction, our hypothesis H is true for all positive values of n.

The advantage of a proof by mathematical induction is clear from this example; the algebra was straightforward. The disadvantage is that the result is not derived as part of the proof (we say that the proof is not *constructive*) and therefore we have to know what the result is before we can prove it.

SUMMARY

Problems do not exist in isolation. When we are given a problem we can usually discover, invent, or construct a related problem that is easier to solve. The solution of the new problem may lead us directly to the solution of the original problem or it may only give us insight into the original problem.

■ *Look for similar problems.* If we know of an equivalent or similar problem for which we already have a solution, we can borrow or adapt the solution and apply it to the given problem. This rule is often applicable and it is the basis of the method by which we learn problem solving: we are shown a problem and its solution and we are then asked to solve a number of similar problems using similar solution techniques.

■ *Look for a standard solution.* Although it is unlikely that the problem in its original form has a standard solution, it is possible that an abstract version of it does. This is because standard solutions are usually expressed in as abstract a form as possible so that they are widely applicable. It is even more likely that the subproblems of a problem have standard solutions; in fact, if possible they should be chosen for just this reason.

■ *Investigate special cases.* Very few problems are so particular that they have no special cases. Examining special cases gives us insight into the problem; solving them is encouraging and may pave the way to a general solution. If the problem is very hard, solving it for a class of special cases may be a worthwhile task even if we do not solve the general problem. If the problem involves an integer n, solving it for small values of n may suggest an inductive solution of the general problem.

■ *Generalize the problem.* Generalizing a problem does not usually help us to solve it. The solution of a generalized problem may be more useful than a solution of the given problem, however, because it is more widely applicable. The most common and useful form of generalization is to replace known quantities by parameters. Numbers may be replaced by letters and the problem solved by algebraic rather than arithmetic methods.

■ *Transform the problem.* Some problems become simpler when they are transformed into a different frame of reference. Geometrical problems, for example, may be transformed into algebraic problems by introducing a coordinate system.

FURTHER READING

The game Hot was invented by Leo Moser. It is described, along with other examples of isomorphic relations between games and problems, by Gardner in *Mathematical Carnival*.

The story of the squared square is narrated by William T. Tutte in Gardner's *More Mathematical Puzzles and Diversions*. It is a fascinating account of the discovery of an isomorphism between dissimilar problems: tiling a square with unequal squares and solving an electrical network using Kirchhoff's laws.

Collision Course is based on a naval anecdote related to me by Bernard Grogono. Polya discusses a more difficult problem which can be solved in the same way in the section "Specialization" of *How to Solve It*. The discussions of *Volume of a Frustrum* and mathematical induction are also adapted from this book.

EXERCISES

3.1 Draw the complete state-action graph for *Margaret and the Fox*.

3.2 Derive the formula for the volume of a frustrum by considering a frustrum as a large cone from which a small cone has been removed.

3.3 Four ships, A, B, C, and D are sailing with constant speed and direction. $A * B$ means that A and B almost collided with one another. If $A * B$, $A * C$, $A * D$, $B * C$, and $B * D$, prove that $C * D$. [*Hint*: assume that the ocean is flat and imagine a time dimension perpendicular to it.]

3.4 A square has four edges and a cube has 12. How many edges does a four-dimensional hypercube have? Generalize to an n-dimensional hypercube and then do the same for the series of objects which starts with a triangle and a tetrahedron.

3.5 Prove by induction that $3^{n+2} + 4^{2n+1}$ is a multiple of 13 for $n \geq 0$. By generalizing your proof, show that for integers $p > 0$ and $n \geq 0$, $p^{n+2} + (p+1)^{2n+1}$ is a multiple of $p^2 + p + 1$.

3.6 Punctuate these sentences using commas and quotes.

a) John where Jane had had had had had had had had full marks.

b) John where Jane had had had had had had had had had had had full marks.

Construct grammatical sentences containing 33 and 36 consecutive *hads* and give a general method of constructing sentences with even greater numbers of consecutive *hads*.

3.7 A number of philosophers have fallen asleep after a night of drunken revelry. While they are asleep a mischievous student paints their faces green. When they wake up they all start laughing at one another. Suddenly they stop laughing, having reasoned as follows.

Let $P(n)$ be the statement: if n philosophers wake up with green faces and laugh at one another, any one of them can deduce that his own face is green. Consider $P(2)$, and call the two philosophers Plato and Socrates. Plato reasons thus:

> if my face were not green, Socrates would not be laughing at me. But Socrates is laughing at me, and therefore my face must be green.

Whereupon Plato stops laughing, and Socrates, who has reasoned likewise, also stops laughing. Thus $P(2)$ is true. Now assume that $P(n - 1)$ is true and consider $P(n)$. Any one of the n philosophers can reason thus:

> if my face were not green, there would be a group of $n - 1$ philosophers all laughing at one another. But according to the assumption that $P(n - 1)$ is true, this cannot happen. Therefore my face must be green.

Consequently $P(n - 1)$ implies $P(n)$ and by the principle of mathematical induction $P(n)$ is true for $n \geq 2$.

Comment on this reasoning.

CHAPTER 4

NOTATIONS

Notation is an important component of abstraction. In the first stage of abstraction we identify the common properties of a class of objects or situations and filter out the differences of detail. In the second stage, we develop a symbolic description or notation that models the common properties we have discovered. Finally, by defining operations that may be applied to these symbols, we complete our notational model of one part of the real world.

It is no exaggeration to say that a good notation enables us to think clearly and a poor notation prevents us from thinking clearly. Consider, for example, the effect that notation for numerals has had on various cultures.

The numeral system that we use today is a powerful and effective notation. This system, the positional decimal system, originated during the Han dynasty in China almost 4000 years ago. We use the same system today, but with Arabic numerals instead of Chinese ideographs. With its aid, we can teach small children to perform arithmetic operations on large numbers. While it is true that division, for example, can be demonstrated by dividing 100 oranges into five equal piles, there is no way that we could demonstrate the division of 1,000,000 oranges into 500 equal piles. A calculation such as $1,000,000 \div 500$ is a highly abstract operation, and in order to perform it we must employ a powerful notation.

What are the factors that make this notation so effective? First, the same ten symbols (0, 1, 2, 3, 4, 5, 6, 7, 8, and 9) are used to represent numbers of any size. This is possible because the value of a digit depends on its position in the numeral: the 2 in 1234 is worth more than the 2 in 321. A positional system requires a symbol for zero so that 30 can be distinguished from 3 and 300.*

An important advantage of a positional system is that the physical size of the numerals increases as the logarithm of the value that they represent: multiplying a number by 10 adds only one digit to its representation. If this were not so, we would be unable to write down and thereby manipulate large numbers. Finally, we can extend a positional number system in a natural way by introducing a decimal point. Digits written after the decimal point are implicitly multiplied by negative powers of 10.

We are so familiar with the decimal system that we can appreciate its power only by comparing it with other numeral systems. The Roman numeral system, for instance, is not positional: V represents 5 wherever it appears in the numeral. The Roman system is not entirely nonpositional, however, because I, which normally represents 1, may also represent −1. For example, IV denotes 4 and IX denotes 9. Similarly, X may represent 10 or −10 and C may represent 100 or −100. Without these conventions the Romans would have written DCCCCLXXXXVIIII rather than CMXCIX to denote the number that we would call 999. This notation hindered the development of Roman mathematics and consequently of Roman engineering. Roman engineers were unable to compute accurate safety margins and used inconsistent building codes; some of their buildings collapsed before they were completed and others are still standing.

Approximately two thousand years before Roman culture reached its zenith, the Babylonians were using a positional notation with a base of 60. Vestiges of this system survive today; we divide the hour and degree into 60 minutes and the minute into 60 seconds. The Babylonians wrote numerals without a symbol corresponding to our decimal point. If we take the liberty of using decimal numbers from 0 to 59 instead of

---

*This is not strictly true because we could use a marker between positions: we could write 123 as 1|2|3 and 1023 as 1||2|3. Apart from the fact that this notation is less concise, there are other applications of the zero symbol; for example, we can write the number zero itself as 0. Until about 1200 A.D., the Chinese did not have a symbol for zero but used a blank. When we study the work of the early Greek arithmeticians, it is important to remember that they considered 1 as somehow different from all other numbers and that they did not consider 0 to be a number at all.

cuneiform symbols, we can say that the number written by the Babylonians as 3|40 might represent either

$$320 = (3 \times 60) + 40$$

or

$$3\frac{2}{3} = 3 + \frac{40}{60}$$

With the aid of this notation, the mathematicians of Babylon were able to construct tables for multiplication and division and to describe sophisticated algorithms. Much later, the Alexandrian mathematician Ptolemy used

$$3 + \frac{8}{60} + \frac{30}{3600} \simeq 3.141667$$

as the value of π; the error is only about 0.000074.

Choice of notation has had important consequences in the development of mathematics. The derivative of a function $f(x)$ was written as $f(x)$ by Newton, df/dx by Leibniz, and later as $f'(x)$ by Lagrange. Today we use all three notations but the differential calculus is usually introduced with Leibniz's notation because it is the most suggestive. In fact, English mathematics lagged behind European mathematics for some time after Newton's death partly because English mathematicians refused to use notations other than Newton's.

Modern mathematicians use many notations. The notations of the differential calculus, integral calculus, tensor calculus, mathematical logic, and others have spurred development in these and related areas of research. Sometimes a spectacular breakthrough in a particular field has been largely due to the evolution of a suggestive notation that changed the way in which people thought about the subject. Heaviside's operational notation had this effect on the field of linear differential equations and control systems.

During the last 30 years, thousands of notations have been invented for one purpose only: programming digital computers. We are slowly acquiring criteria for distinguishing "good" programming languages from "poor" programming languages, thus paving the way for the development of better programming languages in the future.

Many problems can be simplified by the introduction of an appropriate notation. In this chapter we discuss two extremely important systems of notation, diagrams and symbols, and we also outline the concept of formal notation and its function.

4.1 DIAGRAMS

Diagrams are one of the many tools that we can use to obtain insight into the nature of a problem. The relationship between different parts or aspects of a problem may be revealed by a diagram and conversely, a diagram may show ways in which a complex problem can be broken down into simpler problems.

A diagram does not serve the same purpose as a picture. A picture is intended to represent something but a diagram is used to explain something. Some diagrams are obtained from pictures by abstraction. A map of an urban transport system generally shows only the routes and the names of the stations; it is an abstracted form of a detailed map of the city, which nowadays is usually abstracted from an aerial photograph. Experienced photographers use many devices, such as soft focus, restricted depth of field, and overexposure, to the puzzlement of beginners who have been told that sharp focus and correct exposure are the ideal. These photographers are using abstraction techniques to draw attention to certain aspects of a scene and in a sense they are creating diagrams.

Not all diagrams are simplified pictures. A diagram is a useful means of demonstrating a relationship. Figs. 2.1 and 2.2 demonstrate the process of abstraction visually and thereby reveal the solution of *Changing the Guard*. The state-action graph for *Tower of Hanoi* (Fig. 2.4) demonstrates the relationship between the positions and moves of the puzzle. A circuit diagram shows the electrical relationships between the components of the circuit; it is therefore a better aid to understanding the function of the circuit than a picture of the components and wires.

A *Cartesian graph* is a convenient and compact means of expressing the relationship between an independent variable and one or more dependent variables. Fig. 4.1 is a graph of the height s of the ball in *The Throw* (Section 2.2); the ceiling is represented by the line $s = 36$ and the trajectory of the ball is represented by the parabola $s = 80t - 16t^2$. The dotted part of the trajectory is never reached by the real ball because it strikes the ceiling at $t = 0.5$ seconds.

A *Venn diagram* illustrates relationships between sets. In Fig. 4.2, the rectangle represents the set of all cars, C. The circles A, O, and U represent subsets of this set. If we assume that cars in A have automatic transmission, cars in O are more than ten years old, and cars in U are made in the United States, then the shaded area includes all cars that have automatic transmission, are ten years old or more, and were built in the United States. Note that the relative sizes of subsets in a Venn diagram are not proportional to the number of elements they contain,

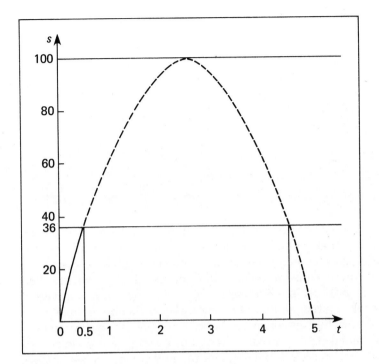

Fig. 4.1
The Throw.

since the purpose of a Venn diagram is to represent merely the logical relationship between subsets.

It is often easier to decide what to include in a diagram than it is to decide what to leave out. A diagram should incorporate features that are relevant to the problem and it should omit features that are not relevant. This seems obvious enough, but nonetheless it comes as a surprise to find that the board can be abstracted from *Changing the Guard*. Symmetries in the problem should be exploited in the construction of the diagram and conversely, the diagram may reveal unexpected symmetries of the problem. For example, the state-action graph of *Jugs* (Fig. 2.6) reveals that we should always pour from the 5-pint jug into the 8-pint jug or *vice versa* but that a mixed strategy does not help.

Psychologists distinguish our spatial ability from our verbal ability; we all have some of each but the actual ratio varies amongst individuals. People with strong spatial ability understand diagrams easily and frequently use diagrams to aid their thought processes. On the other hand,

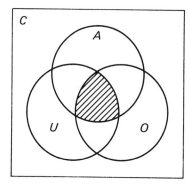

Fig. 4.2
A Venn diagram.

people with strong verbal ability may find that diagrams are not particularly helpful and that verbal reasoning is adequate. The trend towards pictorial traffic signs in many countries may be a mixed blessing because although these signs are in principle independent of written language, they are not deciphered easily by people with strong verbal ability but weak spatial ability. For many years some people have recommended flowcharting as an aid to program design and some people have condemned it; it is possible that both groups are conditioned more by their own spatial/verbal abilities than by the actual advantages and disadvantages of flowcharting. Adapt your problem-solving techniques to your own abilities.

4.2 SYMBOLS

A *symbol* is an abbreviation that stands for a concept. To solve *Annabelle's Uncle Clarence* in Chapter 2 we introduced the symbols A and C to denote Annabelle's age and Clarence's age respectively. These two symbols denote concepts that are specific to the problem. There are other symbols that have conventional denotations. For example, π usually denotes the ratio of the circumference of a circle to its diameter and $\sqrt{}$ indicates that we are dealing with the square root of a quantity.

The choice of appropriate symbols is important in problem solving. The concept denoted by a symbol should be well defined and easy to remember. If possible, the symbol itself should be an aid to memory. We can divide symbols into two classes: symbols that denote objects and quantities, and symbols that denote operations and relations. It is conventional to use letters to symbolize objects and quantities and special signs to symbolize operations and relations.

In many cases the appropriate symbol for a quantity is the first letter of its name. For example, we use t to denote time, F to denote force, V to denote voltage, and v to denote velocity. In other cases, there is a conventional letter that is not the first letter of the name of the quantity: we use i to denote current, s to denote distance, and P to denote momentum. When there is no convention, we can choose any letter we like, but it should have a mnemonic aspect if possible, as in the choice of C for Clarence's age.

Symbols that denote related concepts should have similar characteristics. It is conventional in geometry, for example, to use uppercase Roman letters (A, B, C, . . .) to denote points, lowercase Roman letters (a, b, c, . . .) to denote lines, and small Greek letters (α, β, γ, . . .) to denote angles. Alternatively, we may use the same letter with different subscripts. For instance, a sequence of times might be symbolized by t_0, t_1, t_2, ... We can also use punctuation marks to denote distinct but related concepts. In calculus, for example, we use f' or $\dot{f}$ to denote the derivative of a function f. Similarly the symbol $\vec{x}$ may be used to denote a vector.

Operators may be used to reduce the number of symbols employed. If a problem states that the mass of a planet is 100 times the mass of its satellite, we could write:

1. Let M_p be the mass of the planet.
2. Let M_s be the mass of the satellite.
3. Then $M_p = 100 \times M_s$.

This gives us two unknown quantities, M_p and M_s, and an equation, $M_p = 100 \times M_s$. We could have written instead:

1. Let m be the mass of the satellite.
2. Let $100m$ be the mass of the planet.

This notation requires only one variable, m, and no equations. In some cases the smaller number of distinct symbols may lead to a simpler statement of the problem. It is not always better to have fewer variables, however; sometimes the algebra is easier to understand if each symbol denotes exactly one concept.

Short symbols, consisting of a few characters, are appropriate for problem-solving activities. They enable us to read and write rapidly and we are able to remember the meaning of the symbols without difficulty. When our solutions become computer programs, we need symbols that can be understood by others and that enable us to read programs without confusion. Programs are typically longer and contain more symbols than mathematical derivations, and we must apply different criteria.

4.3 FORMAL SYSTEMS

We are accustomed to associating a meaning with each of the symbols we use. For example, we understand the sequence of symbols 2 + 3 to mean the sum of two and three or perhaps simply two plus three. It is possible, however, to manipulate symbols without regard to their meaning. A notational system in which the permissible symbols and syntactic rules are defined without reference to the meaning of the symbols is called a *formal system*.

By experimenting with the symbols and rules of a formal system, we can discover many different relationships amongst the symbols. If we can demonstrate an isomorphism between the symbols and some other structure, then all the relationships we have discovered within the formal system must apply to this structure. Such a structure is called a *model* for the formal system. The formal system is an abstraction of the model.

The propositional calculus is a formal system that is intended to be an abstraction of a certain kind of reasoning. There is not space here for a rigorous account of the formalization of reasoning that has been achieved by mathematicians and philosophers during the last century, but we will consider the rudiments of the propositional calculus and their relevance to logical argument and problem solving.

The Propositional Calculus

The propositional calculus is a formal system in which expressions containing *propositions* and *connectives* are manipulated. The expressions are called *propositional forms*, and the rules for constructing propositional forms follow.

1. A proposition is a propositional form. Propositions are denoted by uppercase letters such as P, Q, and R.
2. The value of a proposition is either T or F.
3. The connectives of the propositional calculus are $\sim$, $\wedge$, $\vee$, and $\rightarrow$. If X and Y are propositional forms, then the following expressions are also propositional forms:

$$\sim(X)$$
$$(X \wedge Y)$$
$$(X \vee Y)$$
$$(X \rightarrow Y)$$

The following expressions are examples of propositional forms that can be formed in accordance with these rules:

$$P$$
$$\sim(P)$$
$$\sim(\sim(P))$$
$$(P \wedge Q)$$
$$((P \vee Q) \wedge R)$$
$$(((P \vee Q) \wedge R) \rightarrow (P \wedge \sim(Q)))$$

The numerous parentheses make the preceding propositional forms somewhat cumbersome. The following rules are not part of the formal system but are rules of convenience that enable us to omit many of the parentheses without causing ambiguity. In these rules, P is a proposition and X, Y, and Z are propositional forms.

1. The outermost parentheses can be removed: (X) may be written X.

2. Parentheses enclosing a proposition may be removed: (P) may be written P.

3. The connectives are ordered according to their precedence as follows: $\sim$, $\wedge$, $\vee$, $\rightarrow$; that is, $\sim$ has the highest precedence and $\rightarrow$ has the lowest precedence. An expression which contains only connectives of higher precedence than the connectives enclosing it need not be parenthesized.

4. The connectives $\wedge$ and $\vee$ are associative, so that:

$$(X \wedge Y) \wedge Z = X \wedge (Y \wedge Z) = X \wedge Y \wedge Z$$
$$(X \vee Y) \vee Z = X \vee (Y \vee Z) = X \vee Y \vee Z$$

where the symbol $=$ has its usual meaning, is equivalent to.

Using these rules, we may perform simplifications such as these:

$$\sim(\sim(P)) = \sim \sim P$$
$$((P \wedge Q) \vee R) = P \wedge Q \vee R$$
$$(((P \wedge Q) \wedge R) \rightarrow (P \wedge \sim(Q))) = (P \vee Q) \wedge R \rightarrow P \wedge \sim Q$$

Note that $\rightarrow$ is not associative, and therefore $(P \rightarrow Q) \rightarrow R$ is not the same as $P \rightarrow (Q \rightarrow R)$. Consequently we cannot write $P \rightarrow Q \rightarrow R$.

In order to evaluate a propositional form, we need to know the effect of each connective. The value of a proposition is either T or F and so the number of cases to consider is small provided that the number of propositions in the propositional form is small. For the connective $\wedge$, for example, there are only four possibilities. These values and corresponding values for the other connectives are summarized in Table 4.1. The value of a propositional form depends on the value of the propositions of which it is composed. We can tabulate the value of a propositional form for all possible values of its component porpositions just as we can tabulate or plot the graph of an algebraic function. Table 4.2 shows the propositional form $\sim P \vee Q$. It is constructed as follows. First we create a column for each proposition and fill these columns with different combinations of values of the propositions. In this case, there are two propositions and we need four rows. In general, if there are n propositions, we need 2^n rows. Next we assign columns for intermediate results and fill them using Table 4.1 to obtain the appropriate values. In this example the only intermediate result we need is $\sim P$. Finally, we create a column for the complete propositional form and fill it in the same way.

It is possible to construct propositional forms whose values do not depend on their component propositions. Tables 4.3 and 4.4 demonstrate that $P \wedge \sim P$ is always F and that $P \wedge Q \rightarrow (P \rightarrow Q)$ is always T, whatever values we assign to P and Q.

We say that two propositional forms are *equivalent* if they have the same entries in corresponding rows of their tables, or, in other words, if their values are equal for all values of their component propositions. For example, by comparing the sixth column of Table 4.1 with the fourth column of Table 4.2, we can see that the propositional forms $\sim P \vee Q$ and $P \rightarrow Q$ are equivalent. From this and similar observations we can construct rules for replacing propositional forms by simpler equivalent propositional forms without being concerned about the meaning of the symbols.

It is now time, however, to attribute a meaning to these symbols by providing a model for the propositional calculus. The following model is generally accepted.

Table 4.1 Definition of Connectives

P	Q	$\sim P$	$P \wedge Q$	$P \vee Q$	$P \rightarrow Q$
F	F	T	F	F	T
F	T	T	F	T	T
T	F	F	F	T	F
T	T	F	T	T	T

Table 4.2 $\sim P \vee Q$

P	Q	$\sim P$	$\sim P \vee Q$
F	F	T	T
F	T	T	T
T	F	F	F
T	T	F	T

1. Let the values T and F denote *true* and *false* respectively.
2. Let the propositions $P, Q, R, \ldots$ denote statements in English (or any other language) that are either true or false.
3. Let the connectives have the following meanings:

$\sim P$	means	not P.
$P \wedge Q$	means	P and Q.
$P \vee Q$	means	P or Q.
$P \rightarrow Q$	means	if P, then Q.

As an illustration of this model we introduce the following propositions:

A	denotes	Anne wins.
B	denotes	It is before 3 p.m.
C	denotes	There is a fire.
D	denotes	Dick wins.
E	denotes	Ed wins.
H	denotes	I am hungry.
J	denotes	Jane wins.
L	denotes	I have had lunch.
S	denotes	There is smoke.
W	denotes	I will win my bet.

Table 4.3 $P \wedge \sim P$

P	$\sim P$	$P \wedge \sim P$
F	T	F
T	F	F

Table 4.4 $P \wedge Q \rightarrow (P \rightarrow Q)$

P	Q	$P \wedge Q$	$P \rightarrow Q$	$P \wedge Q \rightarrow (P \rightarrow Q)$
F	F	F	T	T
F	T	F	T	T
T	F	F	F	T
T	T	T	T	T

The following sentences can now be represented by propositional forms in the manner indicated.

1. There is no smoke without fire.

$$\sim (S \wedge \sim C) \quad \text{or} \quad S \rightarrow C$$

2. If it is before 3 p.m. and I have had lunch then I am not hungry.

$$B \wedge L \rightarrow \sim H$$

3. If Jane or Dick loses and Anne wins, then Ed also loses and I will have lost my bet.

$$(\sim J \vee \sim D) \wedge A \rightarrow \sim E \wedge \sim W$$

The propositional calculus can be used as an aid to solving problems that involve a certain kind of logical reasoning. Here is a problem of this kind.

Problem 4.1: IN THE SOUP

Algernon invited his erstwhile enemy Egbert to dine at his house. During the soup course, Egbert died. The autopsy showed that he had been poisoned. The detective decided that the poison had been added to the soup, and that this could have been done by the cook who prepared the meal in the kitchen, by the butler who carried it through to the dining room, or by Algernon himself at the table. The detective interviewed the three suspects. Algernon said that he had watched the butler carry the soup and that he knew the cook was honest. The butler said that he had seen the cook prepare the soup. The cook said that he had seen Algernon drink the soup and that he knew that the butler was honest. One person, not necessarily the murderer, is lying. Who killed Egbert?

In order to solve this problem, we must decide whether each participant is a liar, a murderer, or both. Assuming innocence until guilt is proven, we define the following propositions.

$$P = \text{Algernon is telling the truth.}$$

A = Algernon is innocent.

Q = The butler is telling the truth.

B = The butler is innocent.

R = The cook is telling the truth.

C = The cook is innocent.

We can now translate the evidence collected by the detective into propositional forms. In each case we assume that if a witness is telling the truth, then his statement is true.

$P \to B$ Algernon watched the butler carry the soup.

$P \to R$ The cook was honest.

$Q \to C$ The butler saw the cook prepare the soup.

$R \to A$ The cook saw Algernon drink the soup.

$R \to Q$ The butler was honest.

We now require values of these propositions such that all five propositional forms are simultaneously true. That is:

$$(P \to B) \wedge (P \to R) \wedge (Q \to C) \wedge (R \to A) \wedge (R \to Q) = T$$

The complete table for this propositional form has 64 rows because there are six propositions. We do not need to write it out in full, however, because we have some additional information: there is only one liar, and there is only one murderer. Therefore we need consider only those rows of the table for which exactly one of A, B, and C is false and exactly one of P, Q, and R is false. The nine relevant rows are shown in Table 4.5. The first three lines represent the hypothesis that Algernon was the murderer; the second three lines represent the hypothesis that the butler was the murderer; and the last three lines represent the hypothesis that the cook was the murderer. The final column, headed M, is the value of

$$(P \to B) \wedge (P \to R) \wedge (Q \to C) \wedge (R \to A) \wedge (R \to Q)$$

The only row for which M is true is the fourth: the butler poisoned the soup and Algernon is lying.

The advantages of applying a formal system to the solution of *In the Soup* are apparent. As in the solution of *Annabelle's Uncle Clarence*, the manipulation of English phrases and sentences according to nebulous rules is replaced by the manipulation of symbols according to precise rules. We perform mechanical operations instead of constructing confusing arguments.

Table 4.5 $M = (P \rightarrow B) \wedge (P \rightarrow R) \wedge (Q \rightarrow C) \wedge (R \rightarrow A) \wedge (R \rightarrow Q)$

A	B	C	P	Q	R	$P \rightarrow B$	$P \rightarrow R$	$Q \rightarrow C$	$R \rightarrow A$	$R \rightarrow Q$	M
F	T	T	F	T	T	T	T	T	F	T	F
F	T	T	T	F	T	T	T	T	F	F	F
F	T	T	T	T	F	T	F	T	T	T	F
T	F	T	F	T	T	T	T	T	T	T	T
T	F	T	T	F	T	F	T	T	T	F	F
T	F	T	T	T	F	F	F	T	T	T	F
T	T	F	F	T	T	T	T	F	T	T	F
T	T	F	T	F	T	T	T	T	T	F	F
T	T	F	T	T	F	T	F	F	T	T	F

The disadvantage of a formal system is that the precision of the results is limited by the accuracy with which the rules of the system reflect the real situation. It is somewhat disturbing, for example, to find that there is another way of solving *In the Soup* that leads to a different conclusion. Consider the following argument.

1. *Assume that Algernon is telling the truth.* Then the cook is honest, because Algernon says so. Therefore the butler is honest, because the cook says so. Therefore all three are honest, which contradicts the given information.

2. *Assume that Algernon is lying.* Then the cook is lying, because Algernon (who is lying) says he is honest. Therefore Algernon and the cook are both lying, which again contradicts the given information.

3. Thus the information deduced by the detective is inconsistent and there is no solution to the problem.

The discrepancy between the two solutions arises from the sentence, "Algernon said that he knew the cook was honest." We translated this into the propositional form $P \rightarrow R$. Now consider the values of $P \rightarrow R$ as given in Table 4.1. If Algernon is telling the truth, $P = T$, and $P \rightarrow R = R$; in other words, we can believe what he says. On the other hand, if Algernon is lying, $P = F$ and $P \rightarrow R = T$, whether $R = T$ (the cook is telling the truth) or $R = F$ (the cook is lying). In the formal solution, a liar is not constrained to lie: Algernon made a truthful statement about the butler and a false statement about the cook. In the informal solution, having assumed that Algernon was lying, we concluded that both of his statements were false.

There are two potential sources of error in the application of a formal system. First, a formal abstraction may be syntactically correct without necessarily being accurate. The propositional form

$$(P \to B) \wedge (P \to R) \wedge (Q \to C) \wedge (R \to A) \wedge (R \to Q)$$

is syntactically correct but if a liar always lies, it is inaccurate. Second, even if we have constructed an accurate formal abstraction, we will obtain an incorrect answer if we use it with invalid data.

A computer program is a formal abstraction and both of these difficulties occur in programming. A program may be incorrect although it contains no syntax error, and a correct program yields erroneous results if it is presented with invalid data.

SUMMARY

Symbols and diagrams are a powerful aid to problem-solving activities of all kinds. The choice of appropriate symbols requires a balance of personal taste and established convention. We can transform complex reasoning processes into mechanical manipulation of symbols provided that we construct accurate formal abstractions.

FURTHER READING

Knuth discusses Babylonian algorithms in his paper "Ancient Babylonian Algorithms." He also discusses positional number systems in Section 4.1 of his book, *Seminumerical Algorithms*.

For a more complete and rigorous account of the propositional calculus and a discussion of formalization in general, read Stoll's *Sets, Logic, and Axiomatic Theories*.

EXERCISES

4.1   Explain why the bases shown were chosen for the following number systems:

  a) Babylonian (base = 60)

  b) Chinese (base = 10)

  c) Digital computers (base = 2).

4.2 Choose a programming language and comment on its advantages and disadvantages as an expressive notation.

4.3 Solve *In the Soup* by drawing a diagram.

4.4 Construct a formal abstraction of *In the Soup* in which a liar always lies, and show that there is no solution consistent with the given data.

4.5 Does *In the Soup* have a solution if we assume that the murderer and one other person are lying?

PART 2

PROGRAMMING

CHAPTER 5

ALGORITHMS

A computer program is a complex object that contains a large amount of detailed information. The detail is necessary for various reasons but it obscures the structure of the program. In order to write a program or to understand a program written by somebody else, we need a guide to its organization and purpose. Thus although a program is our goal, we usually want to express our solution in an abstract way at first, omitting the irrelevant details. The abstract version of a solution is called an *algorithm*, and the process of creating a program from an algorithm is called *implementation*. We discuss algorithms in this chapter, and various other aspects of program development, including implementation, in the next chapter.

Informally, an algorithm is a collection of instructions which, when performed in a specified sequence, produce the correct result. The study of algorithms is the heart of computer science. Many books have been written about the design and analysis of computer algorithms, and in this chapter we merely take a brief look at algorithms from the problem solver's point of view.

5.1 DESIGN

In order to design an algorithm we need to know the kind of data that will be available to the algorithm and the nature of the result that is required. Using this information, we have to devise a sequence of operations that will produce the correct result for any given values of the data. By way of introduction to the concepts of algorithm design, we briefly examine two early algorithms. The first is Babylonian and it is approximately 3700 years old.

Algorithm 5.1: RECTANGLES

Given that the sum of the length, width, and diagonal of a rectangle is 70 and that the area is 420; find the length, width, and diagonal of the rectangle.

- 70 times 70 is 4900.
- 420 times 2 is 840.
- Take 840 from 4900 leaving 4060.
- One half of 4060 is 2030.
- By what should 70 be multiplied to obtain 2030?
- 70 times 29 is 2030.
- 29 is the diagonal.

This algorithm has several interesting features. The first is that it is actually a worked example, not a general method. The Babylonians who used this algorithm were apparently expected to use the framework as given, substituting different numerical values according to their own requirements. The second interesting feature is that the algorithm uses a rather obscure property of rectangles, which we would express by the formula

$$d = \frac{1}{2}\left(\frac{s^2 - 2A}{s}\right) \qquad (5.1.1)$$

in which d is the length of the diagonal, A is the area of the rectangle, and s is the sum of its length, width, and diagonal. Formulas of this kind are simply algorithms in which an explicit sequence of instructions has been replaced by a string of symbols. Thus (5.1.1) is a modern notation for Algorithm 5.1. Finally, although the opening sentence of the algorithm claims that it will find the length, width, and diagonal of the rectangle, it actually only calculates the diagonal.

The second algorithm is both more recent and familiar than *Rectangles*. It is Euclid's algorithm for finding the greatest common divisor of two positive integers; we state it in modern form.

Algorithm 5.2: GREATEST COMMON DIVISOR

Given two positive nonzero integers, M and N, to find their greatest common divisor.

1. Calculate R, the remainder when M is divided by N.
2. If R is zero, print the result, N, and terminate the algorithm.
3. Set M to N, N to R, and go back to step 1.

This algorithm incorporates the important features of modern algorithms.

1. It is composed of *steps*. Each step is well-defined; we can understand it, and we could program a machine to carry it out if necessary.
2. The *sequence of control* is also well-defined. There is never any doubt as to which step should be executed next, even though this may depend on values of the data. In particular, there is an initial step and a final step; when we have executed the final step, we have obtained the required result.
3. The final step is reached after a *finite number of steps* have been executed.
4. The algorithm represents a *class of computations*, not just a single computation. When it is executed with particular values of M and N, it performs one computation from this class. An algorithm must be given *input data* and it must produce *results*.
5. The values of the input data for which the algorithm is valid are stated: M and N must be positive, nonzero integers.

Note that we do not require that the individual steps of an algorithm be simple or basic. This is because we want to be able to use algorithms as single steps in more complex algorithms. Step 1 of Euclid's algorithm is not a particularly simple step, and if we were implementing this algorithm for a small computer we would probably have to make use of a division algorithm to perform this step. On the other hand, a complex algorithm might reasonably employ Euclid's algorithm as a single step or even as part of a step. The third requirement, that only a finite number of steps need to be executed to complete the algorithm, distinguishes algorithms from *computational procedures*, or *semi-algorithms*, which are not required to terminate.

Here is a computational procedure that prints all the positive integers; it is not an algorithm because it does not terminate.

Computational Procedure 5.1: PRINT POSITIVE INTEGERS

1. Set N to zero.
2. Set N to $N + 1$.
3. Print N and go back to step 2.

Because they do not terminate, computational procedures are more useful as a theoretical concept than as a practical tool. Algorithms should be designed so that they terminate when specified conditions have been established, and we should ensure that these conditions can in fact be established by the execution of a finite number of steps. The following are statements of problems for which the solutions are algorithms.

1. Find the prime numbers of a given number.
2. Find the square root of a given number within a specified precision.
3. Find a path through a given maze.
4. Determine whether or not a bridge will support a given load.

Occasionally the specification of an algorithm contains more information than we need. More often, however, we find that we must supply information that is implicitly required by the specification. A square root, for example, cannot be calculated exactly, and so we need to know how much precision is required. In order to design an algorithm that solves mazes we must know how a maze is represented in the input data. We cannot make calculations about bridges without knowing the theory and practice of structural engineering. Thus we commence by *understanding the problem* and *making implicit data explicit*. Since many thousands of algorithms already exist, the next step is to *look for a standard solution*. There are standard algorithms for simple tasks, such as finding the square root of a number, and also for more complex tasks, such as parsing strings according to the rules of a specified grammar. Standard algorithms are usually expressed in a rather abstract way so that they are widely applicable, and it will often be necessary to adapt them for specific applications.

When we are designing algorithms we may use techniques such as *divide and conquer*. Given a complex problem, we first identify subgoals and then design algorithms to achieve each subgoal. *Balancing* is a useful principle in algorithm design. When we subdivide a problem, we attempt to choose subproblems that are approximately equal in size. This tends to make the resulting algorithm more efficient. Suppose for example that we are designing an algorithm that is to find a specified name in an ordered list such as a telephone directory. If we start by looking at the first name in the directory, we have divided the problem into two parts: "is it the first name?" and "is it in the rest of the directory?" These parts are highly unequal and the solution is poorly balanced. If, instead, we open the directory in the middle, we can immediately decide whether the name we want is in the first or the second half of the directory. If it is in the first half, we can then choose between the first quarter and the second quarter, and so on. At each step we are halving the size of the problem and the resulting algorithm is more efficient because the strategy is better balanced.

In many cases, we cannot achieve the required solution in one step, and in this case we repeat steps, a technique known as *iteration*. The goal of an iterative algorithm is to achieve as much as possible at each step, or to be *greedy*. This, for example, is a simple algorithm that calculates the greatest common divisor of two positive numbers M and N.

Algorithm 5.3: GREATEST COMMON DIVISOR

1. If $M = N$, print the result, M, and stop.
2. If M is greater than N, set M to $M - N$ and go back to step 1, otherwise set N to $N - M$ and go back to step 1.

The following shows what happens when we set $M = 16$, $N = 14$, and execute this algorithm. The calculations are shown on the left and the resulting values of M and N on the right.

	M	N
	16	14
$M = 16 - 14$	2	
$N = 14 - 2$		12
$N = 12 - 2$		10
$N = 10 - 2$		8
$N = 8 - 2$		6
$N = 6 - 2$		4
$N = 4 - 2$		2
Print 2		

The previous version of Euclid's algorithm, Algorithm 5.2, reaches the same result with fewer operations. This is a record of its execution when $M = 16$ and $N = 14$.

	M	N	R
	16	14	
$R = 2$			2
$M = 14$	14		
$N = 2$		2	
$R = 0$			0
Print 2			

The idea used by both algorithms is the same: reduce the value of either M or N without changing the value of $GCD(M, N)$. Algorithm 5.2, however, is greedier: by using remaindering rather than subtraction, it reduces the size of M and N much more rapidly than Algorithm 5.3.

Special cases are of particular importance in algorithm design for two reasons. First, some instances of the problem may be easy to solve and it is often worthwhile to identify these and to employ a special strategy. Second, it is all too easy to devise an algorithm that looks general but that in fact fails in certain cases. Let us assume that we are designing an algorithm to divide one number by another and that both numbers are so large that we cannot use the standard divide instruction. If the divisor is a power of 2, 2^n say, we may be able to find the quotient simply by shifting the dividend n binary places to the right. This is an example of the first kind of special case, an instance of the problem that is particularly simple to solve. If the divisor is zero, we should detect this fact and display an error message; this is an example of the special kind of special case. If the dividend is negative, right shifting might not produce the correct result; this would produce an error due to failure to consider special cases.

We return to the subject of algorithms in Chapters 7, 9, and 10, in which specific algorithms are developed, discussed, and implemented.

5.2 EFFICIENCY

There are very few problems for which exactly one solution is known. There are many problems for which no solution is known; usually, as soon as one solution to a previously unsolved problem is discovered, other solutions follow. Consequently, we are often faced with the problem of deciding which is the most appropriate of several solutions. We can only do this in a rational and consistent way if we have meaningful criteria for comparing solutions. For solutions to puzzles, such as the puzzles of Part 1, the criteria are often vague: elegance, ingenuity, neatness, and so on. When the solution is expressed in the form of an algorithm, however, we can make reliable and quantitative comparisons.

We require finite supplies of two resources, *time* and *space*, to execute an algorithm. Each step of the algorithm requires a certain amount of time for execution and the time required to execute an algorithm is the sum of these amounts. We require space in which to store the data that the algorithm is processing; when a computer is used to execute the algorithm, the space used is simply the amount of memory required to run the program. Time is usually regarded as the more important resource, but in some cases space may be important as well.

Problem 5.1: COILING A ROPE

You are in a room with a pile of rope. Organize the rope into a neat bundle.

The first and simplest solution to this problem is to coil the rope in the traditional manner: take one end in your left hand and add successive loops with your right hand. (You may reverse these directions if you are left-handed.) The time required to coil the rope is proportional to the length of the rope, assuming that each loop is the same size.

Alternatively you could anchor one end of the rope to the center of a board and then turn the board around its central axis with constant angular velocity so that the rope lies on the board in the form of a spiral. At first the rope will move slowly but, as the radius of the spiral increases, the rope will move more rapidly. The length of rope coiled during one complete revolution of the board is approximately proportional to the length of rope already coiled, and the time taken to coil the rope is approximately equal to the square root of the length of the rope. Although progress is slow at first, this method will ultimately be faster than the first method, provided that the rope is long enough.

There is a third method: lay the rope out in a straight line and then carry one end of the rope to the other end so that you have a double rope half as long as the original rope. Double this "rope" again and continue doubling until you have a small bundle. The time taken to complete this operation is approximately equal to the logarithm of the length of the rope, and this method will be the fastest method of the three for sufficiently long ropes. Note, however, that the third method requires that you lay the rope out in a straight line, and therefore its space requirement is greater than that of the other two. It is often true of algorithms that economy of time is only gained by the expenditure of space.

The execution times of algorithms are usually compared theoretically rather than by actual comparison of their running times on a computer. The time is calculated as a function of a small number of variables; if possible, a single variable is used. The function is called the *time complexity* of the algorithm. For example, the time complexity functions of the solutions of Problem 5.1 are functions of the length of the rope. If we assume that the length of the rope is L, the time complexities for the three solutions are $k_1 L$, $k_2 \sqrt{L}$, and $k_3 \log (L)$ respectively, where k_1, k_2, and k_3 are constants. The time complexity of an algorithm that sorts a file is expressed as a function of the number of records in the file.

The space required by an algorithm is called its *space complexity*. It is not usually mentioned unless it has a particularly significant effect on the range of practical application of the program. As an example of a situation in which space complexity might be important, suppose that two algorithms, A and B, perform equivalent operations on $N \times N$ matrices. Algorithm A processes the matrix one row at a time and requires space $N + a$, where a is a constant. Algorithm B runs faster but processes the whole matrix at once and consequently requires space $N^2 + b$, where b is another constant. Our choice of algorithm would depend on the size of the matrices that we wanted to process. If they are small, say $N = 10$, algorithm B would be suitable. If $N = 1000$, however, the space requirement for algorithm B would be excessive and we would have to use algorithm A.

Suppose that we are comparing two algorithms, A and B, which perform certain calculations on N items of data. The results produced by A and B are identical and we must choose between them on the basis of execution time. The times are functions of N, say $T_A(N)$ and $T_B(N)$. How do we go about comparing these times? There is no problem if we have exact expressions. Suppose for instance that we know:

$$T_A(N) = 10N$$

and

$$T_B(N) = 4N + 30$$

Then we can see from Fig. 5.1 that $T_A(N) = T_B(N)$ if $N = 5$ and that if N is greater than 5 then $T_A(N)$ is greater than $T_B(N)$. If we knew that the chosen algorithm would usually be processing more than five items of data at a time, we would have no difficulty in choosing algorithm B.

In most cases, however, our knowledge of the time complexity is vaguer than this. We are more likely to know that, for instance:

$$T_A(N) = aN + b$$

and

$$T_B(N) = cN^2 + dN + e$$

In these equations, a, b, c, d, and e are constants whose values cannot easily be determined because they depend on unknown properties of the environment in which the algorithms will be executed. In this situation we reason in the following way. First we assume that a and c are

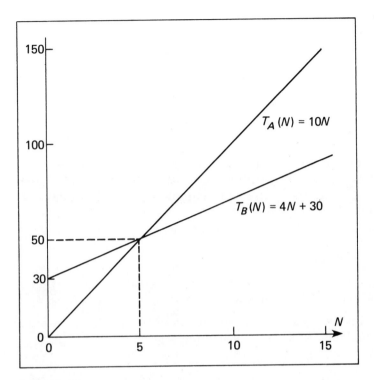

Fig. 5.1
Performance of algorithms A and B.

both greater than zero. Then for large enough N, we can neglect terms other than the first because they will be comparatively small. Thus we compare

$$T_A(N) = aN$$

and

$$T_B(N) = cN^2$$

If N is greater than a/c, then $T_A(N)$ is less than $T_B(N)$ and algorithm A must therefore be faster than algorithm B if N is large enough. We say that algorithm A is *asymptotically* faster than algorithm B. In many situations, the knowledge that one algorithm is asymptotically faster than another is sufficient. Only if the value of a/c in the preceding example is large and we often use the algorithm in cases where N is less than a/c would we consider using algorithm B.

There is a notation, called the *order notation,* for expressing the fact that we are not interested in terms other than the dominant term or the values of indeterminate constants in a complexity function. In the preceding example, we write

$$T_A(N) = O(N)$$

and

$$T_B(N) = O(N^2)$$

These equations are read as: the time complexity of algorithm A is order N, and the time complexity of algorithm B is order N-squared. Alternatively we can read: the time complexity of algorithm A is *big-oh N,* and the time complexity of algorithm B is *big-oh N-squared.*

The concept of order can be given complete mathematical rigor. The following definition of the order notation provides the starting point of a formal analysis.

If the asymptotic value of a function $F(N)$ is specified by $F(N) = O(f(N))$, there exist constants K and N_0, such that if $N > N_0$, then $F(N) < Kf(N)$.

To illustrate this definition, suppose that we have calculated that the exact time complexity of a certain algorithm is given by

$$T(N) = 17N^2 + 45N + 46$$

We can easily see that $T(N)$ is less than $20N^2$ provided that N is greater than 25. Thus we have found constants $K = 20$ and $N_0 = 25$ such that

$$N > N_0 \quad \text{implies} \quad T(N) < KN^2$$

and we are therefore entitled to write

$$T(N) = O(N^2)$$

These are not the only constants that can be found to satisfy the conditions of the definition but since the definition only requires that "there exist" constants, one set of constants is all we need.

In order to apply the order notation successfully we need to know some limiting inequalities. The most important of these appear in the following list. In each case, given any values of the constants a, b, and K, subject to the given constraints, we can satisfy the inequality by making N large enough.

1. If $a > b > 0$ and $K > 0$ then $N^a > KN^b$
2. If $a > 0$, $b > 1$, and $K > 0$, then $N^a > K \cdot \log_b(N)$

3. If $a > 1$, $b > 0$, and $K > 0$, then $a^N > KN^b$

4. If $a > 1$ and $K > 0$, then $N! > Ka^N$

These inequalities are very important. For example, the third inequality tells us that an algorithm of time complexity $O(a^N)$ will ultimately be slower than an algorithm of time complexity $O(N^b)$ even if k is small and b is large. We express this in words by saying that asymptotically an algorithm with *exponential* time complexity is slower than an algorithm of *polynomial* time complexity. The fourth inequality tells us that *factorial* time complexity is the worst of all; this fact severely limits our ability to solve combinatorial problems which require computing all of the permutations of a set. The following are values of $N!$ for N from 9 to 13.

$$9! \ = 362,880$$
$$10! = 3,628,800$$
$$11! = 39,916,800$$
$$12! = 479,001,600$$
$$13! = 6,227,020,800$$

At the other end of the complexity scale the logarithmic functions increase extremely slowly. An algorithm with time complexity $O(\log(N))$ will never be limited by the value of N alone. If a data set containing N items is suitably organized, it is possible to access one item in time $O(\log(N))$. Let us be more specific and suppose that the time is $50 \cdot \log_2(N)$ milliseconds. The following list gives the access time for various values of N:

$N = 10$	$t = 166$ ms
$N = 100$	$t = 332$ ms
$N = 10,000$	$t = 665$ ms
$N = 1,000,000$	$t = 995$ ms $\simeq 1$ second
$N = 1,000,000,000$	$t = 1,495$ ms $\simeq 1.5$ seconds

It is likely that we will run out of space in which to store the data before we run out of time in which to execute the search algorithm.

The speed of electronic computation has affected algorithm design in two ways. First, many things that were hitherto impossible have become possible. The speed of a modern computer is as incomprehensible to us as the size of an atom or the distance to a star. The earliest computers punched their results on paper tape; if we wanted to punch the results generated by a modern computer without slowing it down, we would have to punch several thousand miles of paper tape per second. A generation ago experts announced that one or two large computers would suffice for the computational needs of mankind. They failed to realize that the ability to calculate rapidly and to process large quantities of information would change the fabric of mathematics, physics, engineering, economics, and a variety of other fields so radically that their assessment of what *needed to be calculated* would become entirely invalid.

The second way in which the speed of computation has affected algorithm design is in the number of steps executed. An algorithm for a human processor may contain ten, twenty or at most a few hundred steps. An algorithm for a computer may involve a million, or ten million, or even a billion steps. Each step may introduce a small error and successive errors may accumulate or cancel out. When only a few steps are involved, it may not matter much whether errors get smaller or larger, but when there are a million steps, the difference may be success or disaster.

Some problems require a large amount of computing power. These are problems that skeptics never even conceived as computationally feasible problems, such as forecasting the weather by simulating the motion of the atmosphere or modeling the evolution of a galaxy by simulating the motion of a few thousand stars. There are other problems for which it was once assumed that an efficient solution would eventually be found but none has been found or is likely to be found. An example of this kind is the traveling salesperson problem: a salesperson must visit N towns; how can he or she select the shortest route that passes through each town at least once? There is no known solution for this problem for which the time complexity is not an exponential function of N. (There are faster algorithms that solve the simpler problem of finding a "good" route that is not necessarily the best route.) Consequently the traveling salesperson problem is insoluble by any computer for large values of N.

We cannot neglect the study of efficient algorithms on the grounds that computers are always becoming larger and faster. On the contrary, we will always be short of computing power and there will always be a need for efficient algorithms to solve problems of all kinds.

SUMMARY

Abstraction is as important in programming as it is in problem solving. An algorithm is an abstract form of a program; a program is an implementation of an algorithm.

We can estimate the time and space requirements of an algorithm. The exact time and space requirements of the corresponding program depend on the implementation and so the complexities of two algorithms that solve the same problem are usually compared using the order notation. The order notation also expresses the idea that we are more interested in an improvement from, say, exponential to linear complexity than a change in scale factor.

We have not yet defined a notation for algorithms. This issue is discussed in the next chapter.

FURTHER READING

Algorithm 5.1, *Rectangles*, is adapted from Knuth's fascinating paper, "Ancient Babylonian Algorithms." (If you take the trouble to read this paper, note that Knuth published a correction to it entitled "Reciprocal Table of Inakibit-Anu Incorrectly Rendered.")

There are many books about algorithm design and analysis. Volumes I and II of Knuth's *The Art of Computer Programming* provide a firm foundation. Recommended for further study in this field are *Computer Algorithms* by Baase; *The Design and Analysis of Computer Algorithms* by Aho, Hopcroft, and Ullman; and *Combinatorial Algorithms* by Reingold, Nievergelt, and Deo.

EXERCISES

5.1 Write algorithms for:
   a) getting from your home to your school or place of work by bicycle, by car, and by public transport;
   b) making breakfast;
   c) solving the equation $Ax^2 + Bx + C = 0$;
   d) finding the midpoint of a straight line using a straight edge and a pair of compasses;
   e) finding a book in a library.

5.2 Write algorithms for:
   a) the solution of *Tower of Hanoi*;
   b) the solution of *Jugs*;
   c) the solution of *Students and Professors*.

5.3 You have 500 index cards containing bibliographic references and a table on which to sort them. Describe two methods of sorting and compare their time and space complexities.

5.4 Assuming for each pair of functions $f(N)$ and $g(N)$ that these functions are time complexities for two algorithms F and G that solve the same problem, find out how large N must be to ensure that F is faster than G.

a) $f(N) = 20N^2 + 100$, $g(N) = N^3 + 2N + 17$.

b) $f(N) = 64 \ (\lg N + 4)$, $g(N) = 5\sqrt{N}$.

c) $f(N) = 100N^4$, $g(N) = 10^{(N/10)}$.

(*Note*: in (b) lg denotes logarithm to the base 2.)

CHAPTER 6
PROGRAMS

It is not difficult to write a computer program that performs a simple, well-defined task. Our early experience with writing simple programs leads us to believe that computer programming is straightforward, and once we have written a hundred-line program in a couple of days, we expect to be able to write a thousand-line program in a couple of weeks. This belief is strengthened if we take the trouble to read a long program written by somebody else. If it is well written, it seems to be no more than a collection of simple modules strung together. Unfortunately the simplicity of large programs is deceptive; a large computer program is actually a very complex object. The complexity is hard to see because it lies in the organization of the modules of the program, not in the modules themselves.

The construction of a program can be divided into phases. Program construction is similar in many ways to algorithm design but it is more complicated because there are more issues to be considered. Specifications are more elaborate; input and output, which are of relatively minor importance in algorithm design, play a major role in program construction; and the final product is an executable program expressed in a programming language, with all the detail that this entails.

The first step in program construction is to determine the requirements. Presumably the proposed program is intended to solve a problem. The *requirements analysis* describes the criteria by which the program will be judged. A requirements analysis might reveal, for example, that a solution is only worthwhile if it can be obtained with an outlay of $50,000 or less. If the requirements analysis is done well, the next step, specifying the program, will be straightforward.

The *specification* is a precise statement of what the completed program will do. It is a contract between the author or authors of the program and the people who will eventually use the program.

When everybody has agreed to the specification, the authors *design* the program and then *implement* it. The distinction between design and implementation is not clear cut, but we may say that design consists of choosing an overall structure for the program and selecting appropriate algorithms and implementation consists of writing code in the chosen programming language.

When the program is complete, both its authors and its potential users will require some assurance that it is correct. This assurance may be provided either by *testing* the program or by *verifying* it. We test a program by providing it with carefully chosen input data called *test data*, executing it, and confirming that the results are in agreement with the specification. Testing is of limited value because it is impractical to test the program for anything but a minute fraction of the possible input data. Therefore the fact that a program passes all of its tests by no means guarantees that it will give the correct results for any input data. It is sometimes feasible, however, to demonstrate the correctness of a program by mathematical reasoning. This demonstration, which is called a *verification* of the program, may strengthen our confidence in the correctness of the program more than testing alone can do.

If the program does not work correctly, it must be altered until it does. The correction process is usually called *debugging* when the program is being modified to conform to its original specification, and *maintenance* later on when the original specification has been altered and the program is being revised to conform to the new specification. These two activities are essentially the same, although in practice maintenance tends to be a more systematic operation than debugging. Most large programs have a long lifetime, typically ten years or more. Studies of software projects show that maintenance of a program accounts for more than two-thirds of the total amount spent on the program. For example, if we spend $33,000 to create the first version of a compiler, we should expect to spend a further $67,000 on it before it becomes obsolete. It is therefore important to organize the earlier phases of program construction to minimize maintenance costs.

We have identified eight major steps in the construction of a program: requirements analysis, specification, design, implementation, testing, verification, debugging, and maintenance. In all but the largest projects, these steps tend to overlap. Nevertheless, they exist and are recognizable even in a small project that takes less than a day to complete.

In this chapter, we discuss specifications, describe a systematic method for design and implementation, and consider some aspects of testing, debugging, and maintenance. Finally we look at a technique of program verification and some of its implications.

6.1 SPECIFICATION

The first step in constructing a computer program, after the requirement for it has been established, is to decide what it is that the program is supposed to do. A precise description of what a program should do is called a *specification* of the program. A specification does not describe how a task is to be carried out and it may therefore consist of a description of the output that the program must produce for each possible value of the input. In engineering parlance, the specification treats the program as a "black box" defined solely by its interface with the outside world.

Specifications are often incomplete and ambiguous. Our first task is to examine the specification critically, looking for ambiguities, inconsistencies, omissions, and vagueness. It is pointless to start programming before we know what we are supposed to be doing. The following specification is rather simple but it is typical of the kind of specifications that programmers learn to expect.

Problem 6.1: SQUARE ROOTS

Write a program that reads a list of numbers and prints their square roots.

This specification is so simple that many programmers would start coding without further ado, but we will adopt a more patient attitude and look for some of the difficulties that we may encounter.

Pitfall 1: There is no mention in the specification of how the list of numbers is to be terminated. There are several possibilities: an end-of-file mark, an end-of-line, a special terminating character, a negative number, or zero. The program can easily deal with any of these situations but it is important that we know which to expect.

Pitfall 2: The range of values of the numbers in the list is not specified. Should the program reject negative numbers? What should it do with a number that is too large or too small to process accurately? The program should be able to handle negative numbers, even though negative numbers do not have real square roots, unless the specification states that none will occur in the input, which in this case it does not. The range of values that can be processed accurately is more likely to be determined by the computer on which the program will be run than by the programmer.

Pitfall 3:   The precision required is not specified. This is a common omission because the precision is usually determined by the computer and is outside the programmer's sphere of influence. One way of getting round this problem is to ask for a rather modest precision, such as five decimal places, and hope that the computer can provide it, but this is not very satisfactory.

Pitfall 4:   The specification does not describe the notation in which the numbers are to be expressed, either for input or for output. This may seem to be an unreasonable complaint because we expect numbers to be represented in decimal notation rather than binary or Roman notation, for instance. It does, however, have a practical side: engineers and scientists are accustomed to floating-point number representations, and if the program accepts 1000 as input, they would want it to accept the same number in different forms, such as 1E3 or .1E4.

Pitfall 5:   In the event that an error is discovered in the input data, what should the program do? Presumably an error message of some kind is required, but what should it say, and after reporting an error should the program give up or should it attempt to resume processing?

It is true that these objections are rather unfair when they are applied to such a simple example. They serve to demonstrate, however, that it is not easy to write precise specifications. The following specification of the same program overcomes some of these pitfalls.

Program Specification

Program Name: Square Roots

Function: Read a list of numbers and print their square roots.

Input: A file containing decimal numbers. Each number occupies one line, and the last line is followed by an end-of-file mark. A number consists of one or more digits; there may be a decimal point in the number but it must be preceded by a digit. There may be blanks both before and after a number.

Output: A file containing two items on each line. The first item is the number as read from the input file, with leading and trailing blanks removed, right justified in a field 20 columns wide; and the second item is either the square root of this number or an error message. The square root is printed as a fixed-point decimal number, right justified in a field 30 characters wide. The last line of the output file must be followed by an end-of-file mark.

Description: The program reads one line at a time from the input file and copies each line to the output file. If the number read conforms to the input specifications above, the program computes its square root and writes this value as a decimal string on the same line. The square root must be calculated with a precision of at least six significant decimal digits. The program terminates when it encounters the end of the input file.

Error Handling: If the number read does not conform to the input specification, the program writes one of the following messages immediately after the copy of the input lines:

- Illegal character 'X'
- Number too small (less than *minimum*)
- Number too large (greater than *maximum*)

In the first message, X is to be replaced by the offending character, which might be a plus sign, a minus sign, a second decimal point, a comma, or any other extraneous character. The value of *minimum* should be the smallest value that can be processed accurately by the program and the value of *maximum* should be the largest value that can be processed accurately by the program.

After processing an error, the program continues reading at the beginning of the next line of the input file. In all cases the output file will have the same number of lines as the input file.

If we wrote a program from these specifications, most of the code would be concerned with error checking. Tucked away somewhere, there would be a few statements that actually calculated the square root. This should not surprise us because it is not at all unusual for a program to consist largely of checks for valid input and carefully designed error messages for erroneous input. It is the presence of this code that makes the program into a robust and reliable tool that will be trusted by the people who use it.

Generalizing from this discussion, we see that a specification should include a precise description of the forms of input that must be handled by the program, a precise description of the results that must be produced by the program and their relationship to the input, and a precise description of the action that should be taken by the program in the event of an error in the input. Additional information concerning the particular problem will generally be required as well.

These are some of the things that must be included in a specification but it is also important to consider what should be left out. The specification describes what the program does and does not say anything about how it is to be done. It is useful to think of the specification as a very thorough user manual for the program, and in fact some software companies wisely insist that a user manual be written before programming starts.

Natural languages, such as English, are powerful tools, but they are not altogether suitable for writing specifications because they allow vagueness and ambiguity. As the preceding example demonstrates, efforts to be precise in English tend to lead to verbosity. Mathematicians recognized these defects long ago and invented formal languages that do not suffer from them, as we saw in Chapter 4. More recently, mathematically oriented computer scientists have attempted to design formal specification languages. Although a formal specification is harder to understand than a specification written in a natural language, its greater precision is undoubtedly worthwhile. Perhaps specifications should be written both formally and informally, with the proviso that a discrepancy is always resolved by reference to the formal version. Unfortunately there are currently three different notations for formal specifications (algebraic, logical, and denotational) with many dialects in each notation, and there is as yet no widespread agreement as to which notation is best.

In the meantime, there are many devices that we can use to clarify natural language specifications. Input can be described in terms of its syntax, either by a grammatical notation such as Backus–Naur form or by syntax diagrams. If the program enters various states during processing, state-transition diagrams may be useful. If there are complex interactions between the progress of the calculation and the input data, decision tables may be used for clarification.

6.2 DESIGN AND IMPLEMENTATION

We can think of a computer program at different levels of abstraction. At a high level of abstraction the program is represented by its specification which is a description of what the program does. At a low level the program is represented by a list of instructions in the language of the machine used to execute it. Both of these representations are descriptions of the program but they are so far apart that it is difficult to see how one can be derived from the other. We solve the problem of translating the specification into machine language by introducing descriptions at intermediate levels of abstraction.

One of the intermediate descriptions will be written in a high-level programming language. (The language used in this book is Pascal but the same arguments apply if another programming language is used.) This description is so important that it is usually called the *program*. It is important because it is the level at which the computer can take over the task of translating. Once we have written the program in a high-level language, we can use a compiler to create the machine language version.

In all but the simplest applications, there is still a wide gulf between the specification and the program. To some extent this gulf can be bridged by using the procedure mechanism of the programming language, but in general even this is inadequate. We therefore need a higher level language than the programming language, and we call such a language a programming development language, or *PDL*.

Fig. 6.1 is a diagram of the development process according to this model. The function of design is to translate the specification into a program in the PDL and the function of implementation is to translate from the PDL into the chosen programming language. Compilation, performed by the computer, is the final translation into machine language. Fig. 6.1 also shows that the designer may incorporate standard algorithms into the PDL program and that the compiler may incorporate library procedures, which are merely standard algorithms at a lower level of abstraction, into the machine language program.

Although Fig. 6.1 is accurate in a general way, it is a simplification of what actually happens. Each language used does not occupy a single level but rather occupies a range of levels. Thus we can think of a series of descriptions, each one providing more detail than the previous one.

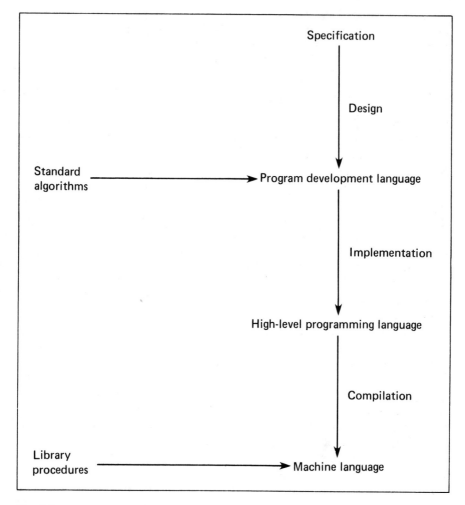

Fig. 6.1
Design and implementation.

Each level has a "how" and a "what" aspect: it describes "how" to perform the operations specified at a higher level of abstraction and "what" is to be done by using operations defined at a lower level of abstraction.

The following example may help to make these ideas more tangible. We consider one component of Problem 6.1: given a number x, greater than zero, we must find $\sqrt{x}$. At the specification level, we have:

$$\text{Specification:}\quad \text{Given } x > 0, \text{ calculate } \sqrt{x}. \qquad (6.2.1)$$

There is a standard algorithm for finding square roots and the next step is merely to mention it:

PDL 1:   Given $x > 0$, use the Newton–Raphson algorithm
           to find $\sqrt{x}$.   (6.2.2)

We can now recall, or look up, the Newton–Raphson algorithm and express it in PDL:

PDL 2: $y := 1$
           repeat

$$y := \frac{1}{2}(\frac{x}{y} + y)$$

           until $y^2 \simeq x$ (6.2.3)

The termination condition, $y^2 \simeq x$, is imprecise and must be improved. We will assume that six decimal digits are required, and accordingly we change $y^2 \simeq x$ to

$$|\frac{y^2}{x} - 1| < 0.000001$$

We have now completed the design and we can start on the implementation. Our program becomes, in Pascal:

var x, y : *real*;

begin

     $y := 1$;

     repeat

         $y := (x/y + y)/2$

         until $abs(sqr(y)/x - 1) < 0.000001$

end   (6.2.4)

In (6.2.1) through (6.2.4) the same task is described with increasing amounts of detail. The last description has sufficient detail for a Pascal compiler although in this form it is not a complete program.

In this example we can distinguish the design phase, which ends at (6.2.3), and the implementation phase, in which (6.2.3) is translated into (6.2.4). In more realistic cases the distinction cannot be made as clearly. We usually split the specification into several components and refine each of them separately. Some components require more refinement than others, and consequently one component may be coded in the target language while other components are still at an abstract level.

The method of moving from an abstract specification to a detailed program is called *top-down design* or *stepwise refinement*. It is not the only method of design but it is one of the most widely used and successful methods.

There are three important points to be made before we describe the PDL in more detail. The first is that stepwise refinement can be carried out with complete rigor. If each description is precise and each step in the translation from the specification to the program is correct in the sense that the meaning of the program is preserved, then the final program must do precisely what the specification says that it ought to do.

The second point is that it is not necessarily easy to recognize the best refinement to make at each stage. An inappropriate refinement made early on may lead to insoluble problems later in the development of the program. When this happens, we *backtrack* to the erroneous refinement and try another refinement. Backtracking impedes progress and is therefore undesirable. Experienced programmers think about more than one level at a time—while they are refining a particular component they are considering the consequences of the refinement and they can thereby avoid making too many wrong decisions. This ability is best acquired by experience.

Finally, the design and implementation of a computer program involve many decisions. We must decide how each part of the program must be split into smaller parts, how these parts relate to one another, and how data structures will be represented in the computer. It is a good idea to defer these decisions for as long as possible. The longer we can postpone making a decision, the more we will know when we come to make it, and the smaller is the probability that we will have to go back and change it later.

6.3 A PROGRAM DEVELOPMENT LANGUAGE

A program development language is a personal tool. Languages such as Pascal and FORTRAN are standardized in order that a program written in one of them can be read by people other than the author, and so that it can be executed on different computer systems. A program written in a PDL is a step in the development of the final program and it is generally read only by its author or perhaps by a small group of people collaborating in its design. In this section, we describe an informal PDL that is suitable for the development of Pascal programs and that is used in subsequent chapters of this book. You should devise your own PDL, perhaps using this one as a guide.

The principle components of the PDL are actions, data, and layout. An *action* specifies that something is to be done, *data* denote objects with values, and *layout* is used to indicate the relationship between different parts of the program. Any part of a PDL program may be written in English, or Pascal, or mathematical notation, or a combination of these. The important point is that detail should not be introduced until it is necessary. For example, we might write this in the PDL:

$$\text{Set all components of } A \text{ to zero} \qquad (6.3.1)$$

The following version of this action contains more information:

$$A[i] := 0, i = 1, 2, \ldots, N \qquad (6.3.2)$$

It is a simple step from this version to the Pascal statement:

$$\textbf{for } i := 1 \textbf{ to } N \textbf{ do } A[i] := 0 \qquad (6.3.3)$$

The idea is to write in English phrases and sentences which are clear and unambiguous and yet which can be written without attending to all the details required by a programming language. In writing (6.3.1), for instance, we do not need to worry about the exact size of A, or whether A is an array or a list or some other kind of structure, or the best kind of loop to use to set its components to zero. In writing (6.3.3), on the other hand, we must have already decided that A is an array with subscripts $1, 2, \ldots, N$; we must have already declared a variable i of the appropriate type; and we are concerned with the syntax of the Pascal **for** statement.

Data

We use simple variables in the PDL just as we use them in Pascal. An integer, real, or boolean variable has a name, may be assigned a value, and may be used in expressions. Whether or not you declare variables in the PDL is a matter of choice; declarations are not necessary but they may be useful if there are many variables or if you are developing a large program over an extended period of time. Structured variables such as arrays and records may also be introduced freely; it is a good idea to write down declarations for structured variables. When you are writing array components in the PDL, it is quicker to use subscript notation, as in A_{ij}, than it is to use the Pascal notation, $A[i,j]$.

Decisions about the representation of more elaborate data objects should be deferred for as long as possible. In the PDL we can refer to objects such as lists, sets, trees, graphs, and tables. We do not choose a representation in Pascal for these objects until we cannot proceed further without doing so.

Expressions

An *expression* represents a value. We can write expressions in the PDL that look like Pascal expressions, such as:

- $x + y$
- 'Pascal'
- $n > 0$

We are not, however, confined to Pascal syntax, and we can also write expressions such as these:

- $e^{x^2 + y^2}$
- $\sum_{i=0}^{n} s_i^2$
- a prime number greater than P_0
- a solution has been found
- there is space in the symbol table

These examples demonstrate that an expression in the PDL need not correspond to a single expression in the Pascal program. Each of the preceding expressions can be evaluated, assuming that it appears in an appropriate context, but the evaluation might require several Pascal statements. We must, however, be careful to ensure that an expression does indeed possess a unique value or we will encounter difficulties later. For example, unless we have good reason to believe that refinement is feasible, we should not write expressions such as:

- x such that $f(x) = 0$
- the matching entry in the table
- a, b, c, d such that $a^2 + b^2 + c^2 + d^2 = N$

Simple Statements

A statement in the PDL describes an action. A *simple statement* is a statement that has no structure of its own although it may describe a complex action. These are examples of simple statements:

- initialize arrays
- sort employees by salary

In many cases the effect of an action is to assign a value to a variable. We use the assignment operator := of Pascal in an *assignment statement* to denote these actions. The general form of an assignment statement is:

$$variable := expression$$

Assignment statements in the PDL are more general than Pascal assignment statements. We can write, for example:

$$prime\ list := \text{first 100 prime numbers}$$

Another important class of statements are those which describe input and output actions. In the PDL, we assume that anything can be read or written and we defer the details of syntax until later. Thus we might write:

- print all solutions
- read *name*, *address*, and *social security number*

Structured Statements

Refinement consists of breaking down complex actions into groups of simpler actions that have the same effect. A group of simple actions is represented by a *structured statement*. The simplest form of structured statement is the *sequence*, which consists of several simple statements that are to be executed one at a time in the order in which they are written. At a late stage in the development of a program we might, for example, refine the simple statement

$$\text{exchange } x \text{ and } y$$

into the sequence

$$t := x$$
$$x := y$$
$$y := t$$

The other forms of structured statement describe *decisions*, in which one of several actions is chosen according to the value of some data, and *repetition*, in which the same action is applied either to different items of data or to data whose value is changing. We borrow control statements from Pascal whenever they are appropriate because in this way we can simplify subsequent refinements. The **if** and **case** statements of Pascal provide a suitable framework for many decisions but it is sometimes useful to use generalized versions of them in the PDL, as this example shows:

case

$$b^2 < 4ac : \text{two complex roots}$$
$$b^2 = 4ac : \text{repeated real roots}$$
$$b^2 > 4ac : \text{two real roots}$$

In a similar way we can use the **while, repeat,** and **for** constructions of Pascal to describe repetition. These constructions are also extended when necessary to obtain clarity and simplicity. For example, we could write in the PDL:

for each vertex v in G do
print edges emanating from v

When we refine this statement, we will have to decide how to traverse the graph G. We will not necessarily use a **for** statement in the Pascal program to do this but we use it in the PDL because it is simple to write, easy to understand, and makes a minimum of unnecessary assumptions about the representation of the graph.

Pascal uses punctuation marks such as **begin, end,** and ";" to define the structure of the program. In the PDL, which is not destined for compilation, these marks are unnecessary. Note, for instance, that semicolons and the final **end** are omitted from the case statement above. Whether you include punctuation or not in your PDL programs is a matter of personal taste.

In this book we use one further convention that helps to clarify the distinction between an algorithm and a program. Algorithms are written in Roman type with identifiers italicized. Programs are written with identifiers italicized and keywords in boldface type.

Refinement

A refinement step consists of taking one statement of the PDL program and transforming it into a collection of simpler statements. Eventually the PDL statements are simple enough to be translated into Pascal. When all of the PDL has been translated into Pascal, the program is complete. Interleaved with the refinement steps we will be making other decisions, such as choosing appropriate representations for data.

The notation that we use for a refinement step is as follows:

statement to be refined ⟶
refined version

The long arrow ⟶ is called the *refinement operator*. Here are two simple examples of refinement.

exchange x and y ⟶
$t := x$
$x := y$
$y := t$

print list ⟶
while list not exhausted do
print one item
advance to next item

We illustrate refinement with the aid of a curious property of the positive integers. We can construct sequences of integers as follows: start with any integer greater than 1, called the *seed*; if it is odd, multiply it by 3 and add 1; if it is even, divide it by two; repeat this operation on the resulting number until the answer is 1. Thus the last number of a sequence is always 1 but the length of the sequence depends in a rather complicated way on the value of the seed. Here are the sequences obtained with seeds 3 and 13:

3 10 5 16 8 4 2 1
13 40 20 10 5 16 8 4 2 1

The problem that we will solve with the aid of a computer program follows.

Problem 6.2: MULTIPLY BY 3 AND ADD 1

What is the smallest seed for which the sequence just defined has more than 100 terms?

We can express the solution to this problem in a single PDL statement:

Print smallest *seed* for which *length* > 100

The obvious way to find this value is to start with a small value of *seed* and to increase it until the condition is satisfied. This leads to our first refinement step:

print smallest *seed* for which *length* > 100 ⟶
seed := 1

```
repeat
  seed := seed + 1
  compute length
until length > 100
print seed
```

The next step is to refine *compute length*. We must initialize the values of the current term of the sequence and the length of the sequence and then calculate terms until the sequence terminates.

```
compute length ⟶
  term := seed
  length := 1
  while sequence not terminated do
    compute next term
    length := length + 1
```

We can now refine the termination condition *sequence not terminated* and the statement *compute next term*; both refinements follow easily from the definition of the sequence.

```
sequence not terminated ⟶
  term ≠ 1

compute next term ⟶
  if term is odd
    then term := 3 * term + 1
    else term := term div 2
```

Our PDL program now has the following form:

```
seed := 1
repeat
  seed := seed + 1
  term := seed
  length := 1
  while term ≠ 1 do
    if term is odd
      then term := 3 * term + 1
      else term := term div 2
    length := length + 1
until length > 100
print seed
```

We can now write a Pascal program from the PDL program.

```pascal
program sequence (output);
  const
    limit = 100;
  var
    seed, term, length : integer;
  begin
    seed := 1;
    repeat
      seed := seed + 1;
      term := seed;
      length := 1;
      while term ≠ 1 do
        begin
          if odd(term)
            then term := 3 * term + 1
            else term := term div 2;
          length := length + 1
        end
    until length > limit;
    writeln(seed)
  end.
```

There are two aspects of this development that you should note. First, this is neither a useful nor a well-written program. It reads no input data and can therefore perform only one computation. At the very least, the value of *limit* could be read rather than being incorporated into the program as a constant. This is a consequence of the limited goals that we set; the object of the exercise was to demonstrate refinement and the program does solve the stated problem. In subsequent chapters we start with more interesting specifications and develop better programs.

The second aspect is more important. The final transformation from PDL to Pascal is very easy. In fact, all we had to do was insert a program heading, some declarations, and some punctuation. There are two reasons for this. The first is that our PDL is designed with Pascal-like features to ease the transition from PDL programs to Pascal programs. The second and deeper reason is that Pascal was itself designed to simplify the translation from abstract algorithm to executable program.

6.4 TESTING, DEBUGGING, AND MAINTENANCE

It is unreasonable to expect that a computer program will contain no errors even if we make careful use of a systematic refinement strategy such as the one just discussed. It follows that as soon as we have finished writing the program, we must try to find out what is wrong with it.

Testing consists of running the program with data for which the expected results are known. The results generated by the program are compared with the results required by the specification, and any discrepancy is an indication of an error in the program.

Debugging consists of locating the error that caused the failure and correcting it. After we have removed a bug, we run the program with the test data set again and check not only that we have eliminated the original discrepancy but also that we have not introduced any new discrepancies.

During all the phases of program construction we have discussed, the program is used only by the person or the group of people directly concerned with its production. When the program has passed all of its tests, it is released to the community of people who will use it. The size of this community depends on many factors; it may be as few as two or three people for a specialized laboratory project or it may be many thousands of people if the program is a utility such as a text editor or a compiler. It is at this time that the program enters its *maintenance* phase. Many people who know no more about the program than what they can find in the user manual are now using it, perhaps in ways not anticipated by the original designers, and if they find faults they complain. The faults they find are of two kinds. First, they may find bugs which were not detected during the testing phase. Second, they may find that the program does not do what they wanted it to do although it behaves correctly according to its specification. Errors of the first kind are treated as bugs; the program is altered and tested until it behaves correctly.

Errors of the second kind indicate that the original specification was at fault. The remedy is to decide whether or not the user is justified in asking for a change, and, if so, revising the specification and then the program accordingly. Thus maintenance involves both debugging and enhancing the original program.

Testing

The completed program is expected to perform according to its specification. In testing it we attempt to discover discrepancies between the specification of the program and its actual performance.

Ideally we would like to ascertain that the output of the program is correct for every possible value of the input, however this is impossible for any nontrivial program. The simplest imaginable program, if it is to be of any use whatsoever, must read at least one number. A large computer can represent perhaps 10^{10} different numbers. Even if we could afford to wait for 10^{10} lines of output to be printed, who would have the patience to read them? Perhaps another computer could read them, but how are we to test its program?

Accordingly, the first axiom of testing is that we can only test the program with an extremely small proportion of the input data that it can accept. The problem of testing is therefore one of deciding how to select test data and how to know when sufficient testing has been done.

There are no general solutions to these problems; all we can do is suggest some basic rules for conducting program tests.

1. The acceptance criteria for a program should be established *before* the program is written. It is a good idea to construct a set of test data in parallel with the specification.

2. The test data should be written by people other than those who are writing the program if the project is large enough to make this feasible. When we are writing test data for our own programs we instinctively avoid tests that are likely to make the program fail; this is human nature.

3. A specification usually partitions the input data into classes. For example, if a program reads a number, that number may be treated differently according to whether its value is positive, negative, or zero; if a program processes commands, there is a class of possible input data for each command. There should be at least one test for each class. This rule is often difficult to apply in practice because the number of possibilities may be too large. If, for example, a program accepts ten different commands, each with three parameters, and there are ten kinds of parameter, we would have to construct 10,000 tests. In these circumstances we must use discretion and judgment: 40 tests, one for each command and one for each kind of parameter, might suffice.

4. It is important to test *boundary conditions*. If a program reads data from a file, it should be tested with an empty file. If it is supposed to perform one kind of transaction for amounts less than $100 and another kind of transaction for amounts equal to or greater than $100, it should be tested at $100 and perhaps at $99 and $101 as well. Numerical programs should be tested with very large and very small numbers and data processing programs should be tested with

names, addresses, and other character data to the full, specified field widths.

5. It is not sufficient to test the program with valid data. We must also construct *invalid* test data in order to ensure that the program generates intelligible error messages. If the specification defines the error messages that the program is supposed to issue, there should be at least one test corresponding to each error message.

6. Quantities that are too large or too small to be processed correctly constitute an important class of invalid data. If a program is supposed to be able to sort a maximum of 1000 items, one test should require it to sort 1500 items. There are four possible responses to this test; in order of decreasing desirability, they are:

    a) the program reports "too many items" and stops;
    b) the program correctly sorts all 1500 items and stops;
    c) the program aborts without an error message;
    d) the program runs without complaining but sorts incorrectly.

7. It may be possible to construct some useful tests by examining the code after the program has been written. For example, the programmer might have decided to use two different algorithms, one for small values and the other for large values. We could devise tests for both algorithms from the code although we could not have done so from the specification.

    This form of testing is unreliable because testing whether the program does what we expect it to do is not the same as testing whether it does what it is supposed to do. The basic tests should always be designed from the specification; if a subsequent examination reveals the need for additional tests, they may be added to the original set of tests.

We have already seen that testing can never be complete, and so the question that arises is: when do we stop testing? The answer is that we stop testing when we are confident that the program is acceptable to its intended users. This does not mean that it is free of errors, for if it is a program of reasonable size, that is extremely unlikely. It means that the error rate is low, that the errors that do occur do not have serious consequences, and that the user will not abandon the program because of the errors. There is a certain amount of arbitrariness in this criterion and judgment and experience are needed to apply it effectively. Most people will use a compiler even though it is known to produce incorrect object code occasionally. Very few people will trust a text editor with known faults because the danger of losing valuable data is too serious. There is an increasing number of situations in which no error is tolerable and yet these seem to be the situations in which reliable testing is hardest to accomplish.

Top-Down Testing

In addition to the kind of testing just described, which we may call *acceptance testing*, a wise programmer will test the program as it is being developed, a kind of testing that we may call *development testing*. If we use top-down design, then at any stage of the development we have a program that is complete but not executable because some of the actions are not yet refined to the level at which they can be coded. An incomplete program in this form can be tested by writing dummy statements in place of actions that have not yet been coded. These statements simulate the effect of the action in as simple a fashion as possible. This technique is called *top-down testing*. The advantage of using it is that early decisions made in the development of the program may be tested as they are made rather than when the program is complete and the reasoning that led to these decisions may have been forgotten.

Debugging

Debugging a program is an excellent exercise for our problem-solving skills. We have a program that produces incorrect results, or perhaps aborts; we know what the program should do; and all the information that we need for finding the error is available. Almost all of the slogans of Chapter 5 are applicable.

The first rule of debugging is to *use all of the available information*. If the program runs to completion but produces incorrect results, then these results are the only information available. It is often possible to diagnose an error simply by examining the results carefully. If we do find a bug by this method, we should determine whether this bug accounts for all the errors in the output or only for some of them.

If the program aborts, the amount and usefulness of the available information depends on the system we are using. We need to know which statement of the program caused the error and the values of the variables at the time of the error. If the error occurred in a procedure, we also need to know from where the procedure was called. Most systems provide this information, but the amount of decoding that will be necessary depends on the system. Early systems merely dumped the contents of memory in some unreadable form, usually octal or hexa-decimal numbers. Such behavior is no longer acceptable. A minimal requirement for high-level language debugging is a report that refers to each variable by its name in the program and gives its value. In addition to helping us locate the bug, the diagnostic printout provides us with a useful opportunity to check the values of all variables: this may reveal other problems which have not yet shown up as bugs.

The second rule of debugging is to *plan test runs*. One run of a program may reveal a bug without providing us with enough information to make the necessary corrections. Altering, recompiling, and re-running the program wastes valuable time—both our own time and machine time. If we think carefully about the effects and possible causes of the bug, we may be able to devise test data which will help us to localize it without recompilation. This is in the spirit of scientific enquiry: formulate a hypothesis about the bug and then devise experiments to test the hypothesis. In this way, we can create more information to help us find the bug.

When we have obtained the information, we can make use of it. The first step is to *localize the bug*, that is, to find out where it is in the program. This is sometimes difficult because it is possible for a fault in one part of the program to cause an error in another part. This is one reason why we should check the values of all variables whenever we have an opportunity to do so, not just the values that seem pertinent to the bug. If the bug cannot be localized easily, we can insert print statements into the program to find out what is going on. For example, if a variable has an incorrect value at the end of the run, we can establish when it first received that value by printing out its value at carefully chosen points in the program.

Frequently we find a small section of the program that looks correct but we strongly suspect that it contains the error. In this case it is best to execute the code by hand, using pencil and paper and being careful to do exactly what the computer would do, not what we think it ought to do.

One of the difficulties of debugging is that we tend to see what we expect to see rather than what is actually there. There are various ways to minimize the effects of this unfortunate tendency. One is to *ignore comments while debugging*. Comments generally are statements about what the program is supposed to do, not what it actually does. When we read comments we are seduced into believing that the program does what the comment claims, and we may miss seeing the bug for the same reason that the author of the program failed to see it. This argument applies even, perhaps especially, when the author and the debugger are the same person.

Debugging is much easier if we have friends to help us. When we are beginners, we are apt to be ashamed of the bugs in our programs and humiliated if someone else has to find them for us. A more enlightened attitude, found among many experienced programmers, is to acknowledge that our friends do not share our prejudices about the program and therefore can look at it more objectively than we can ourselves. Occasionally we can find a bug by explaining the program to someone else. This approach is not always successful, however, because we may confuse the listener with our erroneous concepts. It is better to let the other person attempt to understand the program, asking us for assistance only when necessary. Teams of programmers who cooperate in this way are generally more successful than teams composed of prima donnas who refuse to accept that somebody else could improve their programs.

Finally, it is worth noting that some programming languages are particularly prone to certain kinds of bug. In Pascal, for example, if we omit the final } of a comment, the compiler will skip over code until the end of the next comment, usually without issuing a diagnostic message. This causes very obscure errors because a section of code is not compiled and yet no warning is given of this fact. It is not surprising that different commenting conventions have been adopted in languages descended from Pascal. For example, in Ada, a comment begins with -- and extends to the end of the line.

Another problem in languages descended from Algol is the "dangling else." The following statement has *no effect* if P is *false*:

> if *P* then if *Q* then *S*
> else *T*

P and *Q* are boolean expressions. *S* and *T* are statements. The solution to this problem is to choose a sensible convention for layout and to follow it closely (or use a prettyprinter):

> if *P*
> then
>   if *Q*
>   then *S*
>   else *T*

Bug Prevention

It is better to prevent bugs from occurring in the first place than it is to cure them. The following hints may help you to write programs with fewer bugs.

1. Design programs from the top down, not from the bottom up.

2. Divide your programs into short procedures no more than a page or two long. Each procedure should perform a simple, well-defined task, and have a simple interface to other sections of the program.

3. Use appropriate control structures. In Pascal, **while** is more useful than **repeat**, and **case** statements are easier to understand than deeply nested **if** statements.

4. Use mnemonic variable names.

5. Define symbolic constants rather than using "magic numbers" in the code.

6.5 VERIFICATION

The fact that we cannot test programs completely is disturbing to many people. A similar concern was evidently felt by Euclid. Euclid had discovered or was aware of many empirical facts about geometry. For example, he knew that the sum of the interior angles of a triangle is 180° and that if two sides of a triangle are equal, so are two of the interior angles. These properties of triangles are easily tested, but Euclid was not satisfied with testing and so he developed the concept of *proof*. He showed that if we assume the truth of certain "self-evident" statements and the validity of certain rules of inference, we can demonstrate the truth of propositions such as these for *all* triangles without recourse to measurement. Euclid's *Elements* have been used to instruct people in mathematical techniques for more than 2000 years; we need no further testimony to their importance in mathematics.

Testing a program with different sets of data is like drawing triangles and measuring their interior angles. No matter how patient we are, we can never be certain that there are no data for which the program fails. It would be more satisfying to prove that the program was correct without having to test it at all. Proving that a program is correct is called *verifying* the program.

Before we can verify programs we must make certain concepts precise. Since we are attempting to prove that the performance of the program is in accordance with its specification, we require a precise specification, and hence a method of writing precise specifications. We also require a description of the effect of each statement in the programming language and of the effect of combining statements in various ways. It is also important, although less obvious, that we have a clear idea of what we mean by *correct*.

The proof of a program is usually longer, and often harder to understand, than the text of the program itself. If the proof is constructed by a person, there is no more reason to believe that the proof is free of errors than there is to believe that the program is free of bugs. Consequently the goal of much of the research in program verification is to construct automatic verifiers, which are programs capable of verifying other programs. A verifier can be used to verify both complete programs and partial programs and consequently it can be used as a debugging tool during program development.

Although it is unlikely that we will ever be expected to provide complete proofs of nontrivial programs, an understanding of proof techniques is useful because of the insight it provides into program construction. A detailed treatment of verification is beyond the scope of this book, and so we conclude this section with an outline of one of the several verification techniques currently in use.

When a program is executed by a machine, each statement of the program changes the state of the machine. When the program is started, the machine is in an initial state; when the program terminates, the machine is in a final state. The specification defines which final statements are acceptable for each initial state; the function of the proof is to verify that the program is consistent with the specification.

A machine state is represented by an *assertion* about the variables of the program. Assertions are made in the language of the propositional calculus introduced in Chapter 4. The following are assertions about the variables a and b:

$$a = 0 \, \wedge \, b = 0$$
$$a < b$$
$$0 \le a \le 10$$

An assertion does not define a state completely; it specifies only what we need to know about a state. If we do not know anything about a state at all, the appropriate assertion is simply *true* because this assertion is true regardless of the state of the machine.

If P and Q are assertions and S is a statement or a group of statements, then

$$\{P\}S \, \{Q\}$$

means:

If P is true and S is executed, then if S terminates, Q is true.

P is called the *precondition* of S, and Q is called the *postcondition* of S.

The notation

$$P\{S\}Q$$

is also used, and has certain advantages, but we use the first notation because it allows us to write assertions as comments in a Pascal program.

If S is a single statement, there is an *axiom* relating P and Q. For example, the axiom for the assignment statement is:

$$\{P_e^v\}v := e\ \{P\}$$

The assertion P_e^v is the assertion P with all occurrences* of v replaced by e. We can write, for example:

$$\{x = 1\}\ y := x + 1\ \{y = 2\}$$

This follows because if we replace y by $x + 1$ in the assertion $y = 2$ we obtain $x + 1 = 2$, which we can simplify to $x = 1$. Note that the rule seems to work backwards: we deduce the precondition from the postcondition. This reflects the fact that the postcondition Q is something that we want to establish, and by computing the precondition P we are determining conditions under which the statement S will give us the required result Q. Here are some further examples of assignment statements.

$$\{x = 2\}\ y := x^2\ \{y = 4\}$$
$$\{y > x\}\ y := y - x\ \{y > 0\}$$

Now consider a sequence of two statements, S_1 and S_2. To prove the assertion

$$\{P\}\ S_1 ; S_2\ \{R\}$$

we must prove the two assertions

$$\{P\}\ S_1\ \{Q\} \quad \text{and} \quad \{Q\}\ S_2\ \{R\}$$

for a suitable assertion Q. This rule is expressed as follows:

$$\frac{\{P\}\ S_1\ \{Q\},\ \{Q\}\ S_2\ \{R\}}{\{P\}\ S_1\ ; S_2\ \{R\}}$$

In general, an expression of the form

$$\frac{P_1, P_2, ..., P_n}{P}$$

---

*Actually, P_e^v is the assertion P with all *free* occurrences of v replaced by e. The concept of free and bound variables is required for a detailed treatment of axiomatic semantics, but not for this discussion.

means that we can infer the truth of P from the truth of $P_1, P_2,...,$ and P_n. This means that in practice we first prove $P_1, P_2, ...,$ and P_n, and then we can deduce P.

As a simple example, consider the following statements:

$$u: = x - 1;$$
$$v: = x^2;$$
$$w: = u * v$$

We can prove the postcondition $w = x^3 - x^2$. First we substitute $u * v$ for w, giving the precondition of the last statement:

$$\{u * v = x^3 - x^2\}$$
$$w := u * v$$
$$\{w = x^3 - x^2\}$$

Next we substitute x^2 for v, giving:

$$\{u * x^2 = x^3 - x^2\}$$
$$v := x^2;$$
$$\{u * v = x^3 - x^2\}$$
$$w := u * v$$
$$\{w = x^3 - x^2\}$$

Finally, we substitute $x - 1$ for u to obtain the precondition for the first statement. This gives us the assertion

$$(x - 1) * x^2 = x^3 - x^2$$

which is true for all values of x. Thus we have, after simplification:

$$\{true\}$$
$$u := x - 1;$$
$$\{u = x - 1\}$$
$$v := x^2;$$
$$\{u = x - 1 \wedge v = x^2\}$$
$$w := u * v$$
$$\{w = x^3 - x^2\}$$

The precondition *true* indicates that the postcondition $w = x^3 - x^2$ is true for all values of x. We can do more than this. Suppose, for instance, that we want to know how to ensure that $w > 0$. Making the same substitutions as before, we obtain:

$$\{(x - 1) * x^2 > 0\}$$
$$u := x - 1;$$
$$\{u * x^2 > 0\}$$

$$v := x^2;$$
$$\{u * v > 0\}$$
$$w := u * v$$
$$\{w > 0\}$$

The precondition can be simplified. Since $x^2 \geq 0$, we must have $x - 1 > 0$, or $x > 1$. Thus we have established that $w > 0$ if and only if $x > 1$.

In addition to the proof rule for assignment statements and sequences, there are proof rules for the structured statements of Pascal. For example, the proof rule for the if statement is:

$$\frac{\{P \wedge B\} \, S_1 \, \{Q\}, \{P \wedge \sim B\} \, S_2 \, \{Q\}}{\{P\} \text{ if } B \text{ then } S_1 \text{ else } S_2 \, \{Q\}}$$

provided that B has no side effects. Using these rules, we can verify the following statement:

    $\{true\}$
    if $x \geq 0$
      then $y := x$
      else $y := -x$
    $\{y = |x|\}$

in which $|x|$ denotes the absolute value of x. Using the proof rules for the if statement, we must prove.

$$\{x \geq 0\} \, y := x \, \{y = |x|\}$$

and

$$\{\sim(x \geq 0)\} \, y := -x \, \{y = |x|\}$$

We know, by the rule for assignment statements, that

$$\{x = |x|\} \, y := -x \, \{y = |x|\}$$

and

$$\{-x = |x|\} \, y := -x \, \{y = |x|\}$$

Since $x \geq 0$ is equivalent to $x = |x|$ and $x < 0$ is equivalent to $-x = |x|$, the result follows.

Loops are harder to verify. We will consider the simplest form of loop, using the **while** statement of Pascal. The proof rule for the **while** statement is

$$\frac{\{P \wedge B\} \, S \, \{P\}}{\{P\} \text{ while } B \text{ do } S \, \{P \wedge \sim B\}}$$

The assertion P is called an *invariant* of the loop. The rule shows that the function of a loop is to *maintain* the truth of an assertion P, terminating the iteration when another assertion, B, becomes false. We use this proof rule in the verification of the following program.

$$m := 0;$$
$$f := 1;$$
$$\textbf{while } m \neq n \textbf{ do}$$
$$\quad \textbf{begin}$$
$$\quad\quad m := m + 1;$$
$$\quad\quad f := f * m$$
$$\quad \textbf{end}$$
$$\{f = n!\}$$

The sequence of values taken by f is $1, 1, 2, 6, 24, \ldots$, if n is large enough. This suggests that $f = m!$ is a suitable postcondition for the assignment $f := f * m$. By substitution:

$$\{f * (m + 1) = (m + 1)!\}$$
$$m := m + 1;$$
$$\{f * m = m!\}$$
$$f := f * m$$
$$\{f = m!\}$$

If $f * (m + 1) = (m + 1)!$, then

$$f = \frac{(m + 1)!}{m + 1}$$
$$= m!$$

and so $f = m!$ is the invariant P that we are seeking. We also note that $0! = 1$ and so the initialization statements establish the truth of the invariant. Consequently we have:

$$m := 0;$$
$$f := 1;$$
$$\textbf{while } m \neq n \textbf{ do}$$
$$\quad \textbf{begin}$$
$$\quad\quad \{f = m!\}$$
$$\quad\quad m := m + 1;$$
$$\quad\quad f := f * m$$
$$\quad \textbf{end}$$
$$\{f = m! \; \wedge \; \sim (m \neq n)\}$$

From the postcondition we can deduce that $m = n$ and hence that $f = n!$, as required.

If the initial value of n is negative, on entry to the **while** statement m is greater than n, and within the body of the loop m is incremented. Thus the postcondition $m = n$ is never achieved and the program does not terminate. The proof method that we are using can establish only *partial correctness*. We can prove that if the program terminates, the result is correct. The proof of termination must be provided separately. In this example, the precondition $n \geq 0$ is necessary for the proof of termination.

We can use these methods to establish the correctness of simple programs. This is a useful exercise because the need to prove that the program is correct may force us to find a simple way of writing it. It is very difficult to verify large programs such as compilers and operating systems. The difficulty lies partly in specifying such programs in a formal way and partly in proving the intermediate assertions. Verification will not become standard practice until powerful interactive verifiers become available for widely used languages.

SUMMARY

When we have obtained a precise specification, we have achieved several of the problem solver's goals. We have *stated the problem clearly*, *understood it*, and *made implicit rules and data explicit*. The keys to successful program development by stepwise refinement are: defer decisions whenever possible; do not attempt to do very much in one step; and make sure that each refinement does exactly what it is supposed to do.

The desired end product of all this work is a good program. There follow some of the requirements of a good program.

A good program is correct. Program X may be smaller, faster, more elegant, or better written than program Y, but if X is incorrect and Y is correct, then X is the inferior program of the two. Unfortunately, we all have to work with incorrect programs, and so we cannot say that an incorrect program is useless. Many of us use incorrect programs every day: most compilers, operating systems, and editors have a few bugs. Either we learn to avoid the bugs or they are so obscure that they rarely have any effect. But this is not an alibi; when we are creating software, our first principle must be to ensure that it is correct.

A good program is complete. A good program must do everything that its specification requires it to do. Strictly, of course, correctness implies completeness. Nonetheless, completeness is worth mentioning because it is an important component of correctness.

A good program is adaptable. Surveys have shown that programs have long lives. Even though many programmers prefer to start from the beginning rather than modify another person's work, economics dictate that programmers spend more time changing old programs than they do writing new programs. Consequently, we must write programs that can be adapted to new circumstances.

A good program is extensible. Extensibility is related to adaptability. The difference is simply that a program is adapted to do something else, but it is extended to do something more.

A good program is intelligible. The only conceivable virtue of obscure code is efficiency, and usually it is better to be clear than to be efficient. If efficiency is really a problem, find a better algorithm.

FURTHER READING

The existence of a "software crisis" was formally admitted in 1968. Since that time, many people have written about program construction. The books and articles cited here represent only a small fraction of this work.

Principles of Software Engineering and Design, by Zelkowitz, Shaw, and Gannon, describes techniques for program development and provides examples of both short and long programs in PL/I. *Software Tools*, and *Software Tools in Pascal*, by Kernighan and Plauger, illustrate the application of top-down design in a pragmatic and instructive way. The classic, *Structured Programming*, by Dahl, Dijkstra, and Hoare, clearly outlines the motivation underlying more recent work. Alagic and Arbib explain the verification of Pascal programs in detail in *The Design of Well-Structured and Correct Programs*.

Wirth has written two seminal papers on structured programming: "Program Development by Stepwise Refinement," and "On the Composition of Well-Structured Programs." Ledgard, in his paper, "The Case for Structured Programming," stresses the importance of rigor in program development.

"The Pascal Validation Suite," by Wichmann and Sale, is a collection of some 300 programs designed to test Pascal compilers. This suite should be studied as an example of carefully constructed test data and of the limitations of testing.

Floyd, in "Assigning Meanings to Programs," and Hoare, in "An Axiomatic Basis for Computer Programming," introduced the concept of formal program verification.

Formal specification techniques are surveyed by Marcotty, Ledgard, and Bochman in "A Sampler of Formal Definitions." *Abstract Software Specifications*, edited by Bjørner, contains several interesting, though advanced, papers on specification techniques.

EXERCISES

6.1 Develop a precise specification, choose or design an algorithm, and implement and test a program from each of the following outlines. You should attempt to produce a simple and readable program with no errors (except perhaps keying errors). If there are errors in your program, identify the stage (specification, design, or implementation) at which they first appeared.

a) Determine whether or not a given number is prime.

b) Find the GCD of an arbitrary number of given integers.

c) Balance a bank statement.

d) Count the words in a text.

6.2 Dijkstra has proposed the following control structures:

$$\textbf{if } B_1 \rightarrow S_1 \ \square \ B_2 \rightarrow S_2 \ \square \ldots \square \ B_n \rightarrow S_n \textbf{ fi} \tag{1}$$

and

$$\textbf{do } B_1 \rightarrow S_1 \ \square \ B_2 \rightarrow S_2 \ \square \ldots \square \ B_n \rightarrow S_n \textbf{ od} \tag{2}$$

In each command the B_i are boolean expressions called *guards* and the S_i are *commands*. An S_i may be an **if** or **do** command. (1) is executed as follows: if no guards are true, the program is aborted; if exactly one guard B_i is true, the corresponding command S_i is executed and the **if** command terminates; if more than one guard is true, a command with a true guard is chosen arbitrarily and executed and the **if** command terminates. (2) is executed as follows: if no guard is true, the command terminates; if one guard B_i is true, the corresponding command S_i is executed and the entire **do** command is repeated; if more than one guard is true, a command with a true guard is chosen arbitrarily and executed and the entire **do** command is repeated. For example, we can use the following program to find the GCD of two positive integers m and n:

$$\textbf{do } m \neq n \rightarrow$$
$$\quad \textbf{if } m > n \rightarrow m := m - n$$
$$\quad \square \ m < n \rightarrow n := n - m$$

   fi
od;
print m

We can write the same program more simply in the following way:

do $m > n \to m := m - n$
□ $m < n \to n := n - m$
od;
print m

Design some simple programs using Dijkstra's **if** and **do** commands instead of the conventional **if, case, while,** and **repeat** statements. You will sometimes need a command that does nothing, to prevent **if** commands aborting. (Dijkstra calls this command *skip*.)

CHAPTER 7
SIMPLE EXAMPLES

This chapter illustrates the ideas developed in the previous two chapters by describing in detail the solutions of some simple programming problems. The problems involve either simple calculations or character manipulation and our concern is with the problem solving process rather than with the eventual solution.

The discussion of each problem is in four parts. The first part deals with the statement, or specification, of the problem. Next we discuss the design of the solution, the selection and development of an appropriate algorithm, and the refinements necessary to bring the algorithm to a usable state. We then consider the implementation of the algorithm. Finally we discuss points of interest that have arisen during the presentation of the problem and its solution.

7.1 REMOVING COMMENTS

The program that we design in this section is a simple filter. A *filter* is a program that reads from a single input source and writes a single output stream, performing some transformation on the data. The term filter usually implies that a substantial portion of the input is merely copied to the output, and the transformation is therefore relatively simple. For example, a filter might convert all letters in the input to uppercase, expand specified abbreviations, or, as in this example, remove comments. Here is the specification of the comment removing program.

Problem 7.1: REMOVE COMMENTS

Write a program to read an input text and write an output text that is identical to the input text except that comments have been removed. A comment consists of a left bracket, [, a string of characters, perhaps including comments, and a closing right bracket,].

Note that comments may be nested. Nested comments are not allowed in Pascal and so this program will have more generality than is required to remove comments from a Pascal program. For example, given the input text

$$A\ B\ [\ C\ D\ [\ E\ F\ ]\ G\ H\ ]\ I\ J$$

our program should write

$$A\ B\ I\ J$$

A simple-minded program might assume that the first right bracket encountered signaled the end of the comment. Given the preceding input, it would write

$$A\ B\ G\ H\ ]\ I\ J$$

Design

Our first attempt at writing the program embodies only the most general features of the problem: a text file is to be read from beginning to end.

while not end of input file do
copy everything except comments

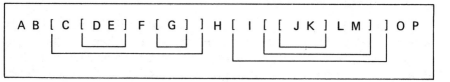

Fig. 7.1
Matching the brackets.

We use *while* rather than *repeat* to control the loop because the file may be empty, and if it is, we do not want to write anything at all. We can recognize the beginning of a comment by its first character, a left bracket. When this character is encountered, we skip over the comment; all other characters are simply written to the output stream.

```
copy everything except comments ———→
   read character
   if character = '['
      then skip over comment
      else write character
```

The action *skip over comment* means to discard characters up to and including the matching right bracket. The difficulty with this is the implementation of *matching*. Before deciding how the program should match a right bracket to the corresponding left bracket, let us see how we do it ourselves. If we consider a simple instance of nested comments such as the one just given, we can solve the problem easily without gaining insight into it, and it follows that to gain insight we must look at a less trivial example. Looking at Fig. 7.1, we find that we can match the brackets by joining corresponding brackets with lines. If we scan this diagram from left to right, we note the following: at each left bracket a new line starts and at each right bracket a line ends. The characters that have no lines underneath them are not inside comments and therefore they are the characters that must be copied. This suggests the following strategy: we introduce a variable *level* to denote the number of lines underneath each character; we increment *level* at each left bracket; and we decrement *level* at each right bracket. When *level* is zero, we have reached the end of a comment. On entry to *skip over comment*, one left bracket has already been read, and so initially *level* is 1. Thus we can write:

```
skip over comment ———→
   level := 1
   repeat
      read character
      if character = '['
         then level := level + 1
         else
            if character = ']'
               then level := level − 1
   until level = 0
```

The complete algorithm now reads as follows:

```
while not end of input file do
  read character
  if character = '['
  then
      level := 1
      repeat
        read character
        if character = '['
          then level := level + 1
          else
            if character = ']'
              then level := level - 1
      until level = 0
  else write character
```

This algorithm will correctly process a file in which left and right brackets are correctly matched. Suppose, however, that we cannot guarantee that this is so. There are two cases to consider: either there is a left bracket without a matching right bracket, or there is a right bracket without a matching left bracket. In the first case, the algorithm we have written will run off the end of the file looking for a right bracket, and in the second case it will not detect an error but will copy a right bracket to the output file.

We can modify the algorithm to take these situations into account by making a single observation: the present version of the algorithm records levels only when *level* is greater than zero. It would be more consistent to maintain the value of *level* all the time, even when *level* is zero and we are copying text. Then a right bracket encountered when *level* is zero is an error, and at the end of the file, if *level* is greater than zero, the file must have contained unmatched left brackets. Thus even the first refinement step was incorrect; it was a mistake to separate copying from skipping before we decided to implement skipping. The revised algorithm looks like this:

```
level := 0
while not end of file do
  read character
  update level
  if level = 0
    then write character
  if level ≠ 0
    then report an error
```

The only statement in this algorithm that requires further refinement is *update level*. We must check for left and right brackets and report an error if a right bracket is encountered when *level* is zero.

update *level* ⟶
  if *character* = '['
    then *level* := *level* + 1
    else
      if *character* = ']'
      then
        if *level* = 0
          then report an error
          else *level* := *level* − 1

There is still one problem. If *update level* reports an error, the current character is a right bracket and *level* is zero. Thus a right bracket will be written to the output file. We do not want this to happen, and consequently we change the condition for writing a character:

if *level* = 0 and *character* ≠ ']'
  then write *character*

Implementation

We are almost ready to write a Pascal program that removes comments. The only thing that the algorithm does not do in its present form is to deal with the line structure of the input file. This is a schema for copying a file with line structure in Pascal:

while not *eof* do
  while not *eoln* do
    read *character*
    write *character*
  readln
  writeln

We can use this schema in our comment skipping program but we do not want to output the line breaks that occur within comments. Consequently we execute *writeln* only when *level* is zero.

```
{ Remove nested comment of the form '[. . .]' from a text }
program skipcomments (input,output);
  const
    opencomment = '[';
    closecomment = ']';
```

```
var
  ch : char;
  level : integer;
begin
  level := 0;
  while not eof do
    begin
      while not eoln do
        begin
          read(ch);
          if ch = opencomment
            then level := level + 1
          else if ch = closecomment
            then if level = 0
              then write ('*** ILLEGAL ', closecomment, '***')
              else level := level - 1;
          if (level = 0) and (ch ≠ closecomment)
            then write (ch)
        end; { of line }
      readln;
      if level = 0
        then writeln
    end; { of file }
  if level ≠ 0
    then writeln('*** EXTRA ', opencomment, '(S) ***')
end. { skipcomments }
```

Discussion

Skipcomments is not intended to be a particularly interesting program. We are concerned with its development, which illustrates that even a simple programming problem must be approached with care and attention. The first design turned out to be unsuccessful because it did not accommodate errors satisfactorily; rather than patching the design up, we started all over again. The reward for this extra effort is a more robust program.

7.2 STORING DISTINCT VALUES

Some programming problems are simple, and we can obtain a solution rapidly. We should not necessarily be content with the first solution that we obtain, however, because there is often something that we can do to improve it. The following problem, although it is relatively simple, demonstrates this.

Problem 7.2: STORING DISTINCT VALUES

Read a list of numbers, storing each distinct value only once. Stop when a specified number *max* of different values has been stored. Assume that there are at least *max* different values in the input stream.

We expect as input a list of numbers such as

$$7 \quad 3 \quad 7 \quad 13 \quad 3 \quad 7 \quad 17 \quad 7 \ldots$$

If *max* = 4, the program should read the first seven of these numbers and then stop, having stored 7, 3, 13, and 17.

Design

The primary function of this program is not to read numbers but to store them, and accordingly the organization of the program should be based on the store. Thus we can write

> store distinct values ⟶
>   initialize store
>   fill store

The second of these actions can be refined to make the reading explicit:

> fill store ⟶
>   while store not full do
>   read *number*
>   if *number* not in store
>   then put *number* in store

We cannot go much further without deciding what kind of store we are going to use. The simplest form of store is an array large enough to hold *max* numbers. Suppose that we declare:

> **var**
>   *store*: **array** [1..*max*] **of** *integer*;
>   *nextentry*: *integer*;

The value of *nextentry* is the location of the next unused component of the array *store* until the program terminates when all the components are in use. We can write:

> initialize store ⟶
>   *nextentry* := 1

and

$$\text{put } \textit{number} \text{ in } \textit{store} \longrightarrow$$
$$store[nextentry] := number$$
$$nextentry := nextentry + 1$$

The next step is to refine *number not in store*. This requires searching the store. Using another index variable, *entry*, we can write the search as a loop:

> *entry* := 1
> while *entry* < *maxentry* and *store*[*entry*] ≠ *number* do
>   *entry* := *entry* + 1

After this search, either we have found that the number was in the store and *entry* < *nextentry*, or it was not in the store and *entry* = *nextentry*. We now have a complete algorithm.

> *nextentry* := 1   (7.2.1)
> while *nextentry* ≤ *max* do
>   read *number*
>   *entry* := 1
>   while *entry* < *maxentry* and *store*[*entry*] ≠ *number* do
>   *entry* := *entry* + 1
>   if *entry* = *nextentry*
>   then
>   *store*[*nextentry*] := *number*
>   *nextentry* := *nextentry* + 1

This solution is the result of refining each step independently and then putting everything together. The algorithm is correct but rather clumsy. We can now work on improving it, being careful not to destroy its correctness.

The first step is to clean up the search. It is well known that we can speed up a linear search by installing a *sentinel* in the array. The value of the sentinel is the value for which we are searching, and it plays two roles. First, it eliminates the need to evaluate the condition *store*[*entry*] ≠ *number* in the inner while loop. Second, it allows us to put the sentinel at *store*[*entry*], thereby eliminating the need for the assignment

$$store[nextentry] := number$$

when we are adding a new value to the store. After making these changes, we have the following algorithm:

$$nextentry := 1 \qquad\qquad\qquad (7.2.2)$$
$$\text{while } nextentry \leq max \text{ do}$$
$$\quad \text{read } number$$
$$\quad entry := 1$$
$$\quad store[nextentry] := number$$
$$\quad \text{while } store[entry] \neq number \text{ do}$$
$$\quad\quad entry := entry + 1$$
$$\quad \text{if } entry = nextentry$$
$$\quad\quad \text{then } nextentry := nextentry + 1$$

Now suppose that we encounter a sequence of numbers whose values are already in the store. The assignment

$$nextentry := nextentry + 1$$

will not be executed, and it is therefore unnecessary to evaluate the condition

$$nextentry \leq max$$

at every cycle of the outer loop. We can make the program tidier by introducing an inner loop to handle numbers that we have seen before, using the outer loop only when we encounter a new value. We can achieve the same insight by considering the program in an abstract way. This is its structure:

$$N := 1 \qquad\qquad\qquad (7.2.3)$$
$$\text{while } N \leq M \text{ do}$$
$$\quad S$$
$$\quad \text{if } B$$
$$\quad\quad \text{then } N := N + 1$$

We have written N for $nextentry$, M for max, S for the statements

$$\text{read } number$$
$$entry := 1$$
$$store[nextentry] := number$$
$$\text{while } store[entry] \neq number \text{ do}$$
$$\quad entry := entry + 1$$

and B for the condition $entry = nextentry$. From (7.2.3) we can deduce the following simpler form of the algorithm:

$$N := 1$$
$$\text{while } N \leq M \text{ do}$$
$$\quad \text{repeat } S \text{ until } B$$
$$\quad N := N + 1$$

Note that this transformation is only legitimate because S does not alter the value of N. Once we have reached this point, it is clear that we can go further:

$$\text{for } N := 1 \text{ to } M \text{ do}$$
$$\text{repeat } S \text{ until } B$$

Now we can make the corresponding changes to (7.2.2) and we arrive at the following algorithm.

$$\text{for } nextentry := 1 \text{ to } max \text{ do} \qquad (7.2.4)$$
$$\text{repeat}$$
$$\text{read } number$$
$$entry := 1$$
$$store[nextentry] := number$$
$$\text{while } store[entry] \neq number \text{ do}$$
$$entry := entry + 1$$
$$\text{until } entry = nextentry$$

Implementation

Writing a Pascal program from this algorithm is straightforward. In the following version of the program, *max* is incorporated as a constant. This is consistent with the specification, which states that the value of *max* is given. A more realistic specification would tell us where to find the value of *max*, and we could modify the program accordingly. The final action of the program is to print the numbers stored.

```
program storenumbers (input,output);
  const
    max = 20;
  var
    number : integer;
    store : array [1..max] of integer;
    entry,nextentry : 1..max;
  begin
    for nextentry := 1 to max do
      repeat
        read(number);
        entry := 1;
        store[nextentry] := number;
        while store[entry] ≠ number do
          entry := entry + 1
```

```
       until entry = nextentry;
       for entry := 1 to max do
          write(store[entry]);
       writeln
     end. { storenumbers }
```

Discussion

This example demonstrates the difficulty of separating design from implementation. We could say that the design was completed when we obtained the first correct and complete version of the algorithm, (7.2.1). Then the cleaning up process leading to algorithms (7.2.2) and (7.2.4) would be part of the implementation. Alternatively we could say that the design was not complete until we arrived at (7.2.4). We are more concerned with the development process, however, than with the names we can give to it.

A more important point is that the improvements we made to (7.2.1) have only a marginal effect on its efficiency. The order of the complexity of the program was determined when we made the decision to use an array for the store and to search it linearly. To improve the performance of this program appreciably, we would have to choose a more elaborate data structure for the store. It is good practice to present our programs in a neat and elegant form, but the effort is wasted if we have made an inappropriate choice of strategy initially.

7.3 INVERTING A FUNCTION

The function $f(m, n)$ defined by

$$f(m, n) = \frac{1}{2}(m + n - 1)(m + n - 2) + n \qquad (7.3.1)$$

for $m = 1, 2, 3, \ldots$ and $n = 1, 2, 3, \ldots$ is a favorite of logicians because it has the curious property that its values are unique integers in the same range as its arguments. If $f(m, n) = f(m', n')$, then $m = m'$ and $n = n'$. Furthermore, for any integer $K \geq 1$, there are integers m and n such that $f(m, n) = K$. The function therefore demonstrates the surprising fact that there are just as many integers as pairs of integers even though from any finite range of N integers, we can construct N^2 pairs of integers. Starting with this function, we can construct other functions such as

$$g(i, j, k) = f(i, f(j, k))$$

which map integer triples onto unique integers. Our interest in this function, however, is confined to the following problem.

Problem 7.3: INVERTING A FUNCTION

Write a program that, given $K \geq 1$, finds $m \geq 1$ and $n \geq 1$ such that $f(m, n) = \frac{1}{2}(m + n - 1)(m + n - 2) + n = K$.

The property just mentioned ensures that this is a fair problem but it does not give us any insight into how to solve it.

Design

We are tempted at first, perhaps, to manipulate the formula algebraically, to rearrange it in such a way that m and n are functions of K. This approach, however, does not get us very far.

The next step is to obtain insight into how the function works. The easiest way to do this is to tabulate it. Table 7.1 shows values of $f(m, n)$ for $m + n \leq 7$. Using this table as a guide, we can restate the problem as follows: given an integer K, find its coordinates m and n in the table. For example, if K is 18, the required values of m and n are 4 and 3, respectively.

Table 7.1   Values of $f(m, n)$ for $m + n \leq 7$

n	m					
	1	2	3	4	5	6
1	1	2	4	7	11	16
2	3	5	8	12	17	
3	6	9	13	18		
4	10	14	19			
5	15	20				
7	21					

We can see from Table 7.1 that the integers are arranged in diagonals starting in the top row ($n = 1$) and running downwards and to the left. For example, starting at $m = 4$ and $n = 1$, we can read the diagonal sequence 7, 8, 9, 10. This suggests a solution in two stages: first identify the diagonal containing the number, and then locate its position in the diagonal.

The key to the first part of the problem is the sequence of numbers in the first column ($m = 1$): 1, 3, 6, 10, ... The first integer in this sequence that exceeds the given integer K is the largest number in the diagonal containing K. For example, if $K = 18$, then we find 21 in the first column and 18 lies on the diagonal containing $16, 17, ..., 21$. Note that we could use the top row in the same way, but if we did this we would have to go past the diagonal that we wanted and then step back one. This is more awkward than the proposed solution.

The value of the nth number in the first column is given by

$$f(1, n) = \frac{1}{2}(1 + n - 1)(1 + n - 2) + n$$
$$= \frac{1}{2}n(n + 1)$$

but we can exploit the fact that these numbers are partial sums of the series $1 + 2 + 3 + \cdots$, as we can see from the following:

$$
\begin{aligned}
1 &= 1 \\
3 &= 1 + 2 \\
6 &= 1 + 2 + 3 \\
10 &= 1 + 2 + 3 + 4
\end{aligned}
$$

...

We can easily generate these numbers by a simple algorithm:

```
diag := 1
sum := 1
while B do
    diag := diag + 1
    sum := sum + diag
```

This loop generates the sequences

$$diag = 1, 2, 3, 4, ...$$
$$sum = 1, 3, 6, 10, ...$$

We can express this more formally by using the axiom of assignment as follows:

```
{ sum = diag(diag + 1)/2 }
diag := diag + 1
{ sum = (diag − 1) × diag / 2 }
sum := sum + diag
{ sum − diag = (diag − 1) × diag / 2 }
```

The postcondition of this sequence of assignments simplifies to:

$$sum = (diag - 1) \times diag / 2 + diag$$
$$= diag(diag + 1)/2$$

and thus the assertion

$$sum = diag(diag + 1)/2$$

is an invariant of the loop. This invariant is established by the initial assignments

$$diag := 1$$
$$sum := 1$$

and it is therefore true when the loop terminates.

We terminate the loop when the value of *sum* is large enough. We require $sum \geq K$, and consequently the condition B for the while loop is $sum < K$. We now have

> $diag := 1$
> $sum := 1$
> $\{K \geq 1 \wedge sum = diag(diag + 1)/2 \}$
> while $sum < K$ do
> $diag := diag + 1$
> $sum := sum + diag$
> $\{1 \leq K \leq sum \wedge sum = diag(diag + 1)/2 \}$

This is the solution of the first part of the problem: we have found the diagonal containing the number K and we have also found the largest number, *sum*, on that diagonal.

The second part of the solution is now straightforward. We move along the diagonal until we reach the desired value. We already know the value of the largest number on the diagonal and so the number of steps that we must make is $sum - K$, which we know to be non-negative. At each step we move up one row, subtracting 1 from n, and across one column, adding 1 to m. Thus we have

$$m := 1 + (sum - K)$$
$$n := diag - (sum - K)$$

When these assignments have been executed, the following assertion is true:

$$1 \leq K \leq sum$$
$$\wedge \ sum = diag(diag + 1)/2$$

$$\land \ m = 1 + sum - K$$
$$\land \ n = diag - sum + K$$

Observing that $m + n = 1 + sum - K + diag - sum + K = diag + 1$, we deduce from this assertion that

$$
\begin{aligned}
f(m, n) &= diag(diag - 1)/2 + diag - sum + K \\
&= diag(diag + 1)/2 - sum + K \\
&= K
\end{aligned}
$$

Also, since $K \le sum$, we know that $sum - K \ge 0$, and consequently

$$
\begin{aligned}
m &= 1 + sum - K \\
&\ge 1
\end{aligned}
$$

We can show that $n \ge 1$ by considering two cases. First, if $K = 1$, the *while* statement does nothing, and $n = diag - sum + K = 1$. Second, if $K > 1$, the *while* statement is executed at least once and it finds the *smallest* value of *sum* for which $sum \ge K$. The previous value of *sum* is $diag(diag - 1)/2$, and this must be less than K. Therefore

$$diag(diag - 1)/2 < K$$

and

$$
\begin{aligned}
n &= diag - sum + K \\
&= diag - diag(diag + 1)/2 + K \\
&= K - diag(diag - 1)/2 \\
&> 0
\end{aligned}
$$

Thus $n \ge 1$, and the complete algorithm is as follows:

```
{ K ≥ 1 }
diag := 1
sum := 1
{ K ≥ 1 ∧ sum = diag(diag + 1)/2 }
while sum < K do
  diag := diag + 1
  sum := sum + diag
{ 1 ≤ K ≤ sum ∧ sum = diag(diag + 1)/2 }
m := sum − K + 1
n := diag − sum + K
{ m ≥ 1 ∧ n ≥ 1 ∧ f(m,n) = K }
```

Implementation

We can easily derive a Pascal procedure from this algorithm.

```
procedure invfunc (K : integer;
                      var m, n : integer);
var
  diag, sum : integer;
begin
  { K ≥ 1 }
  diag := 1;
  sum := 1;
  { K ≥ 1 ∧ sum = diag(diag + 1)/2 }
  while sum < K do
    begin
      diag := diag + 1;
      sum := sum + diag
    end; { while }
  { 1 ≤ K ≤ sum ∧ sum = diag(diag + 1)/2 }
  m := sum − K + 1;
  n := diag − sum + K
  { m ≥ 1 ∧ n ≥ 1 ∧ f(m,n) = K }
end; { invfunc }
```

Discussion

This account demonstrates that the proof of an algorithm can be developed in parallel with the algorithm itself and that the formal assertions lend support to our intuitive arguments. Unfortunately this is not a technique that extends well to larger problems. In this example it is easy to formalize the specification, and the algorithm is very simple. When these conditions are not true, a formal approach may lead to difficult algebra.

7.4 THE QUADRATIC EQUATION

Writing a program to solve a quadratic equation may seem to be a rather mundane problem, however we will see that a careful approach to it yields insight into both program development and the problems of numerical analysis. We start with a specification.

Problem 7.4: SOLVING A QUADRATIC

Write a program that reads the values of three real coefficients, A, B, and C, and then prints the real values of x, if any, such that $Ax^2 + Bx + C = 0$. The program should print explanatory messages in the event that there are not two real roots.

Design

The obvious first step is to use relevant theory. In this case we require algebraic theory; there is a well-known formula for the roots of a quadratic equation. It tells us that the values of x for which

$$Ax^2 + Bx + C = 0$$

are

$$x_1 = \frac{-B + \sqrt{B^2 - 4AC}}{2A}$$

and

$$x_2 = \frac{-B - \sqrt{B^2 - 4AC}}{2A}$$

Whenever we are dealing with an unfamiliar formula, we should first attempt to obtain a feel for its behavior by examining special cases. The quadratic formula is not really unfamiliar but we may approach it as if it is. First we can quickly verify that the formula works well in many simple cases. For example,

$$(x - 2)(x - 3) = x^2 - 5x + 6$$

and setting $A = 1$, $B = -5$, and $C = 6$ in the formula, we obtain

$$x_1 = \frac{5 + 1}{2} = 3$$

and

$$x_2 = \frac{5 - 1}{2} = 2$$

as expected. Next we attempt to exercise the formula more rigorously by selecting cases in which it might break down.

1. What happens if $B^2 - 4AC = 0$? Try, for example, $A = 4$, $B = -12$, and $C = 9$. The formula gives $x_1 = 3/2$ and $x_2 = 3/2$. We should

identify this as a special case and print one value, $x = 3/2$, and a comment such as EQUAL ROOTS.

2. Most formulas fail if they contain a denominator whose value is zero. For example, if $A = 0$, $B = 5$, and $C = -20$, the formula yields $x_1 = 0/0$ and $x_2 = -10/0$. The equation $5x - 20 = 0$, however, can be solved without difficulty to give $x = 4$. We must therefore recognize the case $A = 0$ and return the value of x that satisfies $Bx + C = 0$. This value is $x = -C/B$, and once again we are in trouble if $B = 0$.

   If $A = 0$ and $B = 0$, there are two cases to consider. If $C = 0$, the equation reduces to $0 = 0$ which is satisfied trivially by all values of x. If $C \neq 0$, the equation is $C = 0$ which is meaningless and is satisfied by no values of x. In either case, we will report NO ROOTS.

3. If $C = 0$, the equation is $Ax^2 + Bx = 0$ and the roots are $x_1 = -B/A$ and $x_2 = 0$. The formula gives

$$x_2 = \frac{-B + \sqrt{B^2}}{2A}$$

   and a small error in the calculation of $\sqrt{B^2}$ would produce a non-zero value of x.

4. If B^2 is less than $4AC$, the formula requires us to calculate the square root of a negative number. For example, if $A = 9$, $B = 12$, and $C = 5$, the roots are $x_1 = (-2 + \sqrt{-1})/3$ and $x_2 = (-2 - \sqrt{-1})/3$. The specification asks for real roots and so we should detect this situation and issue the message NO REAL ROOTS.

5. One of the most common problems of numerical analysis is that we may lose precision when we subtract a number from another number that is approximately equal to it. There are two subtractions in the quadratic formula. We will consider first the situation in which B is approximately equal to $\sqrt{B^2 - 4AC}$. This will happen if B^2 is much greater than $4AC$. For instance, suppose that $A = 1$, $B = -10,000$, and $C = 1$. The roots of the equation are approximately 10,000 and $1/10,000 = 0.0001$. The formula gives x_1 accurately but $x_2 = (10,000 - 9,999.9998)/2$. If our computer retains eight decimal digits, the result may be $x_2 = 0$, or even if $x_2 \neq 0$, the result may be considerably in error. In this case, there is a trick that enables us to find the value of the smaller root accurately without performing the subtraction. We can see from the formula that $x_1 x_2 = C/A$. Thus if we know one root, x_1 say, we can find the

other root from the equation $x_2 = C/Ax_1$. In the preceding example, $C/A = 1$ and $x_2 = 1/x_1$.

In order to detect this situation, we check the relative magnitudes of B^2 and $4AC$. If $|B^2 - 4AC| < \epsilon$, where ϵ is a small number related to the precision of the computer, we calculate the value of the larger root first and then deduce the value of the smaller root.

6. We may also lose precision if B is approximately equal to $4AC$. Let $A = 1$, $B = -19,999$, and $C = 99,990,000$. Then $B^2 - 4AC = 399,960,001 - 399,960,000 = 1$. Again we suppose that our computer retains eight decimal digits. It will find that $B^2 - 4AC = 0$ and report equal roots $x_1 = x_2 = 9,999.5$. The *absolute* error in each root is $|10,000 - 9,999.5| = 0.5$. The proportional, or *relative*, error is a more useful measure because it is independent of the magnitude of the particular numbers. In this case the relative error is

$$\epsilon = \left| \frac{10,000 - 9,999.5}{10,000} \right| = 5 \times 10^{-5}$$

We expect errors to be of the order of 10^{-7}, and ϵ is 500 times larger than this. This problem is not easy to correct, and we ignore it.

We are now ready to develop the required program. A sensible first step would be to read the values of the coefficients A, B, and C:

> read coefficients
>
> ...

A natural concluding step would be to print the roots:

> read coefficients
>
> ...
>
> print roots

The intermediate step that we require is clearly *calculate roots*, leading to this version of the program:

> read coefficients
> calculate roots
> print roots

This refinement, however, will lead to problems later. To see why, consider the information that will be passed from each of these steps to the next. The first interface is simple; the values of the three coefficients move across it. The second interface is more complicated because we do not know how many roots there will be, and as we have seen, it will be necessary to print messages as well as roots. It will therefore be easier to combine the special case analysis and the printing in one section of the program, as suggested by the following algorithm:

> read coefficients
> calculate roots and print them

In the calculation phase we will want one branch for each of the special cases previously mentioned and one branch for the normal case in which $A \neq 0$, $C \neq 0$, and $B^2 - 4AC > 0$. These considerations lead us to the following refinement:

> calculate roots and print them $\longrightarrow$
> if $A = 0$
>   then if $B = 0$
>   then NO ROOTS
>   else ONE ROOT: $x := -C/B$
>   else if $C = 0$
>   then TWO ROOTS: $x_1 := 0$ and $x_2 := -B/A$
>   else if $B^2 - 4AC < 0$
>   then NO REAL ROOTS
>   else if $B^2 - 4AC = 0$
>   then EQUAL ROOTS: $x_1 := x_2 := -B/2A$
>   else $\{ B^2 - 4AC > 0 \}$
>   if $B^2 \gg 4AC$
>   then
>   calculate larger root x_1
> $x_2 := C/Ax_1$
>   else calculate x_1 and x_2 from formula

The subsequent refinement steps are simple, except for the case $B^2 - 4AC \gg 0$. (The symbol $\gg$ is read "is much greater than.") In this case we must decide which is the larger root and calculate it first. If $B > 0$, the root

$$\frac{-B - \sqrt{B^2 - 4AC}}{2A}$$

is large and negative, and if $B < 0$, the root

$$\frac{-B + \sqrt{B^2 - 4AC}}{2A}$$

is large and positive. Thus the sign of B determines which root we select:

calculate x_1 $\longrightarrow$
  if $B > 0$
    then $x_1 := (-B - \sqrt{B^2 - 4AC}) / 2A$
    else $x_1 := (-B + \sqrt{B^2 - 4AC}) / 2A$

Implementation

It is now a straightforward matter to write a Pascal program that solves the given problem. There seems to be little point in choosing fancy names for the coefficients, but we introduce *disc* for the value of $B^2 - 4AC$ and *sqrtdisc* for its square root in order to eliminate repeated calculations of these quantities, and we introduce the machine-dependent constant *largeratio*, which we use to ascertain that B^2 is much greater than $4AC$.

```
program quadratic (input, output);
  const
    largeratio = 1E6; { A machine dependent value, large in  }
                      { comparison to the available precision }
  var
    A, B, C, disc, sqrtdisc, root : real;
  begin
    read(A,B,C);
    if A = 0
      then { solve B * X + C = 0 }
        if B = 0
          then writeln('NO ROOTS')
          else writeln('ONE ROOT: ',-C/B)
      else if C = 0
        then { solve A * x * x + B * x = 0 }
          writeln('TWO ROOTS: 0 AND ',-B/A)
        else
          begin
            disc := sqr(B) - 4 * A * C;
            if disc < 0
              then writeln('NO REAL ROOTS')
              else if disc = 0
                then writeln('EQUAL ROOTS: ',- B / (2 * A))
                else { disc > 0 }
                  begin
                    sqrtdisc := sqrt(disc);
```

```
        if abs(sqr(B) / 4 * A * C) > largeratio
          then { Avoid error due to sqr(B) >> 4 * A * C}
            begin
              if B > 0
                then root := (− B − sqrtdisc) / (2 * A)
                else root := (− B + sqrtdisc) / (2 * A);
              writeln('TWO ROOTS: ', root,
                        ' AND ', C / (A * root))
            end
          else { usual case }
            writeln('TWO ROOTS: ', (− B + sqrtdisc) /
                      (2 * A), ' AND ', (− B − sqrtdisc) /
                      (2 * A))
        end
      end
   end. { quadratic }
```

Discussion

A formula by itself, or even a standard algorithm, does not usually provide us with enough information to write a computer program. If there are situations in which the formula does not work, the program must detect them and either use an alternative formula or print an error message. Sometimes the formula may be correct from a mathematical standpoint but nonetheless inadequate computationally; in this case the formula must be modified or an alternative solution found.

In this example our analysis is more detailed than is generally necessary; we have developed a sledgehammer to crack a nut. It is rare in practice that we have to solve a completely general quadratic equation in a computer program. Usually we know something about the values of the coefficients and it is therefore unnecessary to incorporate all the tests and checks of the foregoing program. The point is that any relevant knowledge that we have should be used to simplify the program, but when we do not possess such knowledge, our program should be prepared for the worst.

It is also worth remembering that we may lose accuracy when we calculate the difference between two approximately equal numbers. This is a problem that occurs fairly often, but in many cases we can avoid the subtraction by algebraic manipulation, as we did in this example. It is interesting to note that the reverse situation, in which accuracy can be gained, sometimes occurs. For example, there is a number slightly greater than 2 called the g-factor that is associated with the electron. It is possible to design an experiment that measures $g - 2$ directly with a precision of eight decimal digits. From this value of $g - 2$, which is 0.0023193044, we can obtain the value of g, which is 2.0023193044, with a precision of 11 decimal digits. Not only is there no other physical constant whose value is known with such accuracy, but there is no closer agreement between a measured value and a theoretical prediction in the whole of science.

7.5 THE BISECTION ALGORITHM

In the previous section we considered the problem of finding values of x such that a certain function of x, namely $Ax^2 + Bx + C$, was zero. In this section and the following section we consider related but more general problems in which less is known about the functions whose zeros we seek. The most general form of the problem that we discuss is this:

Problem 7.5: FIND ZEROS

Find values of x such that $f(x) = 0$, given that the numerical value of $f(x)$ may be calculated for any real value of x.

The values of x that we are seeking are referred to either as zeros of the function $f(x)$ or as roots of the equation $f(x) = 0$. Problem 7.5 is too general to use as a starting point and we consider only certain special cases of it. The assumption that we can compute $f(x)$ for any value of x will not be stated explicitly in the problem statements that follow, but we always assume that it is true. First let us suppose that we have discovered an interval that includes the root. The following problem expresses this idea more precisely.

Problem 7.6: FIND AN ENCLOSED ZERO

Given that $f(a) < 0 < f(b)$ and $f(x)$ is continuous in the interval $a \leq x \leq b$, find a value of x such that $a \leq x \leq b$ and $f(x) = 0$.

The easiest way to obtain insight into this problem is to draw a diagram. Fig. 7.2(a) shows the situation described by the problem. In this example, three values x_1, x_2, and x_3 satisfy the conditions of the problem, and to solve the problem as specified we need only find one of them. Note that we are entitled to assume the existence of at least one solution: the situation shown in Fig. 7.2(b) cannot occur because we are told that $f(x)$ is continuous in the interval $a \leq x \leq b$.

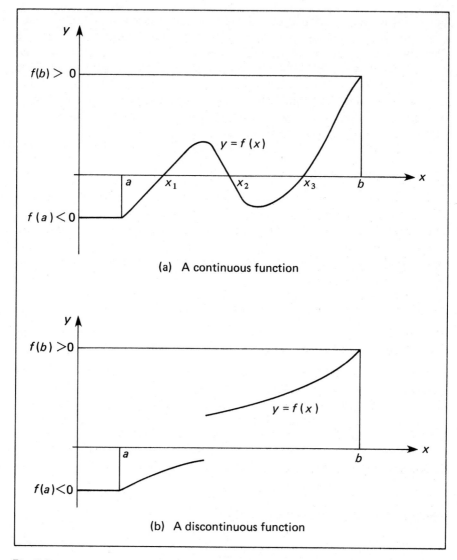

Fig. 7.2
Continuous and discontinuous functions.

   Although drawing the diagram gives us valuable insight into the problem, it does not get us much closer to a solution. We have merely sketched the situation; to find the exact value of x at which $f(x)$ is zero from the diagram, we would have to plot the graph of $f(x)$ with great precision, using many values of x. Solving the problem by plotting a very accurate graph is clearly inefficient, and yet it is evident that we must evaluate $f(x)$ at *some* points in the interval in order to find the true zero. The question is, which points?

Suppose that we start at $x_0 = a$ and increase x in small steps. If the step size is s and s is small compared to $b - a$, we will evaluate the function many times before we reach b. At some point, however, the sign of $f(x)$ must change. In other words, there must be a number i such that

$$f(a + is) < 0$$

and

$$f(a + (i + 1)s) \geq 0$$

When we have found this value of i, we have confined the zero of $f(x)$ to the small interval $a + is < x \leq a + (i + 1)s$, as shown in Fig. 7.3. If we want to find the position of the zero with greater precision, we can repeat the entire operation using $a + is$ as a starting point and an even smaller step size.

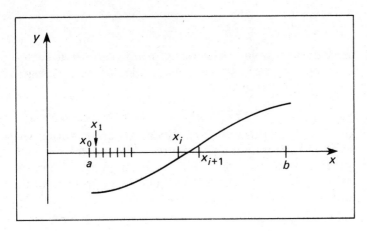

Fig. 7.3
Using small steps.

How small should the steps be? Suppose that we made them very small, allowing perhaps a million steps between a and b. The advantage of small steps is that when we find the small interval, it is a very small interval, and so we are close to the required root. The disadvantage is that, on average, we would calculate $f(x)$ half a million times, and in an unfavorable case, we might evaluate it almost a million times. Not only would the algorithm be very slow, but most of the computation would be wasted, since it contributes nothing to the final result.

If a million steps is too many, we should try fewer. Rather than choosing an arbitrary number, such as 10 or 100, we go straight to the smallest possible number of steps: two. In the following discussion we return to the problem of step size and consider whether there is any reason to believe in an optimal number of steps greater than two and less than a million. Using two steps, we evaluate $f(x)$ at the point $m = (a + b)/2$ midway between a and b. One of three things will happen. If we happen by chance to have found the root exactly, $f(m)$ will be zero. It is more probable that either $f(m) < 0$ and there must be a root between $x = m$ and $x = b$ because $f(m) < 0 < f(b)$, or $f(m) > 0$ and there must be a root between $x = a$ and $x = m$ because $f(a) < 0 < f(m)$. In either of the last two cases, we can repeat the strategy by evaluating $f(x)$ at the midpoint of the new interval, which is half the size of the original interval. Thus after n iterations we will know that the root lies in an interval of length $(a - b)/2^n$ if we have not found it exactly.

Implementation

We can now consider the problem of writing a procedure that corresponds to this algorithm. We use two variables, *lo* and *hi*, and the algorithm maintains the truth of the assertion

$$lo \leq root < hi$$

Initially $lo = a$ and $hi = b$, so this assertion is true. At each iteration we evaluate the function at the midpoint of the interval bounded by *lo* and *hi* and use the sign of its value to change one of the endpoints. We must evaluate the function at least once, and consequently we use *repeat* to control the iteration.

```
lo := a
hi := b
repeat
    mid := (lo + hi)/2
    if f(mid) > 0
        then hi := mid
```

else $lo := mid$
until finished

We must now choose an appropriate condition *finished* to terminate the loop. First, we may be lucky enough to find the root exactly, and the program should recognize this situation. The other criterion is more subtle than this. At each iteration the size of the maximum possible error is halved; in other words, we add one bit of precision to the bits of precision, after *M* cycles we can no longer gain any precision. This provides us with an upper limit to the number of times that we can usefully bisect the interval.

The Pascal procedure *bisect* has as input parameters the function *f* and the endpoints of the interval known to include the root. It returns the value of the root. The variables *lo* and *hi* are value parameters of the procedure and consequently the initial assignments to them which appear in the preceding algorithm are unnecessary in the program. The value of *f* at the point *mid* is saved in the variable *fmid* to avoid evaluating the function more than once at each point.

```
{ Given f(a) < 0 < f(b), find a root of f(x) = 0          }
{ in the interval a < x < b using the bisection algorithm. }
procedure bisect (function f (x : real) : real;
                  lo, hi : real; var root : real);
   const
     maxcycles = 24; { Required precision in bits       }
                     { (machine dependent constant ) }
   var
     cycle : integer;
     mid, fmid : real;
   begin
     cycle := 0;
     repeat
       mid := (lo + hi)/2;
       fmid := f(mid);
       if fmid > 0
         then hi := mid
         else lo := mid;
       cycle := cycle + 1
     until (fmid = 0) or (cycle ≥ maxcycles);
     root := mid
   end; { bisect }
```

Discussion

The bisection algorithm converges slowly because we use only the sign of $f(x)$ at each of the points at which we evaluate it. We are actually using the function $f_{app}(x) = signum(f(x))$ as an approximation to $f(x)$, as shown in Fig. 7.4. Each iteration halves the size of the interval known to contain the root and consequently it contributes one bit to the final result. Since $\log_2(10) \simeq 3.3$, we require 3.3 iterations for each significant decimal digit of the result. Although the rate of convergence is low, it is independent of the nature of the function $f(x)$ and so this algorithm may find roots that faster algorithms cannot find.

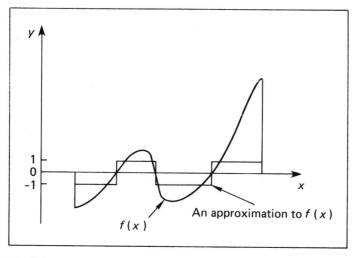

Fig. 7.4
$f(x)$ and an approximation to $f(x)$.

The bisection is pleasantly simple, and it is evident that dividing the interval into more than two sections will make it more complicated. It is conceivable, however, that we might reduce the total amount of work required by dividing the interval into more than two sections at each iteration. The following argument is not rigorous but it does provide some support for the bisection algorithm.

Suppose that we divide the interval into n equal sections. If we assume that the root is equally likely to be in any section, the probability $P(m)$ that we will have to evaluate the function m times is given by

$$P(m) = \frac{1}{n} \quad \text{if} \quad 1 \leq m \leq n - 2$$

and

$$P(m) = \frac{2}{n} \quad \text{if} \quad m = n - 1$$

The average number of evaluations required for one iteration is therefore

$$\frac{1 + 2 + \ldots + (n-2)}{n} + \frac{2(n-1)}{n} = \frac{(n+1)(n-1)}{2n}$$

Each iteration increases the precision of the result by $\log_2(n)$ bits. If the time required to evaluate the function once is T_e, the total time required to achieve M bits of precision is

$$T(n) = \frac{MT_e \ (n+2)(n-1)}{2n \ \log_2(n)}$$

If we tabulate this function, we obtain the following results:

$$T(2) = MT_e$$
$$T(3) \simeq 1.0515 MT_e$$
$$T(4) = 1.25 MT_e$$

$T(n)$ continues to increase for larger values of n. Since we cannot divide the interval into fewer than two sections, we conclude that bisection is optimal given that we are only going to use the sign of the function, not its value. In the next section, we derive an algorithm that does use the value of the function and is consequently faster than the bisection algorithm.

7.6   THE SECANT ALGORITHM

Suppose that we do not know of an interval of the kind required by the bisection algorithm, enclosing a zero. What do we do then? In most practical situations we have some idea about where the zeros of a function might be, and this information is assumed in the following problem.

Problem 7.7:   FIND A ROOT

Given that x_1 and x_2 are approximations to a root of $f(x) = 0$, find the exact root.

Approximation in this case does not necessarily mean that x_1 and x_2 are numerically close to the root. The requirement is that within the interval between an approximation and the root itself the function must be well-behaved. We will consider precisely how well-behaved it has to be after we have derived an algorithm.

Design

We can no longer assume that the required root lies between the given approximations. In fact, all that we know about the function f is summarized in Fig. 7.5(a), which is obtained by evaluating the function at x_1 and x_2 and plotting the points $P_1 = (x_1, f(x_1))$ and $P_2 = (x_2, f(x_2))$. We can discover more about the function by evaluating it at different places and plotting the corresponding points, but the difficulty, as before, is to decide where these places should be. There is clearly no point in evaluating the function at a point midway between x_1 and x_2 because there is no reason to assume that this will give us any more information about the position of the root. We cannot proceed further without making some kind of assumption about the shape of $f(x)$. The simplest assumption that we can make about the function is that it is a linear function; in other words, we assume that its graph is a straight line. We can, in fact, calculate the exact solution of $f(x) = 0$ under the assumption that $f(x)$ is linear. Graphically this solution is the point x_3 in Fig. 7.5(a), obtained by drawing a straight line through P_1 and P_2 and marking its point of intersection with the x-axis. Since the line $P_1 P_2$ passes through the point $(x_3, 0)$, its equation is of the form

$$y = k(x - x_3) \qquad (7.6.1)$$

We already know the coordinates of two points on this line, P_1 and P_2, and we can substitute them into (7.6.1).

$$f(x_1) = k(x_1 - x_3) \qquad (7.6.2)$$
$$f(x_2) = k(x_2 - x_3) \qquad (7.6.3)$$

Eliminating k from (7.6.2) and (7.6.3) by division, we obtain:

$$(x_1 - x_3)/f(x_1) = (x_2 - x_3)/f(x_2) \qquad (7.6.4)$$

We can solve this equation for x_3:

$$x_3 = x_2 - f(x_2)(x_2 - x_1)/(f(x_2) - f(x_1)) \qquad (7.6.5)$$

Now we can calculate $f(x_3)$. If $f(x)$ is actually linear, $f(x_3)$ will be zero, but this is unlikely. It is likely, however, that x_3 will be closer to the true root than x_1 or x_2, and by repeating the calculation using x_2 and x_3 as starting points we can iterate until we are close to the root.

Implementation

We can repeat the calculation without introducing new variables if we carefully cycle the old variables. From x_1 and x_2, we calculate x_3. In the next iteration we use x_2 (renamed x_1) and x_3 (renamed x_2) to cal-

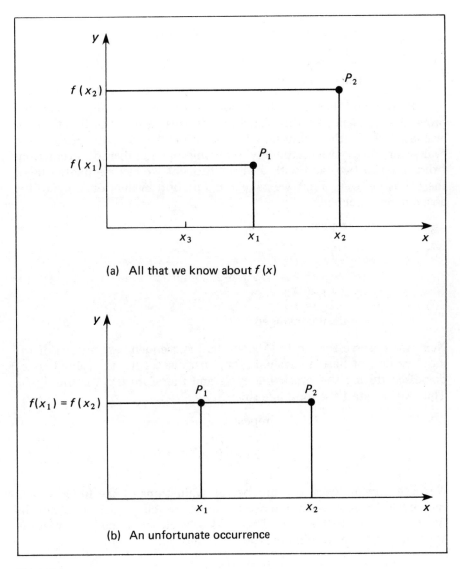

Fig. 7.5
Approximations to a root.

culate a new x_4 (renamed x_3), and so on. Some care is needed to get the assignments in the correct order, but once this has been done it is not hard to derive the following algorithm.

repeat
$$x_3 := x_2 - f(x_2)(x_2 - x_1)/(f(x_2) - f(x_1))$$
$$x_1 := x_2$$
$$x_2 := x_3$$
until converged

Before we attend to the condition for termination, we can improve the efficiency of this algorithm. In this version the function f is evaluated three times during each iteration. We can obviously avoid evaluating $f(x_2)$ twice, thereby reducing the number of evaluations from three to two, and with a bit of thought we can eliminate one of these two as well. First we take the function evaluation outside the assignment statement:

repeat
$$f_1 := f(x_1)$$
$$f_2 := f(x_2)$$
$$x_3 := x_2 - f_2 * (x_2 - x_1)/(f_2 - f_1)$$
$$x_1 := x_2$$
$$x_2 := x_3$$
until converged

Next we observe that in the second and subsequent executions of the loop we do not need to evaluate $f(x_1)$ because x_1 has the value that x_2 possessed during the preceding cycle and therefore $f(x_1)$ is simply f_2. Thus we can start the loop like this:

repeat
$$f_1 := f_2$$
$$f_2 := f(x_2)$$
...

We have now reduced the number of evaluations of the function f in each cycle from three to one but we are in trouble because f_2 is not defined on entry to the loop. This difficulty can be remedied by evaluating $f(x_1)$ before entering the loop, as follows:

$$f_2 := f(x_1)$$
repeat
$$f_1 := f_2$$
$$f_2 := f(x_2)$$
...

It is now time to consider the termination condition. Ideally we would like to iterate until $f(x_2)$ is zero, but this may never happen. It is better to use a criterion based on the value of $|x_2 - x_1|$, based on the assumption that if this amount is very small, we must be in the vicinity of a root. In the following version of the algorithm, ϵ is a small, machine-dependent number approximately equal to the magnitude of the error we can tolerate in the final result.

$$f_2 := f(x_1)$$
repeat
$$\quad f_1 := f_2$$
$$\quad f_2 := f(x_2)$$
$$\quad x_3 := x_2 - f_2 * (x_2 - x_1)/(f_2 - f_1))$$
$$\quad x_1 := x_2$$
$$\quad x_2 := x_3$$
until $|x_2 - x_1| < \epsilon$

Two problems remain. First, we note that the expression $f_2 - f_1$ occurs as a denominator, and therefore we must ensure that it is never zero. The situation in which $f_2 - f_1$ is zero is shown in Fig. 7.5(b). The values of f_1 and f_2 provide no useful information about the location of the root and we simply set x_3 midway between x_1 and x_2. The second problem is that we cannot be certain that the process will converge and so we should limit the number of iterations that are performed. These revisions are incorporated into the following Pascal procedure.

```
{ Find a root of f(x) = 0 close to the given      }
{ values x1 and x2, using the secant algorithm. }
procedure secant (function f (x : real) : real;
                  x1, x2 : real;
                  var found : boolean;
                  var root : real);
const
   maxcycles = 20; { Arbitrary upper bound }
   epsilon = 1E−6; { Convergence criterion   }
var
   cycle : integer;
   x3, f1, f2 : real;
begin
   cycle := 0;
   f2 := f(x1);
   repeat
      f1 := f2;
      f2 := f(x2);
      if f1 = f2
```

```
    then x3 := (x1 + x2)/2
    else x3 := x2 − f2 * (x2 − x1) / (f2 − f1);
  x1 := x2;
  x2 := x3;
  cycle := cycle + 1
  until (abs(x2 − x1) < epsilon) or (cycle ≥ maxcycles);
  root := x1;
  found := cycle < maxcycles
end; { secant }
```

Discussion

This algorithm is called the secant algorithm because it approximates a function $f(x)$ passing through two points by a straight line passing through the same two points, and this line is called a *secant* of the curve whose equation is $y = f(x)$.

If the secant algorithm can find a root, it will do so more rapidly than the bisection algorithm. It cannot find repeated roots, however, because it is estimating the slope of $f(x)$ near the root, and if x is a repeated root of $f(x)$, the slope of f at x is zero.

7.7 A GRAPH PLOTTER ALGORITHM

The graph plotters used in computer systems are either analog or digital. An analog plotter accepts an x-voltage and a y-voltage and uses a feedback mechanism to move the pen to the corresponding position on the graph paper. An analog plotter may be controlled by a digital computer by means of digital-to-analog converters connected to the output ports of the computer. A digital plotter, on the other hand, has two stepping motors. An impulse sent to the x-motor moves the pen one step parallel to the x-axis and an impulse sent to the y-motor moves the pen one step parallel to the y-axis. The size of the step determines the precision of the plot: high-precision plotting requires 800 or 1000 steps to the inch, but for acceptable graphs, 100 or 200 steps to the inch are sufficient.

It is simple to program an analog plotter. The computer merely sends a stream of (x, y) coordinate pairs to the plotter, and the only problem is to avoid sending data so fast that the plotter gets left behind. Programming a digital plotter is more interesting because the computer can only move the plotter one step at a time, and so even a simple operation, such as moving the pen in a straight line that is not parallel to one of the axes, requires the calculation of an appropriate sequence of step operations. We consider the problem of moving the pen in a straight line under the following conditions:

1. The step size is assumed to be 1. This means that the algorithm can use integer arithmetic. The scale of the graph will depend on the step size of the plotter. For example, if there are 100 steps to the inch, 1000 steps must be generated to draw a line 10 inches long.

2. The stepping motors can be operated simultaneously and they can move in either direction. Thus for each motor there are three operations: stay still, step forward, and step backward. A single operation may activate both motors and consequently there are nine operations including the trivial operation in which both motors remain stationary.

From the starting position $(0, 0)$, we can reach any of the points shown in Fig. 7.6 with one operation. We denote a move by the coordinates of the position that the pen would have reached if it had started from the origin $(0, 0)$. Thus $(0, -1)$ is a move in which the x-motor remains stationary and the y-motor moves one step in the negative y-direction. This is a formal statement of the problem we have to solve:

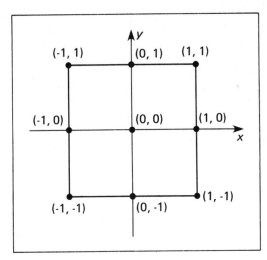

Fig. 7.6
One step from $(0, 0)$.

Problem 7.8:   PLOT A STRAIGHT LINE

The pen of the digital plotter is currently at (x_1, y_1). Construct an algorithm that will generate the steps necessary to move the pen to (x_2, y_2) in such a way that the pen remains as close to the straight line joining (x_1, y_1) and (x_2, y_2) as possible. x_1, x_2, y_1, and y_2 are all integers.

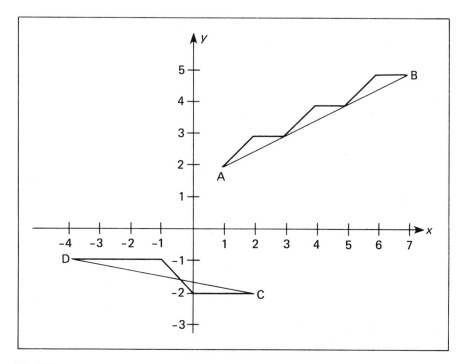

Fig. 7.7
Two plotted paths.

Two examples of the kind of output that we can expect from our algorithm are shown in Fig. 7.7. The line AB runs from $(1, 2)$ to $(7, 5)$ and the line CD runs from $(2, -2)$ to $(-4, -1)$. The dark lines show the path of the pen moving only in the permitted directions.

Design

We start by considering a special case of this problem in which $x_1 = 0$ and $y_1 = 0$. In other words, we consider paths starting at the origin only. We can also regard this special case as a coordinate transformation because the sequence of steps that will move the pen from (x_1, y_1) to (x_2, y_2) is the same as the sequence that will move it from $(0, 0)$ to $(x_2 - x_1, y_2 - y_1)$. Thus if we solve the problem for the path from $(0, 0)$ to any point (dx, dy), we can apply a simple coordinate transformation to obtain the solution for the general case.

We now divide this simplified problem into special cases. If $dx = 0$ and $dy = 0$, no movement is required. If $dx = 0$ or $dy = 0$, only one motor is required; and if $|dx| = |dy|$, the number of steps executed by each motor is the same. Thus there are nine cases in which the problem is easily solved. These nine cases are numbered 2, 4, 6, 8, 9, 10, 12, 14, and 16 in Fig. 7.8 and Fig. 7.9. This leaves eight cases to be considered; these are numbered 1, 3, 5, 7, 11, 13, 15, and 17 in Fig. 7.8 and Fig. 7.9. The numbering is obtained by considering the sign of dx, the sign of dy, and the relative magnitudes of dx and dy; in each case we use the ordering less, equal, and greater.

When we consider any one of these cases, it becomes evident that the others are going to be similar in principle although the details will be different. We select case 15 to study in detail because all the values are positive and it is easier to work with positive numbers than with negative numbers. Consequently we assume that $dx > 0$, $dy > 0$, and $dy > dx$.

This is an appropriate point at which to pause and see what we have accomplished. We have selected a special case of the original problem and we have divided this special case into 17 subcases, nine of which are easily solved. We are now investigating one of the remaining eight subcases: move the pen from $(0, 0)$ to (dx, dy), given that $dx > 0$, $dy > 0$, and $dy > dx$. This problem is very much simpler to solve than the original problem and yet when we have solved it most of the work is done.

We denote the point $(0, 0)$ where the pen starts by O and the point (dx, dy) which it eventually reaches by P. The path of the pen must remain as close to the line OP as possible. To move the pen from O to P, we must step the x-motor dx times and the y-motor dy times. Since we know that $dy > dx$, it seems reasonable to step the y-motor at every move and the x-motor at some moves and not others. Thus the path will consist of dy moves of type $(1, 1)$ and $dy - dx$ moves of type $(0, 1)$. The only remaining problem is to arrange these moves in a suitable order.

The strategy that we use is to build the path step by step, keeping as close to the line OP as possible. There are only two possible moves at each step and all we have to do is choose the move that leaves us closer to OP. Suppose that the pen has reached the point A with coordinates (X, Y), as shown in Fig. 7.10. Then the next move will take it either to B at $(X, Y + 1)$, or to C at $(X + 1, Y + 1)$. The distances of B and C from OP are BD and CF respectively. Calculating these distances requires finding square roots, which we prefer to avoid because we are

Case			
1			$|dX| < |dY|$
2	$dX < 0$	$dY < 0$	$|dX| = |dY|$
3			$|dX| > |dY|$
4		$dY = 0$	
5			$|dX| < dY$
6		$dY > 0$	$|dX| > dY$
7			$|dX| > dY$
8		$dY < 0$	
9	$dX = 0$	$dY = 0$	
10		$dY > 0$	
11			$dX < |dY|$
12		$dY < 0$	$dX = |dY|$
13			$dX > |dY|$
14	$dX > 0$	$dY = 0$	
15			$dX < dY$
16		$dY > 0$	$dX = dY$
17			$dX < dY$

Fig. 7.8
Seventeen special cases.

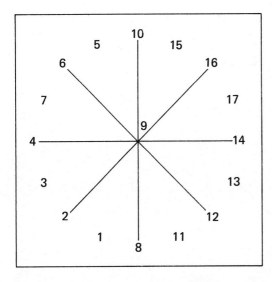

Fig. 7.9
The regions defined by Fig. 7.8.

using integer arithmetic. Since the triangles BDE and CFE are similar, we can compare the distances BE and EC instead. The equation of the line OP is

$$y = (dy/dx)x$$

and at E we have

$$y = Y + 1$$

and hence

$$x = (dx/dy)(Y + 1)$$

The distances BE and EC are therefore given by

$$BE = (dx/dy)(Y + 1) - X$$

and

$$EC = (X + 1) - (dx/dy)(Y + 1)$$

We should move the pen to B if BE $<$ EC and to C if BE $>$ EC. If BE $=$ EC, either move leaves us exactly half a step from the line (this is the maximum possible error) and the choice of moves can be made arbitrarily. The test that we must make is

$$|(dx/dy)(Y + 1) - X| < |(X + 1) - (dx/dy)(Y + 1)| \quad (7.7.1)$$

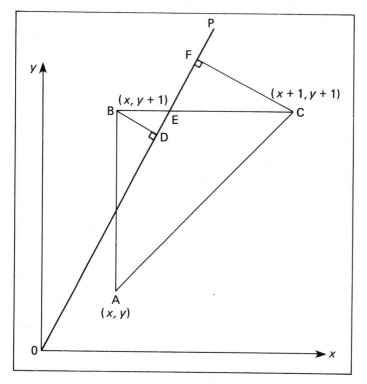

Fig. 7.10
Choosing the next move.

In the program this condition is evaluated at every step, and it is there-fore important that we simplify it as much as possible. E must lie be-tween B and C and consequently:

$$(dx/dy)(Y + 1) - X > 0$$

and

$$(X + 1) - (dx/dy)(Y + 1) > 0$$

Thus we can remove the absolute value signs from (7.7.1), obtaining:

$$(dx/dy)(Y + 1) - X < (X + 1) - (dx/dy)(Y + 1)$$

which can be simplified to:

$$2(X \times dy - Y \times dx - dx) + dy > 0$$

We can now write down an algorithm for the special case we are considering. If $dx > 0$, $dy > 0$, and $dy > dx$, then the correct sequence of moves is given by the following algorithm:

$X := 0$
$Y := 0$
for $step := 1$ to dy do
   if $2(X \times dy - Y \times dx - dx) + dy > 0$
     then
       move(0,1)
       $Y := Y + 1$
     else
       move(1,1)
       $X := X + 1$
       $Y := Y + 1$

It is straightforward, though tedious, to complete the solution by analyzing the other cases.

Implementation

If we replace each $>$ in Fig. 7.8 by $\geq$ and ignore the cases containing $=$, we can reduce the number of special cases to eight without impairing the validity of the algorithm. This revision shortens the program considerably without significantly reducing its efficiency.

The Pascal procedure *plot* generates a sequence of commands for a digital plotter that moves the pen from the point (*xstart*, *ystart*) to the point (*xfinish*, *yfinish*). The procedure first moves the origin to (*xstart*, *ystart*) and then generates commands to move the pen from the new origin to the point (*dx*, *dy*), where

$$dx = xfinish - xstart$$

and

$$dy = yfinish - ystart$$

It then calculates the number of steps that are required, which is

$$max(|dx|, |dy|)$$

because this simplifies the construction of the **for** loops.

The procedure *move* is called to generate the actual plotter commands. *Move* also updates the current position (x, y); this shortens the text of the procedure considerably.

{ Move plotter from (*xstart*,*ystart*) to (*xfinish*,*yfinish*) }
procedure *plot* (*xstart*, *ystart*, *xfinish*, *yfinish* : *integer*);
  var
    x, *y*, *dx*, *dy*, *p*, *step*, *length* : *integer*;
  { Move one step and update global coordinates (*x*,*y*) }
  procedure *move* (*xinc*, *yinc* : *integer*);
    begin
      x := *x* + *xinc*;
      y := *y* + *yinc*
      { Send appropriate plotter command }
    end; { move }
  begin { plot }
    { Transform coordinates }
    x := 0;
    y := 0;
    dx := *xfinish* − *xstart*;
    dy := *yfinish* − *ystart*;
    { Calculate path length }
    if *abs*(*dx*) < *abs*(*dy*)
      then *length* := *abs*(*dy*)
      else *length* := *abs*(*dx*);
    { Case analysis }
    if *dx* < 0
      then if *dy* < 0
        then if *abs*(*dx*) < *abs*(*dy*)
          then
            for *step* := 1 **to** *length* **do**
              if 2 * (*x* * *dy* − *y* * *dx* + *dx*) − *dy* > 0
                then *move*(0,−1)
                else *move*(−1,−1)
          else { *abs*(*dx*) ≥ *abs*(*dy*) }
            for *step* := 1 **to** *length* **do**
              if 2 * (*x* * *dy* − *y* * *dx* − *dy*) + *dx* < 0
                then *move* (−1,0)
                else *move*(−1,−1)
        else { *dy* ≥ 0 }
          if *abs*(*dx*) < *abs*(*dy*)
            then
              for *step* := 1 **to** *length* **do**
                if 2 * (*x* * *dy* − *y* * *dx* − *dx*) − *dy* < 0
                  then *move*(0,1)

```
                else move(−1,1)
          else { abs(dx) ≥ abs(dy) }
            for step := 1 to length do
              if 2 * (x * dy − y * dx − dy) − dx > 0
              then move (−1,0)
              else move(−1,1)
    else { dx ≥ 0 }
      if dy < 0
        then if abs(dx) < abs(dy)
          then
            for step := 1 to length do
              if 2 * (x * dy − y * dx + dx) + dy < 0
              then move(0,−1)
              else move(1,−1)
          else { abs(dx) ≥ abs(dy) }
            for step := 1 to length do
              if 2 * (x * dy − y * dx + dy) + dx > 0
              then move(1,0)
              else move(1,−1)
    else { dy ≥ 0 }
      if abs(dx) < abs(dy)
        then
          for step := 1 to length do
            if 2 * (x * dy − y * dx − dx) + dy > 0
            then move(0,1)
            else move(1,1)
        else { abs(dx) ≥ abs(dy) }
          for step := 1 to length do
            if 2 * (x * dy − y * dx + dy) − dx < 0
            then move(1,0)
            else move(1,1)
end; { plot }
```

Discussion

The procedures of a graph-plotter library may be executed either by a
large processor running in time-sharing mode or by an off-line microprocessor used exclusively for plotting. In the first case the program
should use as little processor time as possible. In the second case speed
is less important because the microprocessor should be able to generate
moves faster than the plotter can respond to them even if the plotting

algorithm is inefficient. In both cases it is desirable to use integer arithmetic to avoid rounding errors.

The procedure we have developed has one advantage and two disadvantages. Its advantage is that it is accurate; the maximum error is only half the step size. Its two disadvantages are that it performs two multiplications for each step of the pen, and that the intermediate products of these multiplications are sometimes large. The algorithm is inconvenient for microprocessor implementation because 32-bit integers are required.

In Bresenham's algorithm the only multiplications required are multiplications by 2, which can be implemented by shift operations. Thus Bresenham's algorithm is easier to implement than this one, but it is less accurate; the maximum error is equal to the step size.

SUMMARY

Although we can construct programs in a rigorous and systematic way, it is inevitable that problems will arise during their development. We can solve these problems by applying the techniques described in Part 1.

Specification requires stating the problem clearly and making implicit rules and data explicit. There are many ways of obtaining insight into the problems of design and implementation. We can investigate special cases, look for standard solutions and related problems, and apply the technique of divide and conquer to split the problem into subproblems.

We make many decisions while developing a program. It is important not to make decisions until enough evidence is available for us to make them correctly; we must leave our options open for as long as possible.

A solution obtained by the systematic application of simple rules is likely to be correct but it may not be elegant or concise. This is true of the first version of *Storing Distinct Values*, for example. This is as it should be; if we try to tidy up as we go along, we are likely to make mistakes. When we have obtained a solution, there is no harm in reorganizing it to make the finished program more readable. We should not expect significant gains in efficiency, however, nor should we incorporate clever tricks that make the program slightly faster or slightly shorter at the risk of making it harder than necessary to understand.

FURTHER READING

The problem *Storing Distinct Values* is based on a discussion by Wirth in his paper, "On the Composition of Well-Structured Programs."

Aspects of the problem of finding zeros of a given function are considered in three sections of this chapter. This problem is considered in greater depth in books on numerical analysis, such as *Numerical Analysis* by Johnson and Riess, and *Numerical Methods* by Dahlquist and Björck.

The experimental determination of the g-factor of the electron, mentioned in the discussion of the quadratic equation, is described in "The Isolated Electron" by Ekstrom and Wineland.

Bresenham described his plotter algorithm in "Algorithm for the Computer Control of a Digital Plotter." It is discussed, along with other algorithms, in *Principles of Interactive Computer Graphics* by Newman and Sproull.

EXERCISES

7.1 Write a program according to the specification of *Remove Comments* which assumes that comments are introduced by /*, terminated by */, and may be nested.

7.2 Modify program *storenumbers* of Section 7.2 so that it stores a number only if the number is larger than all the numbers currently stored.

7.3 Write a program that accepts as input an integer $N \geq 1$ and returns three integers i, j, and k, such that $i \geq 1, j \geq 1, k \geq 1$, and $f(i,f(j,k)) = N$ where f is the function defined by (7.3.1).

7.4 Is it possible to solve Problem 7.3, *Inverting a Function*, without iteration?

7.5 Fig. 7.11 shows the graph of a function $f(x)$ in the interval $a \leq x \leq b$ and $f(a) < 0 < f(b)$. We can estimate the root of the equation $f(x) = 0$ which lies in the interval $a \leq x \leq b$ by the method of *regular falsi* which generates x_1, x_2, and x_3 as successive approximations to the root. Write a procedure that uses this method to find the root.

7.6 Write a program that estimates the area enclosed by the lines

$x = a$, $x = b$, $y = 0$, and $y = f(x)$, where f is a given function. This area is shaded in Fig. 7.12. [This area is the value of $\int_b^a f(x)\, dx$. There are several standard solutions of this problem, but the point of the exercise is that you should develop a solution of your own.]

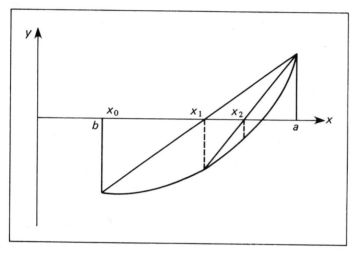

Fig. 7.11
Finding a root with regular falsi.

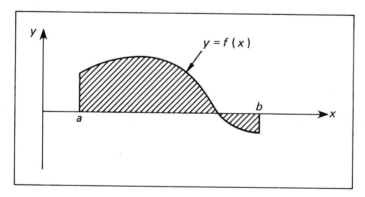

Fig. 7.12
Estimating an area.

7.7 If we use the graph-plotter algorithm of Section 7.7 to move the pen from A to B and then back again from B to A, the pen does not always retrace its steps. Can you alter the algorithm so that the pen passes through the same points in both directions?

7.8 We can program a computer to draw lines using a dot-matrix printer or a raster-scan display. In each case, the line is approximated by points selected from a rectangular array. Is the algorithm of Section 7.7 suitable for this application? Can you suggest an alternative algorithm?

CHAPTER 8

ABSTRACTION TECHNIQUES

We have seen that choice of notation is an important component of abstraction. A programming language is a notation for expressing algorithms and it is not surprising that the most successful programming languages are built from carefully chosen abstractions. In Chapter 6 we developed a programming methodology built on a small set of control structures: sequence, decision, and repetition. In this chapter we introduce the procedure as an abstraction mechanism and discuss means of abstracting properties of data.

A computer program is an abstraction both of the world of the problem it is intended to solve and of the machine by which it is executed. Consider, for example, an accounting program for a small business. In the business, a sum of money such as $19.95 is a collection of bank notes and coins, or perhaps a check. This sum of money is represented in the computer by a collection of electronic signals or charges in an integrated circuit chip. In the program, the same sum of money is represented by a number, 19.95. This number is an abstraction; it is the only common property of a pile of notes and coins and a collection of electronic signals. Thus the program straddles the complex worlds of financial transactions and electronic components, but it is only concerned with certain abstract properties of each.

In a technical sense, all programming languages are equally powerful. Any computation that can be described in one language can be described in any other general-purpose programming language. In practice, then, the usefulness of a programming language depends not on its power but on its ability to express solutions in a problem-oriented rather than a machine-oriented way. Many years of research were required to discover abstractions that are both helpful to programmers and efficient to implement. Much work remains to be done.

8.1 PROCEDURES

The principle role of a procedure in a computer program is to separate specification from implementation: *what* is to be done from *how* it is to be done. It is only by using procedures in this way that a long program can be made intellectually manageable. In this role, the procedure is simply a physical realization of the technique of stepwise refinement. When we have performed a refinement step such as

$$S \longrightarrow$$
$$S_1$$
$$S_2$$
$$S_3$$

we have the choice of further refining statements S_1, S_2, and S_3, or of simply declaring them to be procedure invocations (answering the question *what?*) and later on writing the procedure bodies (answering the question *how?*). The importance of the procedure in this context is that it enables us to think about one thing at a time; this applies whether we are writing the program, altering it, or merely reading it. We can see from this reasoning that the choice of appropriate names for procedures is very important. We should be able to deduce from its name what a procedure does without having to look for the body of it in the text of the program.

When procedures are used in this way, as a step in the refinement process, the finished program has a tree structure. For example, if we start with a statement S and refine it using three procedures S_1, S_2, and S_3, we obtain the tree of Fig. 8.1. A more elaborate statement ES might be refined into a larger tree, such as the one shown in Fig. 8.2. The importance of the tree structure is that the role of each procedure is clearly defined by its position in the tree.

The other role of procedures in programming is to permit *factorization*. In algebra, the expression $a \times x + b \times x$ can be factored into the form $(a + b) \times x$. The second form is easier to understand because x occurs only once, and if x is a complicated expression, the second

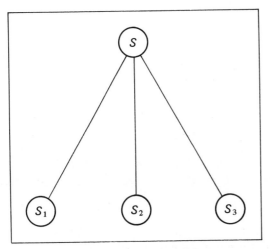

Fig. 8.1
A simple tree-structured program.

form is also more efficient computationally. In a similar way, we encounter situations in program development in which the same refinement is used more than once. Suppose, for example, that in Fig. 8.2 it turns out that procedures C, E, and I perform the same task. It would be tiresome to write out the same procedure three times, and of course we do not have to because we can factor the procedure C. The resulting program no longer has a tree structure, as we see from Fig. 8.3.

Factorization is a useful technique, but it must be applied with care. Whereas in Fig. 8.2 we can alter C to suit the requirements of A, or E to suit the requirements of D, we can alter C in Fig. 8.3 only after checking that the changes are compatible with the expectations of procedures A, D, and H. When we use procedures in this way, we must provide them with clean and simple interfaces to ensure that they are used correctly.

The tree structure of a program is represented in block-structured languages, such as Pascal, by nested procedures. The tree of Fig. 8.2, for example, corresponds to the following program structure:

```
program ES
  procedure A
    procedure B
      { Body of B }
    procedure C
      { Body of C }
    { Body of A }
```

(8.1.1)

```
procedure D
  procedure E
    { Body of E }
  { Body of D }
procedure F
  procedure G
    { Body of G }
  procedure H
    procedure I
      { Body of I }
    { Body of H }
  { Body of F }
{ Body of ES }
```

Observe, however, that Pascal and other programming languages allow procedure invocations that are not shown in the tree diagram. For example, B can invoke C and I can invoke G. This is the loophole that permits factorization. The Pascal program corresponding to Fig. 8.3 has the following structure:

```
program ES                                          (8.1.2)
  procedure C
    { Body of C }
  procedure A
    procedure B
      { Body of B }
    { Body of A }
  procedure D
    { Body of D }
  procedure F
    procedure G
      { Body of G }
    procedure H }
      { Body of H }
    { Body of F }
  { Body of ES }
```

In this program, the procedure C is a utility that can be invoked from any part of the program. Utilities of this kind are needed frequently in large programs. Since they can be accessed from anywhere, they should be kept as simple as possible and particular care should be taken in coding them.

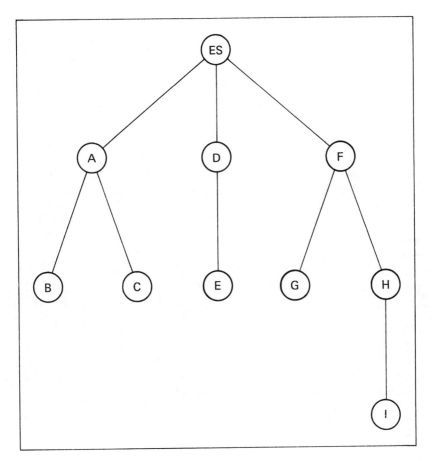

Fig. 8.2
A more elaborate tree-structured program.

Parameters

A procedure communicates with its environment by means of parameters. Parameters are used both to pass information to a procedure and to receive results from it. In some programming languages, including Pascal, procedures may also access and alter variables in enclosing scopes. For example, procedure B in program (8.1.2) can access the local variables of procedure A, and any procedure in a Pascal program can access the global variables of the program.

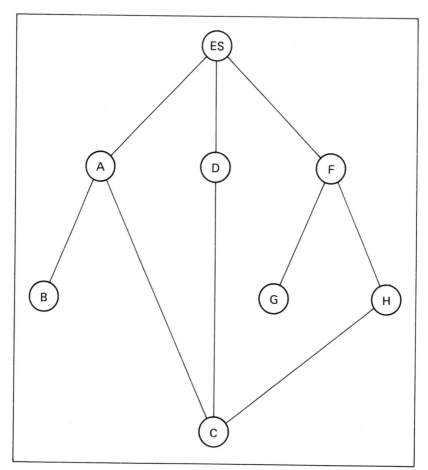

Fig. 8.3
Tree structure lost.

There is a strong argument for prohibiting the use of global variables in procedures. If a procedure refers only to its own local variables
and its parameters, every variable used by it is defined within it. The
procedure is then easy to read and understand because it is a self-
contained module. Although this is in many ways a desirable way of
programming, it is not always a practical way with a language such as
Pascal. There are situations in which we can only avoid using global
variables by introducing unwieldy parameter lists.

We can distinguish two kinds of program. The first kind might be
called action-oriented programs; the flow of control is primary and data
is subordinate to control. In this style of programming, procedures
operate with a small number of variables and the information that they

need can be passed by parameters. The second kind is a data-oriented program; there is a large body of data and different parts of the program act on this in various ways. In this kind of programming, which Bachman has colorfully described as "navigating in a sea of data," a low-level procedure might need to access large parts of the data, and it is highly inconvenient to pass all the global data down through many levels of intermediate calls in the form of parameter lists.

Notation

The notation we use for procedures in the program development language conveys the important features of the procedures but need not conform to the detailed syntax required for the final program. It is important to specify the name of the procedure and its parameters. Although we always distinguish value and variable parameters in the program development language, we do not mention the types of parameters unless the context requires that we do so. For example, a procedure that skips over blanks in the input file might appear in the program development language in this form:

> procedure *skip* (var *ch*)
>   repeat
>   read(*ch*)
>   until *ch* ≠ blank or end of file

This procedure would eventually be refined into a Pascal procedure something like this:

> **procedure** *skip* (var *ch* : *char*);
>   **begin**
>   **repeat**
>   *read*(*ch*)
>   **until** (*ch* ≠ ' ') **or** *eof*
>   **end**;

Functions perform for data the role that procedures perform for actions. A function is invoked in an expression; it should return a value and preferably it should not do anything else. In the program development language we identify the type of a function with a notation that is similar to Pascal's notation. This is a function in the program development language:

> function *cube* (*x*) : real;
>   *cube* := *x* * *x* * *x*

The result of refining this function would be the following Pascal function:

```
function cube (x : real) : real;
  begin
    cube := x * sqr(x)
  end;
```

8.2 DATA

To solve problems we must manipulate many different kinds of data. Some data, such as lengths, masses, times, and sums of money, are numerical. Data also occur in the form of characters. A short string of characters may represent a name or a part-description, and a long string of characters may represent an entire book. Another form of data is binary data. Binary data items are two-valued; a switch, for instance, may be on or off.

All of these forms of data are represented in a digital computer by binary digits, or *bits*. Each bit may have one of two possible values, and we use the symbols 0 and 1 to denote these values. Before we present data to the computer we must *encode* them into strings of bits, and when the computer informs us of its results, we must *decode* them. At the level of the user of a program, the encoding and decoding processes are usually implicit because they are performed partly by the processor and partly by the peripherals. When we are programming, we work at an intermediate level at which we must be aware that the encoding and decoding take place, but we need not be concerned with the way in which they are implemented. In high-level programming languages this intermediate level is defined by the concept of *type*.

When we say that a value is an integer, a real, or a character, we are referring to its type. Since it is not possible to determine the type of a value by examining the bits that represent it in the machine, the type is an abstraction. The type of a value determines the way in which we interpret the bits that represent it. For example, the bits 01100001 may represent either the integer 97 or the ASCII character "a".

The type of a value has a further role: it determines the operations we can meaningfully apply to the value. For example, the operation of addition is meaningful when applied to integers but not when applied to characters. Moreover, although we may add both integers and reals, the algorithms—and hence the instruction codes—used are different. The compiler of a high-level language must therefore both reject meaningless operations and disambiguate operators such as + which may be used with different types.

Types have both machine-oriented and problem-oriented aspects. For example, when we use real numbers to represent lengths, we are exploiting their problem-oriented properties; they behave in the way that we expect real numbers to behave when we add them, multiply them, and find their square roots. On the other hand, if we worry about rounding errors and overflow, we are concerned with machine-oriented properties. The problem of language designers is to balance these aspects of the types they select for the language. Types that are too machine-oriented may be inconvenient to use and types that are too problem-oriented may be inefficient to implement.

Integer arithmetic is simple to implement and the results are exact. When we use integers to solve problems, we need not be concerned about their representation by the machine unless their values are very large. Real arithmetic is much less satisfactory from the point of view of the problem solver. When we manipulate algebraic expressions, we frequently assume the truth of axioms of number theory, such as the associative and distributive laws. These laws state that for all real numbers X, Y, and Z, the following equalities are true:

$$(X + Y) + Z = X + (Y + Z)$$
$$X \times (Y + Z) = X \times Y + Y \times Z$$

These axioms are not satisfied by the real arithmetic instructions of most computers. In the terminology of Section 4.3, the formal system of real arithmetic is an inadequate abstraction of the real arithmetic of actual computers. Unfortunately it is quite difficult to construct axioms for the arithmetic of computers that are precise and yet not too complicated to use. Consequently we must take great care in simplifying the expressions we intend to use in our programs.

When we compare Pascal with its predecessor, Algol 60, and with other programming languages, we find that the greater expressive power of Pascal owes much to its provision of problem-oriented types. In fact, we can illustrate the distinction between machine-oriented and problem-oriented types by considering the enumerated and set types of Pascal.

In an enumerated type definition, the values of the type are listed explicitly, as in this example:

type
    color = (*red, orange, yellow, green, blue, violet*);

A similar effect can be obtained by a set of constant definitions of the following form:

const
    red = 0;   *green* = 3;

$$orange = 1; \qquad blue = 4;$$
$$yellow = 2; \qquad violet = 5;$$

The advantage of the enumerated type definition over the list of constant definitions is that the enumerated type definition does not permit accidental or intentional abuse of the type. For example, we cannot write expressions such as *blue + yellow* or use 6 as an additional color. Moreover, any abuses can be detected by the compiler and so no run-time overhead is incurred by the use of an enumerated type. Enumerated types are problem oriented because they allow us to state our requirements very precisely; this simplifies both the programming task and the subsequent reading of the program.

The advantages of the Pascal set type are similar but even more significant. Most compilers have instructions that perform logical operations on strings of bits. For example, if the operands are the bit strings

$$1\ 0\ 1\ 0\ 1\ 0\ 1\ 0$$

and

$$1\ 1\ 1\ 1\ 0\ 0\ 0\ 0$$

then the *and* operation applied to these strings would produce a string containing 1 where both operands contained 1, and 0 elsewhere. In this example, the result is the string:

$$1\ 0\ 1\ 0\ 0\ 0\ 0\ 0$$

One common use of this instruction in assembly language programming is to test for a particular bit. For example, if any bit string is *and*ed with the string

$$0\ 0\ 1\ 0\ 0\ 0\ 0\ 0$$

the resulting string will be nonzero if and only if the third bit of the given string is 1.

In some high-level languages, these operations and operands are abstracted in an obvious way from the machine language. In these languages, we can declare variables whose values are bit strings and we can write literal bit strings. The languages also provide operations that take bit strings as operands. The preceding test, for instance, might be written in the following way:

$$X \text{ and } `00100000' \neq 0$$

Although it is useful to be able to do things like this in a high-level language, the notation is not problem oriented. There is nothing, for example, in the preceding expression that tells us the significance of the third bit. All we have gained is the ability to represent low-level operations in a high-level language.

We use bit strings in low-level languages to record the presence or absence of an object that belongs to a particular universe. A string of eight bits represents a universe in which eight objects can be distinguished. From this viewpoint, we can see that the use of a bit string corresponds closely to the mathematical concept of a *set*.* In Pascal, the notation used for operations on bit strings is derived from the mathematical notation used for sets, and it is a powerful and suggestive notation for the programmer. Individual objects have names; a constant set is represented by a list of its members; and set membership is denoted by the operator **in** used between an object and a set rather than by the operator *and* used between two bit strings. We can write, for example, boolean expressions such as

> *endfile* **in** *status*

rather than obscure expressions involving bit strings. Thus although the implementation of bit string operations and sets is the same, sets provide a problem-oriented interface to the machine whereas bit strings provide a machine-oriented interface.

8.3 STRUCTURED TYPES

An object whose type is structured has more than one component. The important properties of a structured type are the relationship between the components of the type and the means by which the individual components are accessed. The structured types provided by Pascal are *arrays* and *records*. The components of an array are all of the same type, and a component is selected by an index expression. If we have defined

> **type** *vector* = **array** [1..3] **of** *real*;

and we have declared

> **var** *v* : *vector*;

then the components of *v* are *v*[1], *v*[2], and *v*[3]. The components of a record need not be of the same type, and a component is selected by name. We can define, for example, a record describing the identity, position, and velocity of an airplane as follows:

---

*To be more precise, each bit string is a member of the power set of a given set.

```
type
  airplane = record
                identity : 1..100;
                position, velocity : vector
            end;
```

We can declare a variable of this type, as in:

var *jumbo* : *airplane*;

The components of *jumbo* are *jumbo.identity*, *jumbo.position*, and *jumbo.velocity*. The third component of the velocity of *jumbo* is *jumbo.velocity*[3].

There are important parallels between control structures and data structures. The control structure corresponding to the array is the **for** statement. It is natural, for example, to process the components of a vector by a statement such as

```
for i := 1 to 3 do
  v[i] := 0
```

The control structure corresponding to the record is the *sequence*. When we initialize or otherwise process a record, it is natural to process each component in turn, as in this example:

```
jumbo.identity := 76;
for i := 1 to 3 do
  begin
    jumbo.position[i] := 0;
    jumbo.velocity[i] := 0
  end
```

Records with variants may be defined in Pascal using the keyword **case**. The corresponding control structure is a **case** statement. We encounter examples of this correspondence in Chapter 10.

The components of arrays and records in Pascal may themselves be arrays and records and consequently we can construct elaborate data structures. We cannot, however, define operations that accept objects with structured types as operands. All operations, except copying and comparison for equality, are permitted only for the primitive components of structured objects. There are other languages, Algol-68 for instance, in which operations can be defined for structured types.

The fact that we can define our own structured types in Pascal has a significant effect on the ease with which we can solve programming problems. It is easier to write a large program in Pascal than in FORTRAN, for example. Despite their usefulness, however, the structured types of Pascal are abstractions of the addressing modes of typical modern computers, and as such they are machine oriented. In order to define problem-oriented structured types we require a means of specifying both a set of values and a set of operations for a structured type. Moreover, operations other than the specified operations must not be permitted. These goals are achieved by *encapsulating* the implementation details of the type and *exposing* only the specification of the type to other parts of the program in the same way that a procedure is known to other parts of the program only by its name and parameter list. Types defined in this way are called *abstract data types*.

A large number of languages provide data abstraction facilities of this kind, although none is yet in widespread use. In most of these languages, abstract data types (variously called classes, clusters, capsules, envelopes, and modules) can be defined. These types incorporate both data structures and procedures, and the data structures may only be accessed by invoking the procedures. Thus abstract data types serve to combine procedural abstraction and data abstraction.

SUMMARY

Abstraction is an important technique both in problem solving and in programming. The function of a programming language is to bridge the gap between the world of the problem and the world of the machine. All programming languages provide a procedural mechanism that enables us to encapsulate and name a sequence of actions. The provisions for data abstraction vary from one language to another. The languages that provide complete facilities for data abstraction are of recent vintage and have yet to be fully evaluated. Although Pascal does not provide for encapsulation of data structures, we can write robust and adaptable programs in Pascal if we understand the concept of abstract data types. The next chapter contains examples of this programming style.

FURTHER READING

Bachman introduced the concept of "navigating in a sea of data" in his Turing Award lecture, "The Programmer as Navigator."

Hoare gives a lucid explanation of the principles of data abstraction in the book *Structured Programming* by Dahl, Dijkstra, and Hoare. Wirth incorporated these principles into Pascal, which was originally described in his paper, "The Programming Language Pascal."

The idea that the type of an object determines more than the set of permissible values of an object possessing the type is explored by Morris in "Types Are Not Sets."

Languages incorporating abstract data types are described in the papers "Abstraction Mechanisms in CLU" by Liskov, Snyder, Atkinson, and Schaffert; and "Early Experience with Mesa" by Geschke, Morris, and Satterthwaite. The book *Structured System Programming* by Welsh and McKeag describes the language Pascal-Plus, which incorporates an abstract data type facility called an *envelope*.

Wirth has proposed an alternative kind of data abstraction to the one described in this chapter. He calls it a *module*, and the concepts are expounded in a group of papers about the language *Modula*.

Further information about types in Pascal may be obtained from Chapters 5 and 6 of *Programming in Pascal* by Grogono.

EXERCISES

8.1 What are the desirable abstract properties of a file? Do you think that Pascal provides a useful file abstraction?

8.2 Compare the abstraction facilities of two programming languages you know well. [Suggestions: BASIC, FORTRAN, PL/I, Pascal, LISP, APL.]

8.3 What are the differences between the implementations of linked lists in Pascal and LISP? If you do not know LISP, you could answer this question by considering strings in SNOBOL or arrays in APL.

8.4 In what ways do global variables subvert modularity? We could eliminate nested scopes from Pascal (and similar block-structured languages) by allowing a procedure to access only its parameters and its local variables, but the resulting language would be hard to use. Can you suggest an intermediate solution to this problem?

8.5 Suggest syntax for an extension to Pascal that would allow true encapsulation of a type descriptor and permitted operations for the type. Would nested scopes be useful in your language? Outline the changes that would have to be made to the Pascal compiler to implement your extension.

CHAPTER 9
REPRESENTATION

In simple problems, such as those of Chapter 7, we are not concerned with the issue of representation; at such a low level the programming language and the machine handle the problem of representation for us. We merely specify that we want to use an integer, a real, or an array, and everything happens automatically.

It is important to realize that although there are conventional representations for these simple objects, there are nonetheless opportunities for choice of representation at this level. Most computers, for example, represent integers and reals by binary strings. This is merely an electronic convenience, however, and some early computers represented numbers by decimal strings, using dekatron vacuum tubes. Today binary storage is ubiquitous and true decimal representations are not used, although binary coded decimal representation is still in use. An array is usually represented by a set of contiguous locations in primary storage, but again this is not the only possible representation. A large array may be split into pages, and some of these pages may be moved onto a disk from time to time.

These variations in representation are usually invisible to the programmer. When we require elaborate data structures, however, we must design our own representations for them. Appropriate choice of representation for data structures is a major aspect of the design of large programs. An algorithm does not, and should not, specify the representation of data, and consequently the choice of representation is an important component of implementation.

In this chapter we consider four problems. The problems are simple to solve in that algorithms for their solution are easy to find. The interesting part of each solution is the implementation which requires us to discover a suitable representation for the data.

9.1 THE TOWER OF HANOI

The problem *Tower of Hanoi*, introduced in Section 2.3, provides a simple example of the problem of representation. In this section we develop a program that prints the moves required to transfer a pile of *numdisks* disks from the left peg to the right peg, using the center peg when necessary. The design of the program is based on features of the known solution and the data structure that we use is a straightforward model of the physical system.

The state-action graph of *Tower of Hanoi*, shown in Fig. 2.4, reveals properties of the solution that apply to any number of disks, although Fig. 2.4 only shows the possible states for a system with three disks. First, we observe that the small disk moves at the odd-numbered (first, third, fifth, ...) steps. Second, the small disk moves cyclically. If we number the pegs 1 (left peg), 2 (middle peg), and 3 (right peg), the small disk visits pegs

$$1, 2, 3, 1, 2, 3, \ldots$$

if *numdisks* is even, and pegs

$$1, 3, 2, 1, 3, 2, \ldots$$

if *numdisks* is odd. There are two ways to model the cyclic motion of the smallest disk. One way is to use modular arithmetic; the statements

$$peg := peg \ \textbf{mod} \ 3 + 1$$

and

$$peg := peg \ \textbf{mod} \ 3 + 2$$

can be used repeatedly to generate the sequences $1, 2, 3, \ldots$ and $1, 3, 2, \ldots$ respectively. Looking ahead, however, we see that this approach will lead to difficulties when we want to refer to pegs other than the one holding the smallest disk, and accordingly we choose another way to model the cyclic motion. We use three variables, *peg1*, *peg2*, and *peg3*, and we perform a *cyclic assignment*:

$$peg1$$

$$peg2 := peg3$$

We can implement these assignments in a linear way by introducing a temporary store called *peg*:

$$peg \ := peg1 \qquad\qquad (9.1.1)$$
$$peg1 := peg2$$
$$peg2 := peg3$$
$$peg3 := peg$$

If *numdisks* is odd, we perform the initialization

$$peg1 := 1$$
$$peg2 := 3$$
$$peg3 := 2$$

and the first move is

$$move(peg1, peg2)$$

in which we assume the existence of a procedure *move* that prints an appropriate message. If *numdisks* is even, we perform the initialization

$$peg1 := 1$$
$$peg2 := 2$$
$$peg3 := 3$$

and the first move is again

$$move(peg1, peg2)$$

Before each subsequent move of the smallest disk, we perform the assignments (9.1.1). Then if *numdisks* is odd, the moves generated for the smallest disk are

$$move(1,3)$$
$$move(3,2)$$
$$move(2,1)$$
$$...$$

and if *numdisks* is even, the moves are

$$move(1,2)$$
$$move(2,3)$$
$$move(3,1)$$
$$...$$

We can now turn our attention to the larger disks. Since the odd-numbered moves leave the smallest disk on *peg2*, the even-numbered moves are of the form:

$$move(peg1,peg3)$$

or

$$move(peg3,peg1)$$

because we can neither move the smallest disk nor put another disk on top of it. We can decide between these by examining the sizes of the top disks on these pegs and moving the smallest disk; no other move is possible. Suppose that we have a function *top* that tells us the size of the top disk on a given peg. Then we can write the even-numbered moves in this way:

> if *top(peg1)* < *top(peg3)*
> then *move(peg1,peg3)*
> else *move(peg3,peg1)*

We note that *top* will sometimes examine a peg with no disks on it, and in this case it must return a size larger than the size of any actual disk so that we do not attempt to move a disk that does not exist.

Finally, we need a termination condition. Clearly we have finished when there are *numdisks* on the right peg. In the following algorithm we assume the existence of a function *height* that returns the number of disks on the given peg.

```
peg1 := 1
if odd(numdisks)
  then
    peg2 := 3
    peg3 := 2
  else
    peg2 := 2
    peg3 := 3
move(peg1,peg2)
while height(3) < numdisks do
  if top(peg1) < top(peg3)
    then move(peg1,peg3)
    else move(peg3,peg1)
  peg := peg1
  peg1 := peg2
```

$$peg2 := peg3$$
$$peg3 := peg$$
$$move(peg1,peg2)$$

We cannot derive a program directly from this algorithm as we did in the examples in Chapter 7 because we have not yet chosen a data structure to represent the state of the system. We can represent a pile of disks using an array. Assuming that we will never encounter a pile of more than *maxdisks* disks, we can define a type *pile*:

type
    diskindex = 0..*maxdisks*;
    pile = **record**
           ht : *diskindex*;
           size : **array** [*diskindex*] **of** *integer*
       end;

The sizes of the disks may be represented by numbers ranging from 1, the size of the smallest disk, to *maxdisks*, the size of the largest possible disk. When a pile p contains no disks, we will ensure that $p.ht$ is zero and that $p.size[0]$ is *maxint* so that when *top* looks at an empty pile it will return a large number, as required.

We can represent the state of the complete system by an array of three piles:

var
    state : **array** [1..3] **of** *pile*;

Since the program models one system only, we make *state* a global variable that is altered by *move* and examined by *top* and *height*. We initialize the state in two steps. First, we establish three pegs with no disks on them and then we put *numdisks* disks on the left peg. This is the first step:

          for *peg* := 1 **to** 3 **do**
            state[*peg*].*ht* := 0
            state[*peg*].*size*[0] := *maxint*

This statement, and several statements that we write later, can be expressed more succinctly using the **with** notation of Pascal. We have not used **with** in the development language previously, but its introduction is consistent with the policy that notation may be introduced freely provided that it clarifies the development. We can write the preceding statement in this way:

```
for peg := 1 to 3 do
  with state[peg] do
    ht := 0
    size[0] := maxint
```

We can now place the stack of disks on the left peg, with the largest disk at the bottom:

```
with state[1] do
  for disk := 1 to numdisks do
    size[disk] := numdisks − disk + 1
  ht := numdisks
```

We can define the functions *height* and *top* as follows:

```
function height (peg) : diskindex
  height := state[peg].ht
```

```
function top (peg) : integer
  with state[peg] do
    top := size[ht]
```

The function *top* appears as a Pascal function in the final program. The function *height* is trivial and, since it is only required once, we do not use it explicitly in the final program.

The procedure *move* both prints the move and updates the state. Since it knows the size of the disk that it is moving, it prints that too. The **with** statement helps to make it clearer.

```
procedure move (pegf,pegt)
  print 'Move disk' top(pegf) 'from' pegf 'to' pegt
  with state[pegf] do
    s := size[ht]
    ht := ht − 1
  with state[pegt] do
    ht := ht + 1
    size[ht] := s
```

We now have all the components we need for a Pascal program. The program that follows reads a value of *numdisks* from *input*, verifies that $0 < numdisks \leq maxdisks$, and prints the moves required to move a stack of *numdisks* disks from the left peg to the right peg.

```
program hanoi (input,output);
  const
    maxdisks = 10;
```

```
    maxpegs = 3;
type
  diskindex = 0..maxdisks;
  pegindex = 1..maxpegs;
  disksize = 0..maxint;
  pile = record
          ht : diskindex;
          size : array [diskindex] of disksize
        end;

var
  state : array [pegindex] of pile;
  numdisks : integer;
  disk : diskindex;
  peg, peg1, peg2, peg3 : pegindex;
{ Return size of top disk in given pile }
function top (peg : pegindex) : disksize;
  begin
    with state[peg] do
      top := size[ht]
  end; { top }
{ Move a disk from pegf to pegt }
procedure move (pegf, pegt : pegindex);
  var
    s : disksize;
  begin
    writeln('Move disk ',top(pegf),' from ',pegf,' to ',pegt);
    with state[pegf] do
      begin
        s := size[ht];
        ht := ht - 1
      end; { with }
    with state[pegt] do
      begin
        ht := ht + 1;
        size[ht] := s
      end { with }
  end; { move }
begin { Hanoi }
  { Establish initial state }
  for peg := 1 to maxpegs do
    with state[peg] do
```

```
    begin
      ht := 0;
      size[0] := maxint
    end; { with and for }
{ Read number of disks to be moved }
read(numdisks);
if numdisks = 0
  then writeln('No disks')
else if numdisks > maxdisks
  then writeln('Too many disks')
else
  begin
    { Put disks on left peg }
    with state[1] do
      begin
        for disk := 1 to numdisks do
          size[disk] := numdisks - disk + 1;
        ht := numdisks
      end; { with }
    { Set up smallest disk for cycling }
    peg1 := 1;
    if odd(numdisks)
      then
        begin
          peg2 := 3;
          peg3 := 2
        end
      else
        begin
          peg2 := 2;
          peg3 := 3
        end;
    { Move the disks }
    move(peg1,peg2);
    while state[3].ht < numdisks do
      begin
        if top(peg1) < top(peg3)
          then move(peg1,peg3)
          else move(peg3,peg1);
        peg := peg1;
        peg1 := peg2;
```

```
        peg2 := peg3;
        peg3 := peg;
        move(peg1,peg2)
    end { while }
  end
end. { Hanoi }
```

This program is a rather complex solution to a problem that is actually quite simple. It does more than is required, in that it actually simulates the entire system of pegs, disks, and moves although we only need to list the moves. In this respect, it can be called a naive solution. The amount of detail that we incorporate into a data structure should be related to the amount of information that we intend to derive from it, and in this solution we have incorporated more information in the data structure than we require to solve the problem. In the next chapter we examine ways of solving *Tower of Hanoi* with a less elaborate data structure.

9.2 A GRAPH ALGORITHM

We encountered graphs in Chapter 2, in which state-action graphs helped us to understand the problems *Tower of Hanoi* and *Jugs*. There are many other applications of graphs. In some situations it is natural to apply graph theory; for example, in the analysis of electrical networks, the organization of the components of an integrated circuit, or the analysis of the flow of control in a computer program. There are many other less obvious applications of graph theory in diverse areas such as grammar analysis and resource scheduling.

Graph algorithms are usually formulated in an abstract way in terms of the set of nodes and the set of edges of a graph. A graph can be represented in a program in several ways, and the choice of representation can significantly affect the efficiency of the program. It is therefore important that we select a representation of a graph that is appropriate to the problem being solved. In general, we need to know the operations that must be performed on the graph, and it is also useful to have some idea of the frequency with which they will be used.

Suppose that we have succeeded in expressing a problem space in the form of a graph, as we did in Chapter 2. That is, we have defined a set of states, including an initial state and a goal state, and a set of actions that enable us to move between states. The nodes of the graph represent the states of the problem and its edges represent the actions.

The problem is solved if we can find a path along the edges of the graph that joins the initial state to the goal state; the solution is optimal if we can find the shortest such path.

The problem of finding the shortest path between two specified nodes of a graph is one of the many problems with which graph theory deals. The solutions of these problems have many applications and consequently a number of graph algorithms have been developed to solve them in the general case. For example, the *shortest paths* algorithm, which we consider in more detail in the following discussion, finds the shortest path or paths between two given nodes of a graph.

Graph algorithms are usually stated in such a way that they are independent of the way in which the graph is represented. This means that choosing a suitable representation for a graph is an important step in the implementation of a graph algorithm. We will follow the process through in detail for the problem of the shortest paths. We start with a formal statement of the problem.

Problem 9.1:   SHORTEST PATHS

Given a graph G and two nodes *initial* and *goal* of G. Construct the subgraph of G that contains the shortest paths connecting *initial* to *goal*.

A *subgraph* of a graph G is a graph that contains some of the nodes and edges of G but not necessarily all of them. The solution of the problem is a subgraph rather than a list of edges because in general the shortest path is not unique. The problem is illustrated in Fig. 9.1. Fig. 9.1(a) shows the original graph and Fig. 9.1(b) shows the graph of shortest paths between the nodes A and K. The solution contains two paths of length 4 from A to K. There are other paths joining A to K but they are longer than 4 edges and consequently they are not included in the solution.

The principle of the shortest paths algorithm is simple. We construct the set S_k of nodes that can be reached from *initial* by traversing k edges, for $k = 0, 1, 2, \ldots$. If there is a path of length k from *initial* to *goal*, then *goal* will be a member of the set S_k. If there is no value of k for which *goal* is a member of S_k, then *goal* cannot be reached from *initial*. We can think of the sets $S_0, S_1, S_2, \ldots$ as the front of a "wave" that starts from *initial* and spreads through the graph. The construction of the sets S_k is called the *label phase* of the shortest paths algorithm. Once we have reached *goal*, we work our way back to *initial* using information accumulated during the label phase to ensure that we stay on the shortest paths. This is called the *return phase* of the algorithm.

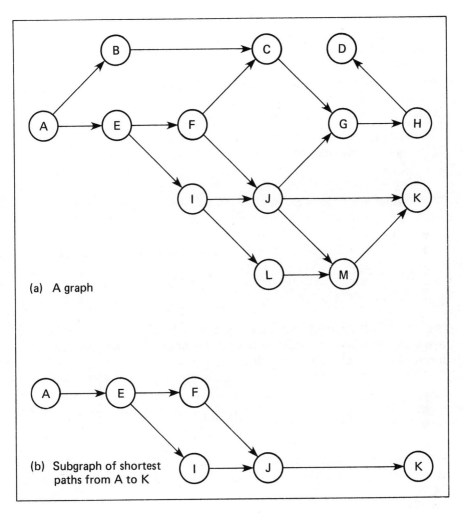

(a) A graph

(b) Subgraph of shortest
paths from A to K

Fig. 9.1
Shortest paths.

The algorithm maintains a record of its progress by labeling the nodes that it visits. Only unlabeled nodes are added to the sets S_k, and consequently the algorithm terminates when every node that can be reached from *initial* has been labeled and it does not loop indefinitely if the graph contains cycles. We can improve its efficiency by terminating the label phase as soon as we have found a set S_k containing the node *goal*.

We use set notation in the following refinement of the label phase. ϕ is the empty set, ϵ denotes set membership, and $\cup$ denotes set union. We use brackets [...] rather than braces {...} to denote sets because we are already using braces in our development languages to enclose comments. Moreover, the brackets are in accordance with Pascal usage. The boolean function *joined* (G,X,Y) returns *true* if there is an edge in the graph G that joins the node X to the node Y.

label phase ⟶   (9.2.1)
  label *initial* with '0'
  $k := 0$
  $S_k := [initial]$
  while not $(goal \ \epsilon \ S_k$ or $S_k = \phi)$ do
    $S_{k+1} := \phi$
    for each node $X \ \epsilon \ S_k$ do
      for each unlabeled node Y such that *joined*(G,X,Y) do
        $S_{k+1} := S_{k+1} \cup [Y]$
        label Y with '$k+1$'
    $k := k + 1$

The effect of the label phase on the graph of Fig. 9.1 is shown in Fig. 9.2 in which the labels are written beside the nodes. The sets S_k generated during the label phase are as follows:

$$S_1 = [B,E]$$
$$S_2 = [C,F,I]$$
$$S_3 = [G,J,L]$$
$$S_4 = [H,K,M]$$

At this point the algorithm terminates because the goal node K belongs to the set S_4. If we ignored this and continued, we would obtain the sets

$$S_5 = [D]$$
$$S_6 = \emptyset$$

indicating that every node that can be reached from A is labeled.

We now know that the shortest paths from A to K contain 4 edges but we do not yet know which edges lie on these paths. We can obtain this information by working backwards from K. Since the node K is labeled 4, the only neighboring nodes that lie on the shortest paths to K must be labeled 3. Thus J lies on one of the shortest paths but M does not in Fig. 9.2. This idea is embodied in the following algorithm for the return phase. Note that at the beginning of the return phase k has

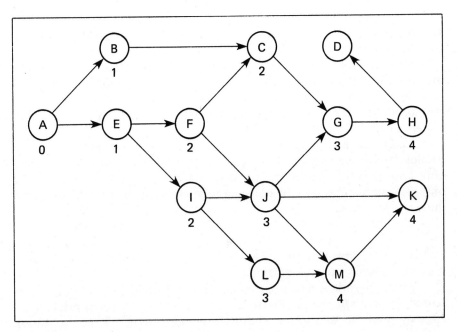

Fig. 9.2
Conclusion of the label phase.

the last value that it achieved in the label phase. The sets T_k contain the
nodes that lie on the shortest paths and that can be reached in k steps
from *initial*. The subgraph H of the shortest paths is constructed during
this phase; it is initially empty, and the operation *join*(H,X,Y) creates
an edge joining the nodes X and Y in H.

(9.2.2)

       return phase $\longrightarrow$

         $H :=$ empty graph
         $T_k := [goal]$
         while $k > 0$ do
            $T_{k-1} := \phi$
            for each node $Y \in T_k$ do
               for each node X labeled '$k-1$' such that *joined*(G,X,Y) do
                  $T_{k-1} := T_{k-1} \cup [X]$
                  join(H,X,Y)
         $k := k - 1$

When the return phase has finished, the subgraph H has the form shown
in Fig. 9.1(b) and $T_{k-1} = [A]$, the initial node.

Further refinement of this algorithm is impossible without some knowledge of the way in which operations such as *join* are implemented, and this in turn depends on the way in which the graph is represented.

The number of edges that we expect a graph to have will influence the way in which we represent it and process it. A graph with N nodes may have as few as zero edges and as many as N^2 edges, but these bounds are too far apart to guide us without some further knowledge of the application.

There are many structures in which the average number of edges leading from a particular node is small. If we know, for example, that only two or three edges leave most nodes, we need provide storage for only $3N$ edges. This may be considerably less than the theoretical maximum of N^2 edges.

We can divide the problem of representing a graph into two subproblems: how to represent the edges and how to represent the nodes. The issues are not entirely separate, but this discussion of the problem provides us with a useful starting point.

First, there is a naive representation in which each node is represented by a node containing pointers and each pointer represents an edge by pointing to another node. The advantage of this representation is that information associated with a node can be stored in the corresponding record. This form of representation is sometimes used for parse trees, and Fig. 9.3(b) shows the expression of Fig. 9.3(a) represented in this way. For general graph applications, however, this representation has a major disadvantage: we can only access the nodes of the graph by traversing its edges. Not only is this inefficient, but if we delete an edge, we may lose part of the graph altogether!

The other representations do not immediately reveal the topology of the graph. We can represent the set of nodes by a vector or by a list, and we can represent the set of edges emanating from a node by a vector or by a list. Of these four representations, the most useful are the two obtained by representing the set of nodes by a vector because they permit rapid access to specified nodes. If the edges emanating from a node are also represented by a vector, the graph is represented by a vector of vectors, or, in other words, a matrix. This matrix is called the *adjacency matrix* of the graph. If we are interested only in the presence or absence of edges and not the cost associated with an edge, the adjacency matrix has *boolean* components. If we call it *adj*, then *adj*[X, Y] is *true* if the graph contains an edge from node X to node Y, and *false* otherwise. Fig. 9.4(b) shows the boolean adjacency matrix of the graph depicted in Fig. 9.4(a).

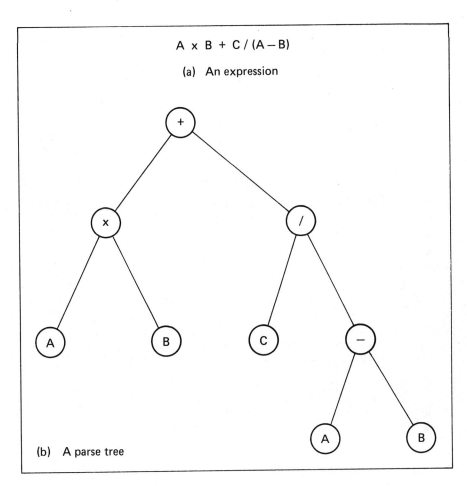

A x B + C / (A − B)

(a)   An expression

(b)   A parse tree

Fig. 9.3
An expression and its parse tree.

An advantage of the adjacency matrix is that if cost information is associated with the edges, this information can be stored in the matrix. The value of $adj[X,Y]$ is then *integer* or *real* rather than *boolean*. If there is an edge from X to Y, its cost is $adj[X,Y]$, and if there is no edge from X to Y, then $adj[X,Y]$ is given some readily identifiable value such as *maxint*. There are also disadvantages with the adjacency matrix. One is its size: the adjacency matrix of a graph with N nodes contains N^2 components regardless of the number of edges in the graph.

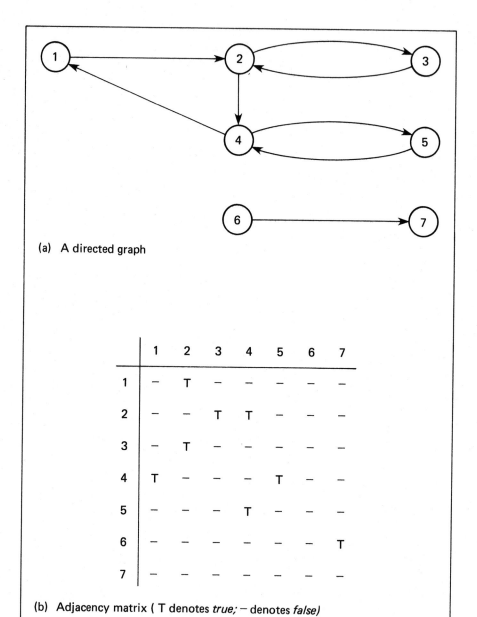

(a) A directed graph

	1	2	3	4	5	6	7
1	–	T	–	–	–	–	–
2	–	–	T	T	–	–	–
3	–	T	–	–	–	–	–
4	T	–	–	–	T	–	–
5	–	–	–	T	–	–	–
6	–	–	–	–	–	–	T
7	–	–	–	–	–	–	–

(b) Adjacency matrix (T denotes *true;* – denotes *false)*

Fig. 9.4
Graph representation.

If the number of edges is likely to be closer to N than to N^2, the adjacency matrix will be sparse and space will be wasted. A further disadvantage of the adjacency matrix is the time required to enumerate the edges emanating from a given node: N operations are necessary although in many cases the number of edges emanating from a particular node will be much less than N.

Summing up the merits and demerits of the adjacency matrix, we can say that the operation *join* and the function *joined* are fast, but that enumeration of edges is slow and a large amount of storage is required for the graph.

The last representation, and the one that we use in the examples that follow, has a vector of nodes, and each node is the starting point of a list of the edges that emanate from that node. Fig. 9.5 illustrates this representation of the graph of Fig. 9.4(a).

The space used by this representation is proportional to $N + E$, where n is the number of nodes in the graph and E is the number of edges. If E is a small multiple of N, say kN, the space required to store the graph is proportional to $(k + 1)N$, which is likely to be much smaller than N^2. The operation *join* is still efficient because *join* merely has to insert an item into a list. We can also rapidly find a node and enumerate the edges leading from it. The function *joined*, on the other hand, is slower because it has to perform a linear search of a list of nodes to find whether a particular edge exists or not. The average length of this search is $k/2$ steps. This representation is more suitable for directed than for undirected graphs, but we can represent undirected graphs by storing each edge twice, once in each of the lists corresponding to the nodes that it joins.

The type declarations required to represent graphs in this way in a Pascal program follow. *Maxnodes* is an integer whose value is chosen to suit the application; it defines the largest number of nodes that a graph may possess. A record of type *graphtype* contains two fields. The first field is the size of the graph expressed as a number of nodes and the second field is an array of pointers. Each component of the array represents a node of the graph and points to a list of the nodes that can be reached by traversing one edge.

```
type
  nodeindex = 0..maxnodes;
  nodeptr = ↑ noderec;
  noderec = record
                 node : nodeindex;
                 next : nodeptr
```

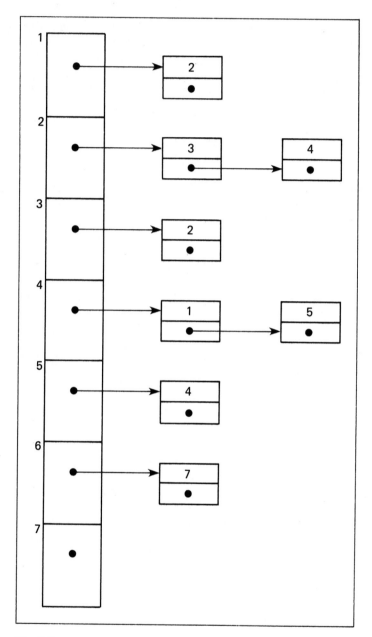

Fig. 9.5
Vector/list representation of a graph.

```
      end;
graphtype = record
              size : nodeindex;
              desc : array [1..maxnodes] of nodeptr
            end;
```

The graph *G* is initialized by setting *G.size* to zero and *G.desc*[*i*] to nil for *i* = 1, 2, ..., *maxnodes*. The procedure *join* adds a new edge to the graph and updates its size if necessary. It does not look to see if the edge is already present; in many situations this is not necessary, and when it is necessary it should be done by the calling program. The function *joined* looks in the appropriate list of edges for an edge leading to the target node.

```
procedure initialize (var graph : graphtype);
  var
    node : nodeindex;
  begin
    graph.size := 0;
    for node := 1 to maxnodes do
      graph.desc[node] := nil
  end;

procedure join (var graph : graphtype;
                start, finish : nodeindex);
  var
    ptr : nodeptr;
  begin
    if graph.size < start
      then graph.size := start;
    if graph.size < finish
      then graph.size := finish;
    new(ptr);
    ptr↑.node := finish;
    ptr↑.next := graph.desc[start];
    graph.desc[start] := ptr
  end;

function joined (graph : graphtype;
                 start, finish : nodeindex) : boolean;
  var
    ptr : nodeptr;
```

```
    state : (searching,found,endlist);
  begin
    ptr := graph.desc[start] ;
    state := searching;
    repeat
      if ptr = nil
        then state := endlist
        else if ptr↑.node = finish
          then state := found
        else ptr := ptr↑.next
      until state ≠ searching;
    joined := state = found
  end;
```

It is possible to implement the shortest paths algorithm using only the procedures *initialize* and *join* and the function *joined*. The procedure that follows uses an array of Pascal sets, *nodeset*, to represent the sets S_k of the label phase and the sets T_k of the return phase. It is a direct translation of algorithms (9.2.1) and (9.2.2), in which each abstract operation is transformed into a Pascal operation in a naive manner.

```
    procedure shortestpaths (graph : graphtype;
                             initial, goal : nodeindex;
                             var subgraph : graphtype);
  const
    unlabeled = maxint;
  var
    node, xnode, ynode : nodeindex;
    dist : integer;
    nodeset : array [nodeindex] of set of nodeindex;
    labels : array [nodeindex] of integer;
  begin
    for node := 1 to graph.size do
      labels[node] := unlabeled;
    {Label Phase}
    labels[initial] := 0;
    dist := 0;
    nodeset[dist] := [initial] ;
    while not ((goal in nodeset[dist] ) or (nodeset[dist] = [ ] )) do
      begin
        nodeset[dist + 1] := [ ] ;
        for xnode := 1 to graph.size do
```

```
          if xnode in nodeset[dist]
          then
             for ynode := 1 to graph.size do
               if labels[ynode] = unlabeled
               then
                  if joined(graph,xnode,ynode)
                  then
                     begin
                        nodeset[dist + 1] := nodeset[dist + 1]
                                                      + [ynode];
                        labels[ynode] := dist + 1
                     end;
          dist := dist + 1
       end; {while}
{ Return Phase }
initialize(subgraph);
nodeset[dist] := [goal];
while dist > 0 do
   begin
      nodeset[dist − 1] := [ ];
      for ynode := 1 to graph.size do
        if ynode in nodeset[dist]
        then
           for xnode := 1 to graph.size do
             if labels[xnode] = dist − 1
             then
                if joined(graph,xnode,ynode)
                then
                   begin
                      nodeset[dist − 1] := nodeset[dist − 1]
                                                    + [xnode];
                      join(subgraph,xnode,ynode)
                   end;
      dist := dist − 1
   end {while}
end; {shortestpaths}
```

Unfortunately this implementation is too inefficient to be of any practical use. The inefficiency comes about in the following way. In algorithm (9.2.1) we wrote

$$\text{for each node } X \in S_k \text{ do}$$

In the Pascal procedure, this statement becomes:

```
for xnode := 1 to graph.size do
   if xnode in nodeset[dist]
      then ...
```

The following line of the algorithm is:

for each unlabeled node Y such that $joined(G,X,Y)$ do

and in the procedure this becomes:

```
for ynode := 1 to graph.size do
   if labels[ynode] = unlabeled
      then
         if joined(graph,xnode,ynode)
            then ...
```

In each case the algorithm processes the members of a set that will usually contain only a small fraction of the nodes of the graph, but the procedure examines every node of the graph and then rejects those that do not fulfill the given conditions.

We can improve the efficiency of procedure *shortestpaths* by approaching the problem of representation more cautiously. We can eliminate the inefficiency of statements of the form:

```
for xnode := 1 to graph.size do
   if xnode in nodeset[dist]
      then ...
```

by using a linked list instead of a Pascal set. The list can be traversed by a loop of the following form:

```
x := nodeset[dist];
while x ≠ nil do
   begin
      ...;
      x := x↑.next
   end
```

In a similar fashion, we can use our knowledge of the representation of the graph to speed up searches of the form:

```
for ynode := 1 to graph.size do
   if joined(graph,xnode,ynode)
      then ...
```

These statements can be written more efficiently in this way:

```
x := graph.desc [xnode] ;
while x ≠ nil do
  begin
    ...;
    x := x↑.next
  end
```

These changes have been incorporated into the following version of *shortestpaths*. The new version is longer and harder to understand than the first version but it is considerably more efficient.

```
procedure shortestpaths (graph : graphtype;
                         initial, goal : nodeindex;
                         var subgraph : graphtype);

const
  unlabeled = maxint;
var
  x, y : nodeptr;
  node, xnode, ynode : nodeindex;
  dist : integer;
  nodeset : array [nodeindex] of nodeptr;
  labels : array [nodeindex] of integer;
  reached : boolean;
begin
  for node := 1 to graph.size do
    labels[node] := unlabeled;
  {Label Phase}
  labels[initial] := 0;
  dist := 0;
  nodeset[0] := nil;
  insert (nodeset [0], initial);
  reached := false;
  while not (reached or (nodeset[dist] = nil)) do
    begin
      nodeset[dist + 1] := nil;
      x := nodeset[dist] ;
      while x ≠ nil do
        begin
          ynode := x↑.node;
          y := graph.desc[ynode] ;
```

```
                while y ≠ nil do
                  begin
                    if labels[y↑.node] = unlabeled
                      then
                        begin
                          insert(nodeset[dist+1],y↑.node);
                          labels[y↑.node] := dist + 1;
                          if y↑.node = goal
                            then reached := true
                        end;
                    y := y↑.next
                  end; {while}
                x := x↑.next
              end; {while}
            dist := dist + 1
          end; {while}
        {Return Phase}
        initialize(subgraph);
        nodeset[dist] := nil
        insert(nodeset[dist],goal);
        while dist > 0 do
          begin
            nodeset[dist − 1] := nil;
            y := nodeset[dist];
            while y ≠ nil do
              begin
                for xnode := 1 to graph.size do
                  if labels[xnode] = dist − 1
                    then
                      if joined(graph,xnode,y↑.node)
                        then
                          begin
                            insert(nodeset[dist − 1],xnode);
                            join(subgraph,xnode,y↑.node)
                          end;
                y := y↑.next
              end; {while}
            dist := dist − 1
          end; {while}
      end; {shortestpaths}
```

We can see from this example that there is a tradeoff between a simple and clean implementation that corresponds closely to the abstract algorithm, and a somewhat more complicated implementation that is considerably more efficient in typical cases. This is a problem that occurs frequently in situations where we can choose between different levels of abstraction. The choice between the two versions of *shortestpaths* is comparable to the choice between a high-level programming language and an assembly language, between automatic and standard transmission, between a sewing machine and a needle, or between a food processor and a sharp knife. In each case we gain some kind of power with the higher level approach but at the same time we lose some precision of our control of the situation.

We can consider the two versions of *shortestpaths* as the result of an exercise in *program transformation*. The first version is easy to write because it corresponds closely to the algorithm, and it is therefore likely to be correct. Although it is inefficient, it is a working program and consequently we can test it if we so desire. We can also determine where the inefficiencies are by counting the number of statements executed. Once we have a working version of the program, we can transform it in small, systematic steps, being careful that we do not destroy its correctness. The advantage of developing a program in this way is that we do not have to worry about many levels of detail at the same time. Program transformation is a variety of top-down design, and it is successful for the same reasons. We concentrate first on developing a sound overall architecture for the program, and then we can afford to worry about the details.

9.3 EQUIVALENCE RELATIONS

The two preceding examples of this chapter demonstrate that we can design algorithms without being concerned with the separate issue of data representation. Sometimes it is helpful to turn this technique around by choosing a representation and then designing algorithms that manipulate it. This technique is appropriate when a particular representation is forced on us or when an abstract algorithm gives us no clues that lead to a simple implementation. In this section, we compare two algorithms that perform equivalent operations on equivalent data structures and yet differ substantially in efficiency.

Suppose that we define a boolean valued function $PF(i, j)$ for integers i and j greater than one: $PF(i, j)$ is *true* if and only if i and j have the same number of prime factors. Then we can say, for example, that

$PF(10, 49)$ is *true* because $10 = 2 \times 5$ and $49 = 7 \times 7$
$PF(16, 54)$ is *true* because $16 = 2 \times 2 \times 2 \times 2$ and $54 = 2 \times 3 \times 3 \times 3$
$PF(5, 13)$ is *true* because both are prime
$PF(6, 8)$ is *false* because $6 = 2 \times 3$ and $8 = 2 \times 2 \times 2$

We call *PF* a *relation*. Given any two integers i and j we can determine whether or not the relation holds between them (that is, that $PF(i, j)$ is *true*) by counting their prime factors. If i and j are integers greater than one, *PF* has the following properties:

1. $PF(i, i)$
2. If $PF(i, j)$, then $PF(j, i)$
3. If $PF(i, j)$ and $PF(j, k)$, then $PF(i, k)$

These properties are called *reflexivity*, *symmetry*, and *transitivity*, respectively. A relation that is reflexive, symmetric, and transitive is called an *equivalence relation*. An equivalence relation divides the set over which it applies into subsets called *equivalence classes*. The relation *PF* divides the integers into classes $F_1, F_2, F_3, \ldots$ in which the class F_k contains all the integers that have exactly k prime factors. Thus we have

$$F_1 = [2, 3, 5, 7, 11, \ldots]$$
$$F_2 = [4, 6, 9, 10, 14, \ldots]$$
$$F_3 = [8, 12, 18, 20, 27, \ldots]$$
$$F_4 = [16, 24, 36, 54, 81, \ldots]$$

The problem we now consider is the representation of equivalence classes in a computer program. We assume that we are given a list of pairs of numbers (i, j) for which a certain equivalence relation is true and that we must maintain a data structure that can be used to determine whether other pairs of numbers are related. We require a data structure *DS* and three algorithms:

1. *initialize(DS)* sets *DS* so that it contains no related objects;
2. *update(DS, i, j)* informs *DS* that the relation holds between i and j;
3. *examine(DS, i, j)* returns *true* if the relation holds between i and j and returns *false* otherwise.

These algorithms will only be useful if they implement the full definition of an equivalence relation correctly. Thus the following conditions must always be satisfied:

1. *examine(DS, i, i)* always returns *true*;
2. *examine(DS, i, j)* = *examine(DS, j, i)*;
3. If we have executed *insert(DS, i, j)* and *insert(DS, j, k)* then *examine(DS, i, k)* must return *true*.

For example, if we have executed the following statements:

$$insert(DS, 2, 7)$$
$$insert(DS, 5, 13)$$
$$insert(DS, 5, 7)$$

then *examine(DS, 7, 2)* and *examine(DS, 2, 13)* should both return *true*.

We will assume in the development that the set of objects on which the relation is defined is a set of integers 1, 2, 3,..., N, where N is known and may be quite large, perhaps several thousand. In general, an equivalence relation may be defined over pairs of objects of any kind, and so we are considering only a limited class of equivalence relations.

As we have seen, the equivalence relation divides the set into equivalence classes. Let *class(i)* be the set to which the object i belongs. Then *insert* and *delete* can be refined as follows:

$$insert(DS, i, j) \longrightarrow$$
$$\text{if } class(i) \neq class(j)$$
$$\text{then } merge(class(i), class(j))$$

$$examine(DS, i, j) \longrightarrow$$
$$class(i) = class(j)$$

We can represent the equivalence classes by trees of the form shown in Fig. 9.6(a) and Fig. 9.6(b). These trees are organized in such a way that it is possible to find the root of a tree from any node in the tree. We use the value of the root of the tree to denote the value of the class. For example, in Fig. 9.6(a), 2, 3, 7, and 11 all belong to the same class and the value of this class is 7. Consequently, *class(2)* = *class(3)* = *class(7)* = *class(11)* = 7. The function *class* is easy to implement: all it has to do is climb down the tree to the root and return the value it finds at the root.

Now suppose that we have the two classes of Fig. 9.6(a) and Fig. 9.6(b) and we have to perform *insert(DS, 5, 11)*. First we find the roots of the trees containing 5 and 11. Since they are not the same, we must merge the classes. This we can do by adding one extra link, as shown in Fig. 9.6(c).

The tree can conveniently be represented by an array *parent*, arranged so that *parent*[*i*] is the parent of node i in the tree. (By convention, the root of a tree is the ancestor of all nodes. Thus the parent of a

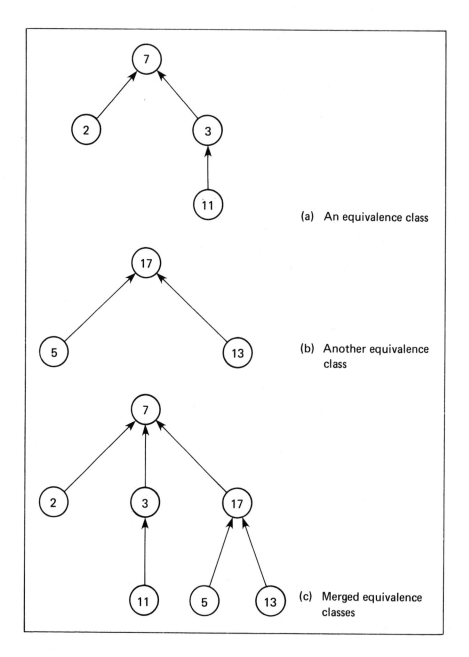

(a) An equivalence class

(b) Another equivalence class

(c) Merged equivalence classes

Fig. 9.6
Equivalence classes represented by trees.

node is reached by moving along one link of the tree in the direction of the root. Since there is exactly one link leading from a node towards the root, the parent of a node is defined uniquely.) If i is the root node of a tree, then we set $parent[i] = i$. In Fig. 9.6(a), we have:

$$parent[2] = 7$$
$$parent[3] = 7$$
$$parent[7] = 7 \quad \text{(because 7 is the root of a tree)}$$
$$parent[11] = 3$$

Using this representation, we can define *class* and *merge*:

$$class(i) \longrightarrow$$
$$\text{while } parent\ [i] \neq i \text{ do}$$
$$i := parent\ [i]$$
$$class := i$$
$$merge(class(i),class(j)) \longrightarrow$$
$$parent[class(i)] := class(j)$$

We initialize the array *parent* by setting $parent[i] = i$ for all values of i, indicating that initially each class contains only one object. Here are Pascal declarations of the data structure and operations.

```
type
  index = 1..N;
  table = array [index] of index;

procedure initialize (var parent : table);
  var
    i : index;
  begin
    for i := 1 to N do
      parent[i] := i
  end;

procedure update (var parent : table, i, j : index);
  begin
    while i ≠ parent[i] do
      i := parent[i];
    while j ≠ parent[j] do
      j := parent[j];
    if i ≠ j
      then parent[i] := j
  end;
```

```
function examine (parent : table; i, j : index) : boolean;
  begin
    while i ≠ parent[i] do
      i := parent[i];
    while j ≠ parent[j] do
      j := parent[j];
    examine := i = j
  end;
```

The work is nicely divided between *update* and *examine*; in fact, *update* and *examine* are the same except for the last statement. Suppose, however, that we have an application in which *examine* is used much more frequently than *update*; then it would be desirable to shorten the loops of *examine*. To do so, we must make the trees "bushier" by shortening the average distance from a node to the root. There are various ways in which *update* can be made to flatten the trees; the following solution is particularly elegant.

```
procedure update (var parent : table; i, j : index);
  var
    x, y : index;
  begin
    x := parent[i];
    y := parent[j];
    while x ≠ y do
      if x < y
        then
          begin
            parent[j] := x;
            j := y;
            y := parent[y]
          end
        else {x > y}
          begin
            parent[i] := y;
            i := x;
            x := parent[x]
          end
  end;
```

The algorithm used by this procedure is subtle and it is not easy to see how it works by examining its text. Fig. 9.7 may help to clarify matters. In Fig. 9.7(a) there are two trees rooted at 2 and 3 respectively and *update* has been invoked with $i = 19$ and $j = 11$. The statement controlled by *while* is executed five times; at each cycle its effect is to move one edge of a tree, and this edge is shown in Fig. 9.7 as a dotted line. The first action, shown in Fig. 9.7(a), is to change the value of *parent*[19] from 10 to 4. The final configuration is shown in Fig. 9.7(f).

9.4 TABLES

A *set* is a collection of objects chosen from a predetermined universe of objects. A set either contains a particular object or it does not; an object cannot occur twice in the same set. The set operations in which we are interested are the following:

insert: add an object to a set;

delete: remove an object from a set;

member: return *true* if a given object belongs to a set, otherwise return *false*.

Set is a reserved word of Pascal, and to avoid confusion with Pascal sets we use the term *table* to denote a set in this section. This usage corresponds to the term look-up table in programming jargon.

The tables that we consider are characterized by a large universe of objects and the need to associate information with an object. Telephone directories are typical, though large, examples of the kind of table we are considering. The universe consists of all names and addresses but a particular telephone directory contains only a very small proportion of this universe. A typical telephone directory includes the names, addresses, and telephone numbers of the people who live in a certain area, possess a telephone, and do not request to be unlisted. Insertion and deletion of entries is carried out by the telephone company, and subscribers to the system perform membership tests whenever they use a directory to look up a telephone number.

This example shows that only a part of the stored information is required to identify uniquely a member of the table. We call this part the *key* and we call the rest *additional information*. In a telephone directory the name and address constitute the key and the telephone number is additional information. Thus the additional information is by no means superfluous or uninteresting; it is often the reason for the existence of the table.

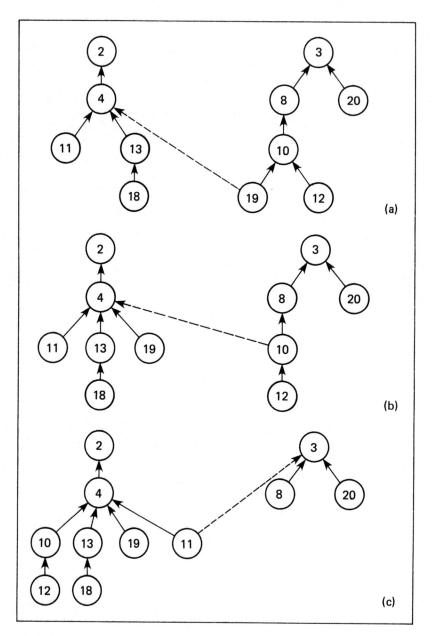

Fig. 9.7
Processing of
update (*parent*, 19, 11).

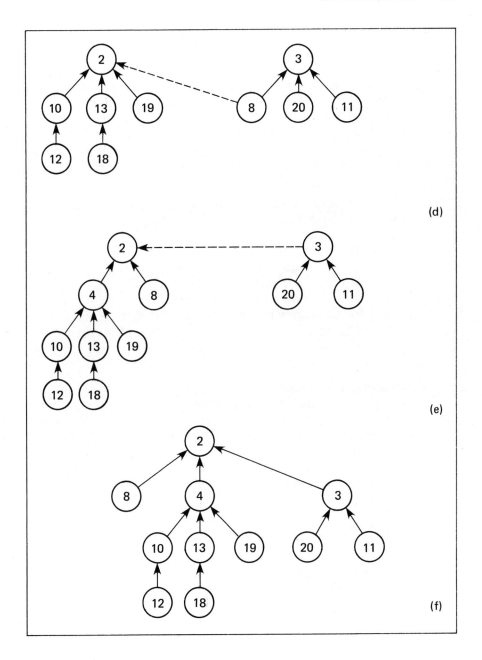

(d)

(e)

(f)

We will find, as we found with equivalence relations, that effort expended in organizing a table may improve the efficiency of accessing it. The telephone company would probably prefer to organize directories by placing the telephone numbers in numerical sequence instead of by placing the names in alphabetical order, but the resulting directories would be less useful to the subscribers. We cannot decide on a suitable representation for a table without knowing something about the way in which it will be used. We can, however, decide on an interface between the table and the rest of the program. We will need four procedures.

procedure *initialize* (**var** *table* : *tabletype*);
   {Create an empty table.}

procedure *member* (*memkey* : *keytype*;
                 var *present* : *boolean*;
                 var *entry* : *entrytype*;
                 var *table* : *tabletype*);
   { Look for an entry with the given key. If such an entry exists, set *present* to *true* and *entry* to the value of the entry. Otherwise, set *present* to *false* and do not change the value of *entry*. }

procedure *insert* (*newentry* : *entrytype*;
              var *reply* : *replytype*;
              var *table* : *tabletype*);
   { Attempt to insert *newentry* into the table. The *reply* is *entered* if the insertion is successful, *full* if there is no room in the table for the new entry, or *duplicate* if there is already an entry in the table with the same key.}

procedure *delete* (*delkey* : *keytype*;
             var *reply* : *replytype*;
             var *table* : *tabletype*);
   { Attempt to delete the entry with the given key *delkey*. The *reply* is *deleted* if the entry is removed or *nokey* if there was no entry with the given key. }

We have distinguished the types *entrytype* for an entire table entry and *keytype* for the key field of an entry only. The simplest way of representing the table is to put the entries into an array and to record the current number of entries. We define the following types:

```
type
  entrytype = record
                  key : keytype;
                  data : datatype
              end;
  tabletype = record
                  entrycount : 0..tablesize;
                  contents : array [1..tablesize] of entrytype
              end;
  replytype = (entered,full,duplicate,deleted,nokey);
```

The procedure *initialize* is straightforward.

```
procedure initialize (var table : tabletype);
  begin
    table.entrycount := 0
  end;
```

Member has to search the table. Since the table is not ordered, we must use a linear search. Linear search is inefficient but the inefficiency can be mitigated if we use a sentinel, as we did in the solution of *Storing Distinct Values* in Section 7.2. The sentinel occupies one location of the table and therefore the capacity of the table is reduced by one entry. We can create a special location *table.contents*[0] for the sentinel or we can put it at the top of the table at *table.contents*[*entrycount* + 1]. We choose the second alternative because *insert* can then use *member* to do the actual insertion. Since *member* has the side effect of altering the table, *table* is a variable parameter.

```
procedure member (memkey : keytype;
                    var present : boolean;
                    var entry : entrytype;
                    var table : tabletype);
  var
    index : 1..tablesize;
  begin
    table.contents[entrycount + 1].key := memkey;
    index := 1;
    while table.contents[index].key ≠ memkey do
      index := index + 1;
    present := index ≤ entrycount;
    if present
      then entry := table.contents[index]
  end;
```

The procedure *insert* uses *member* to find out whether or not the new entry is already in the table. If *member* reports that the entry is not present, then *insert* merely increments *entrycount* since *member* has already inserted the new entry in the table. If we were actually implementing these versions of *insert* and *member*, we would carefully document this relationship between them, of course.

```
procedure insert (newentry : entrytype;
                  var reply : replytype;
                  var table : tabletype);
var
  oldentry : entrytype;
  present : boolean;
begin
  if table.entrycount ≥ tablesize − 1
    then reply := full
    else
      begin
        member(newentry.key,present,oldentry,table);
        if present
          then reply := duplicate
          else
            begin
              entrycount := entrycount + 1;
              reply := entered
            end
      end
end;
```

The procedure *delete* cannot use *member* to locate the entry to be deleted because *member* does not return the position of the entry in the table. Consequently it does the search itself; having found the entry, it moves other entries down in the table to fill the gap created by the deletion.

```
procedure delete (delkey : keytype;
                  var reply : replytype;
                  var table : tabletype);
var
  t, index : 1..tablesize;
begin
  table.contents[entrycount + 1].key := delkey;
  index := 1;
```

```
while table.contents[index].key ≠ delkey do
  index := index + 1;
if index > entrycount
  then reply := nokey
  else
    begin
      for t := index to entrycount − 1 do
        table.contents[t] := table.contents[t + 1];
      reply := deleted
    end
end;
```

When we are writing procedures that perform operations on data structures, it is extremely useful to define properties of the data structures that may be assumed to be true on entry to a procedure and that must be true when the procedure has performed its function. We can define the following properties for a data structure *table* of type *tabletype*:

1) table.contents[i] is a current entry for $\qquad\qquad$ (9.4.1)
$1 \leq i \leq$ table.entrycount;

2) $0 \leq$ table.entrycount $<$ tablesize.

Properties of this kind are called *invariants* of the data structure although they are not always true. They are only false, however, before *initialize* has been executed and during the execution of *insert* and *delete*. To guarantee the security of our tables, we must ensure that the following conditions are always satisfied.

1) The first operation applied to a table is *initialize*. $\qquad\qquad$ (9.4.2)

2) If the invariants of (9.4.1) are true on entry to *member*, *insert*, or *delete*, they must also be true on exit.

3) No other access to components of the table is possible.

In Pascal, we can satisfy the first two of these conditions but not the third. If the procedures are going to work, the definition of the type *tabletype* must be global and therefore accessible throughout the program. In some languages defined more recently than Pascal, this definition can be *encapsulated* in a module that also contains declarations of the four procedures. Moreover, initialization can be performed automatically by this module. When this is done, the *only* means of accessing a table is by means of the chosen interface, and the conditions of (9.4.2) can be satisfied.

The principle of encapsulation has a number of advantages. One of the more important of these advantages is that we can change the representation of a data structure without changing the interface. Thus we can achieve modularity by encapsulation. We demonstrate this by changing the representation of tables without changing the interface that we have defined.

The time required to find an object using linear search is proportional to *entrycount*, the number of objects stored in the table. This is not a serious problem if the number of objects to be stored is small but it becomes intolerable when the number of objects is large. We have seen that telephone directories can be used efficiently because the entries are arranged in alphabetical order. The same technique can be used by a computer. If we order the entries in the table, *insert* becomes a little slower because it must maintain the ordering, but *member* becomes much faster. We assume that the type *keytype* is an ordered type (that is, the operator $<$ may be used with operands of this type). The new procedures will maintain the additional invariant

$$i < j \quad \text{if and only if}$$
$$table.contents[i].key < table.contents[j].key$$

which asserts that the keys are stored in increasing order. *Insert* finds the appropriate place for the new entry and moves the entries above it up to make space. The procedures all use a new operation that we will call *find*, and so we consider *find* first.

The binary search algorithm provides an efficient means of finding an item in a sorted list. It is essentially a discrete version of the bisection algorithm of Section 7.5, but with the difference that the root may not exist. In the following version, we are given the key *givenkey* in a set containing *entrycount* objects stored in an array *contents*.

```
find(givenkey) ⟶
  low := 1
  high := entrycount
  repeat
    middle := (low + high) div 2
    if contents[middle].key < givenkey
      then low := middle + 1
      else high := middle − 1
  until contents[middle].key = givenkey or high < low
```

When this algorithm terminates, either *high* is less than *low* and there is no entry with the given key, or *middle* is the index of the required key.

Furthermore, if *high* is less than *low*, then

$$contents[high].key < givenkey < contents[low].key$$

and thus we know where the new entry must be inserted. One of the problems with this version of the binary search algorithm is that *middle* may be set to *entrycount* + 1. Thus we must ensure that *entrycount* is less than *tablesize*, just as we did when we used linear search. Moreover, if *entrycount* is zero, *find* will attempt to access *contents*[0], which does not exist, and we must therefore check for this situation explicitly.

The procedure *find* must return all three index values, *low*, *middle*, and *high*, so that the caller can determine the exact state of affairs. Note too that *find* is used only by *member*, *insert*, and *delete*, and it is therefore a "private" component of the table module. We need a new type, *tableindex*, for the parameters *low*, *middle*, and *high*, defined by:

```
type
    tableindex = 1..tablesize;
procedure find (givenkey : keytype;
                var low, middle, high : tableindex;
                table : tabletype);

begin
  low := 1;
  if entrycount = 0
    then high := 0
    else
      begin
        high := entrycount − 1;
        repeat
          middle := (low + high) div 2;
          if table.contents[middle].key < givenkey
            then low := middle + 1
            else high := middle − 1
        until (table.contents[middle].key = givenkey)
              or (high < low)
      end
end;
```

The new version of procedure *member* consists of little more than a call to *find*.

```
procedure member (memkey : keytype;
                  var present : boolean;
                  var entry : entrytype;
                  var table : tabletype);
```

```
    var
      low, middle, high : tableindex;
    begin
      find(memkey,low,middle,high,table);
      if high < low
        then present := false
        else
          begin
            entry := table.contents[middle];
            present := true
          end
    end;
```

The new version of *insert*, which also uses *find*, is straightforward, and the new version of *delete* is the same as the old one except that we use *find* to locate the entry to be deleted. Here is the new *insert*:

```
    procedure insert (newentry : entrytype;
                      var reply : replytype;
                      var table : tabletype);
    var
      index, low, middle, high : tableindex;
    begin
      if table.entrycount = tablesize − 1
        then reply := full
        else
          begin
            find(newentry.key,low,middle,high,table);
            if high ≥ low
              then reply := duplicate
              else
                begin
                  for index := table.entrycount downto low do
                    table.contents[index + 1]
                      := table.contents[index];
                  table.contents[low] := newentry;
                  table.entrycount := table.entrycount + 1;
                  reply := inserted
                end
          end
    end;
```

There are several other ways in which a table can be represented without changing the interface we have proposed. We consider some of these representations briefly, but we do not consider their implementation in detail.

First we consider *hash tables*. A hash table uses an array of fixed size S to store the entries and a *hashing function* that maps the keys onto the numbers 1, 2, ... , S. Ideally the hashing function should be simple to evaluate and its values should be randomly distributed over the interval 1, 2, ... , S. As more entries are added to the table, the probability that more than one key will be transformed to the same value by the hashing function increases and *collisions* occur. There are a number of ways of resolving collisions; the simplest is to search the table linearly for the next free space. Hashing becomes less efficient as the table fills up, and eventually the table must be enlarged. This is a potentially inefficient operation because it is usually necessary to re-hash all the existing entries. There have been many proposals for ameliorating the difficulties of hash table management, however, and hashing is the optimal choice of set representation in many applications.

The table can also be represented by a *linked list*. Insertions are made at the front of the list and are fast; deletion and membership tests require a linear search of the list and are slow. Additional space is required to store the links between list items, but there is no need to place an upper bound on the number of objects that can be stored in a list because the list will share space with other dynamic data structures.

The *self-organizing list* is a refinement of the basic list organization. Whenever a successful membership test is performed, the object accessed is placed at the front of the list. This trick reduces the average length of a search in situations in which objects are often accessed several times in succession or when a small group of objects is active for a time. Self-organizing lists are sometimes used for the symbol tables of simple compilers: the local variables of a procedure migrate towards the front of the list and can be found rapidly whereas variables in enclosing scopes are not accessed so often and their entries drift towards the tail of the list.

Objects can also be stored in *trees*. Trees have space requirements that are comparable to lists, and although they can be searched more rapidly, they are harder to maintain. A considerable amount of research has been devoted to the representation of sets by trees and several kinds of tree have been defined.

SUMMARY

The stages of design and implementation must be kept separate. An algorithm should not be cluttered with unnecessary details of representation. The choice of appropriate representation is an important part of implementation.

In most cases it is advisable to design the algorithm and then to choose appropriate representations for its data structures. In this way, we can ensure that the operations that are required frequently by the algorithm will be executed efficiently by the program. Occasionally a particularly appropriate data structure may suggest an algorithm, or even several different algorithms. For example, the inverted tree structure motivated two algorithms for the operation *update* of Section 9.3.

Equivalent representations may differ in their level of abstraction. We see a data structure through an interface. The interface may be high level, in which case it only allows us to perform abstract operations on the data structure, or it may be low level, in which case operations on the data structure are unrestricted. The two versions of *shortestpaths* in Section 9.2 illustrate the difference between the two kinds of interface. The table example of Section 9.4 illustrates that the definition of an interface does not determine the representation.

High-level interfaces lead to secure and robust programs. Low-level interfaces are less secure and must be used with care. The importance of efficiency depends on the application. The prevailing trend is that processors are becoming faster and cheaper and software is becoming more complex and more expensive. Moreover, the use of computers is increasing in situations where a software error may have disastrous consequences. For these reasons, we should be more concerned with the reliability of our software than with its efficiency.

We can combine the advantages of reliability and efficiency by systematic program transformation if we are working on small programs. A program written at a high level of abstraction is likely to be correct. By applying careful transformations to the representations of its data structures, we may be able to reduce its time and space requirements. This approach is not usually applicable to large programs written by teams of programmers. In large projects it is essential that interface designs are completed at an early stage and are not changed thereafter; they must also be simple.

FURTHER READING

An iterative solution of *Tower of Hanoi*, similar to the solution of Section 9.1, is described in "A Note on the Towers of Hanoi Problem" by Hayes.

Graph algorithms, including the shortest paths algorithm, are discussed by Baase in her book, *Computer Algorithms: Introduction to Design and Analysis*.

The first version of *update* in Section 9.3 is by Fischer and Galler. It is described, together with some improvements, in *The Art of Computer Programming*, Vol. I: *Fundamental Algorithms* by Knuth. The second version is by Rem and its history is narrated by Dijkstra in *A Discipline of Programming*.

Data Structure Techniques by Standish is an excellent source of information on methods of representation. Representation issues in Pascal are discussed by Tenenbaum and Augenstein in their book, *Data Structures Using Pascal*.

EXERCISES

9.1 Suggest a suitable representation for the state-action graph of *Students and Professors* (Section 2.3). Use it in a program that solves this problem.

9.2 Suggest other ways in which the procedure *update* of Section 9.3 can make the trees "bushier," thereby improving the performance of the function *examine*.

9.3 We could represent an equivalence class by a closed ring of linked nodes. What effect does this have on the performance of *update* and *examine*? Would it help to use a ring *and* a tree?

9.4 Tables are used by compilers to store identifiers and information pertaining to them. Suggest suitable representations for symbol tables for (a) BASIC, (b) FORTRAN, and (c) Pascal compilers. Specify the operations that must be performed on the symbol tables.

9.5 An $m \times n$ array A is usually mapped into a linear store S by storing $A[i,j]$ at the location $S[A_0 + n(i - 1) + (j - 1)]$. We could also store $A[i,j]$ at the location $S[A_0 + f(i,j)]$, where f is the function defined in Section 7.3. The second method has an important advantage over the first. What is this advantage, and why is the first method almost always used in spite of it?

9.6 We can represent a binary tree using a vector T in the following way: the left and right sons of the node stored at $T[n]$ are stored at $T[2n]$ and $T[2n + 1]$ respectively. What are the advantages and disadvantages of this representation?

9.7 *Concatenation* and *finding a substring* are operations that can usefully be applied to character strings. Can you think of other useful operations? Propose a representation for strings that allows these operations to be performed with reasonable efficiency.

9.8 Design algorithms for adding and multiplying polynomials with integer coefficients. For example, if $P(x) = x^3 + 3x^2 + 1$ and $Q(x) = x^2 + 5x$, your algorithms should be able to evaluate

$$P(x) + Q(x) = x^3 + 4x^2 + 5x + 1$$

and

$$P(x) \times Q(x) = x^5 + 8x^4 + 15x^3 + x^2 + 5x$$

Select two different representations for polynomials, assuming that polynomials are (a) dense (most coefficients are nonzero), and (b) sparse (most coefficients are zero; for example, $x^{50} + x^5$ is a sparse polynomial). Write programs for polynomial addition and multiplication using both representations.

CHAPTER 10
RECURSION

We are motivated to split problems into subproblems by the likelihood that the subproblems will be easier to solve than the original problem. In many circumstances a subproblem turns out to be similar to the original problem, differing only in that it is smaller in scale.

Consider, for example, the problem of paying an exact sum of money, such as $6.31, in bills and coins. This problem may be split into subproblems "pay $5" and "pay $1.31." The first of these is easily solved by paying $5 with a $5 bill, and the second is similar to the original problem except that the amount of money is smaller. If we denote the problem of paying an amount A exactly by $P(A)$, we can write down a tentative solution of $P(A)$ in this way.

1. Choose the highest valued bill or coin whose value is less than or equal to A, and let its value be B.

2. Pay B and solve $P(A - B)$ using this solution.

This solution is not yet complete because it does not terminate. We must specify that when the amount to be paid is zero, there is nothing to do. This is the complete solution:

$$\text{solve } P(A) \longrightarrow$$
$$\text{if } A = 0$$
$$\text{then do nothing}$$

else
    choose $B \le A$ as described above
    pay B
    solve $P(A - B)$

This is a typical *recursive solution*. It has three components that occur in one form or another in all recursive solutions. First, there is a *test* that determines whether or not the problem is simple enough to be solved directly. Second, there is a solution to this simple problem. Finally, there is a solution to the problem that contains one or more *recursive calls*.

Recursion is a powerful problem-solving tool and a useful programming technique. It is unfortunate that recursive methods are not used as much as they should be. There are two reasons for this. First, it is not easy to implement recursive solutions in some of the most widely used programming languages, including FORTRAN, COBOL, and BASIC. Second, many people believe that recursive solutions are hard to understand and inefficient.

In this chapter, we examine recursive solutions to a variety of problems. Although we identify situations in which recursion is not an appropriate strategy for implementation, we demonstrate that recursion is indispensable to the serious programmer.

10.1 SIMPLE RECURSIVE ALGORITHMS

Many problems have both recursive and nonrecursive solutions. The simplest problem for which recursive solutions are appropriate is the evaluation of recursively defined functions. Mathematicians use recursive definitions extensively because it is often simple to prove properties of recursively defined functions using mathematical induction. The first three examples that follow discuss algorithms for evaluating recursively defined functions and the last two examples describe recursive solutions to more complex problems.

The Fibonacci Numbers

The Fibonacci numbers are the members of an infinite sequence of increasing integers that begins with the numbers:

$$1 \; 1 \; 2 \; 3 \; 5 \; 8 \; 13 \; 21 \; ...$$

The rule for constructing this sequence is very simple: each number, except for the first two, is the sum of its two immediate predecessors. If we call the $(n + 1)$th Fibonacci number F_n, we can define all of the Fibonacci numbers by the following equations:

$$F_0 = 1$$
$$F_1 = 1$$
$$F_n = F_{n-1} + F_{n-2} \quad (n \geq 2)$$

For example, we have

$$F_2 = F_1 + F_0$$
$$= 2$$

and

$$F_3 = F_2 + F_1$$
$$= 3$$

We can construct a function that computes F_n directly from this definition:

> function $F(n)$: integer
>   if $n = 0$
>   then $F := 1$
>   else if $n = 1$
>   then $F := 1$
>   else $F := F(n - 1) + F(n - 2)$

The function F is called a *recursive function* because it contains calls to itself. This example demonstrates that recursive solutions are easy to write. It is not quite so easy to see how they work and this is an issue to which we return.

It is not difficult to see that the function F is very inefficient. The evaluation of $F(5)$, for example, proceeds as follows:

$$
\begin{aligned}
F(5) &= F(4) + F(3) \\
&= F(3) + F(2) + F(2) + F(1) \\
&= F(2) + F(1) + F(1) + F(0) + F(1) + F(0) + 1 \\
&= F(1) + F(0) + 1 + 1 + 1 + 1 + 1 + 1 \\
&= 1 + 1 + 1 + 1 + 1 + 1 + 1 + 1 \\
&= 8
\end{aligned}
$$

The inefficiency arises because each evaluation of $F(n)$ for $n \geq 2$ greater than or equal to 2 requires two further evaluations, $F(n - 1)$ and $F(n - 2)$. Moreover, the same evaluations are performed over and over again. In the preceding example, $F(0)$ is evaluated three times and $F(1)$ is evaluated five times.

We can improve the performance of the function F by giving it a memory so that it does not have to calculate the same value more than once. Assume that we have declared

var
  $memo$: **array** [1..max] **of** $integer$;

and that each component of $memo$ has been initialized to zero. We can revise F as follows:

```
function F (n) : integer
  if n > max
    then F := F(n − 1) + F(n − 2)
  else if memo[n] > 0
    then F := memo[n]
  else
    if n = 0
      then memo[n] := 1
    else if n = 1
      then memo[n] := 1
    else memo[n] := F(n − 1) + F(n − 2)
    F := memo[n]
```

Max is a positive integer, and $memo$ contains max components. If the argument n is within the bounds of $memo$, the algorithm looks in $memo$ to see if the result is already there. If it is not there, or if n is greater than max, the value of the function is computed recursively, as before. The array $memo$ may be local to the function or global. If it is local to F, it must be reinitialized at each call; if it is global, it is initialized once only, but F has side effects.

A function that is evaluated in this way is sometimes called a *memo-function*. The memo-function F is neither a practical nor a desirable function because it requires a large amount of space and it has side effects. It is nonetheless a significant improvement over the purely recursive version of F because it reduces the time to evaluate $F(n)$ from $O(2^n)$ to $O(n)$ in the worst case. Of course if $memo$ is global and $F(n)$ has already been evaluated, then subsequent evaluations require only $O(1)$ time.

There is a more practical way of improving the efficiency of F than this. We can easily construct the Fibonacci sequence from left to right, performing one addition for each term, thus:

$$1 \quad 1$$
$$1 + 1 = 2$$

$$1 + 2 = 3$$
$$2 + 3 = 5$$
$$\cdots$$

The following function evaluates F_n using this method.

```
function F (n) : integer
    a := 1
    b := 1
    for m := 2 to n do
        t := b
        b := a + b
        a := t
    F := b
```

In this version, a, b, m, and t are local integer variables. We now have the following results for the evaluation of the Fibonacci numbers.

1) The recursive solution is easily written from the definition of the Fibonacci numbers but is unacceptably inefficient.

2) The efficiency of the recursive solution can be improved by using a memo array but this requires a large amount of space.

3) The problem can be solved without recursion in linear time.

We can in fact do even better than this because F_n is the integer closest to $\phi^n/\sqrt{5}$, where $\phi = (1 + \sqrt{5})/2$. We can compute ϕ^n, and hence F_n in time $O(\log n)$.

Binomial Coefficients

The binomial coefficients are the numbers that appear in Pascal's triangle. The first few rows of Pascal's triangle are as follows:

```
1
1 1
1 2 1
1 3 3 1
1 4 6 4 1
```
$$\cdots$$

The binomial coefficient $C(n, k)$ is the kth number in the nth row of the triangle, numbering rows and columns from zero. Thus the top row tells us that $C(0, 0) = 1$, and the next row tells us that $C(1, 0) = C(1, 1) = 1$. $C(n, k)$ is pronounced "n choose k," and it may also be written in either of the forms ^nC_k or $\binom{n}{k}$. Each number in the tri-angle is the sum of two numbers in the row above it, unless it is in the leftmost column, in which case its value is 1. Thus the binomial coefficients are defined by the following recursive equations:

$$C(n, 0) = 1 \quad (n \geq 0)$$
$$C(n, k) = 0 \quad (n < k)$$
$$C(n, k) = C(n - 1, k) + C(n - 1, k - 1) \quad (0 \leq k \leq n)$$

These definitions lead naturally to a recursive function that evaluates $C(n, k)$.

```
function C (n,k) : integer
  if k = 0
    then C := 1
  else if n < k
    then C := 0
  else C := C(n − 1,k) + C(n − 1,k − 1)
```

Once again the recursive function is very inefficient because a call may invoke two further calls. Furthermore, the binomial coefficients can easily be evaluated iteratively by the following algorithm:

```
num := 1
den := 1
for j := 1 to k do
    num := num * (n + 1 − j)
    den := den * j
C := num div den
```

In these two examples, the Fibonacci numbers and the binomial coefficients, the recursive solution is simple and intuitive but too inefficient to be of any use. There are faster methods of evaluating Fibonacci numbers and binomial coefficients, and we do not need to resort to recursion.

Ackermann's Function

Ackermann's function A is a function of two positive integer arguments defined as follows:

$$A(0, n) = n + 1 \quad (n > 0)$$
$$A(m, 0) = A(m - 1, 1) \quad (m > 0)$$
$$A(m, n) = A(m - 1, A(m, n - 1)) \quad (m > 0, n > 0)$$

There is no difficulty in constructing a recursive function from this definition:

> function $A\ (m,n)$: integer
> if $m = 0$
>   then $A := n + 1$
> else if $n = 0$
>   then $A := (m - 1,1)$
> else $A := A(m - 1, A(m,n - 1))$

Ackermann's function takes a long time to evaluate unless the arguments are very small. It is impossible to appreciate the tediousness of evaluating Ackermann's function without attempting some simple examples by hand. The evaluation of $A(2, 1)$ proceeds as follows:

$$
\begin{aligned}
A(2, 1) &= & \text{(10.1.1)}\\
&= A(1, A(2, 0))\\
&= A(1, A(1, 1))\\
&= A(1, A(0, A(1, 0)))\\
&= A(1, A(0, A(0, 1)))\\
&= A(1, A(0, 3))\\
&= A(1, 3)\\
&= A(0, A(1, 2))\\
&= A(0, A(0, A(1, 1)))\\
&= A(0, A(0, A(0, A(1, 0))))\\
&= A(0, A(0, A(0, A(0, 1))))\\
&= A(0, A(0, A(0, 2)))\\
&= A(0, A(0, 3))\\
&= A(0, 4)\\
&= 5
\end{aligned}
$$

It is evident that $A(m, n)$ cannot be evaluated by this method in a reasonable amount of time even for small values of m. In fact, $A(3, 1) = 13$ and $A(4, 1) = 32765$.

We can see by inspecting the preceding evaluation that some of the operations are repeated. $A(1, 1)$, for instance, is evaluated twice. This suggests that a memo array might help. A detailed study shows that a memo array does not help, however, for two reasons. First, there are fewer repeated evaluations than we expect from a superficial look at simple examples. Second, the evaluation of $A(m, n)$ requires the evaluation of $A(p, q)$ for which $q > n$. For example, to evaluate $A(3, 3)$ we need to know the values of $A(0, 59)$, $A(1, 59)$, and $A(2, 29)$.

Ackermann's function is interesting because its evaluation is inherently difficult. The preceding algorithm is not slow because it is recursive but because there is no fast way to evaluate Ackermann's function.

The Tower of Hanoi

The problem *Tower of Hanoi* can be solved by simple recursive reasoning. In developing the iterative solution of Section 9.1, we considered the smallest disk first. We derive the recursive solution by considering the largest disk instead. We denote the problem of moving N disks from peg 1 to peg 3 by the procedure call

$$move(N, 1, 3)$$

This problem can be solved in three steps. These three steps are shown in Fig. 10.1, and we can describe them as follows:

1. $move(N - 1, 1, 2)$
2. $move(1, 1, 3)$
3. $move(N - 1, 2, 3)$

We can obtain a general recursive solution of the problem in two more steps. The first step is to specify the peg that is to be used to store the pile consisting of all disks except the largest. When we are moving the largest disk from peg 1 to peg 3, for example, the other disks must all be on peg 2. *Move* therefore requires four parameters altogether. The second step is to provide an "escape clause" for the trivial problem of moving no disks. After carrying out these two steps, we arrive at the following recursive procedure for *Tower of Hanoi*.

```
procedure move (N,a,b,c)
   if N > 0
      then
         move(N − 1,a,c,b)
         print a '→' b
         move(N − 1,c,b,a)
```

The following Pascal program is derived from this algorithm.

```
program Hanoi (input,output);
   var
      numdisks : integer;
   procedure move (N, a, b, c : integer);
      begin
```

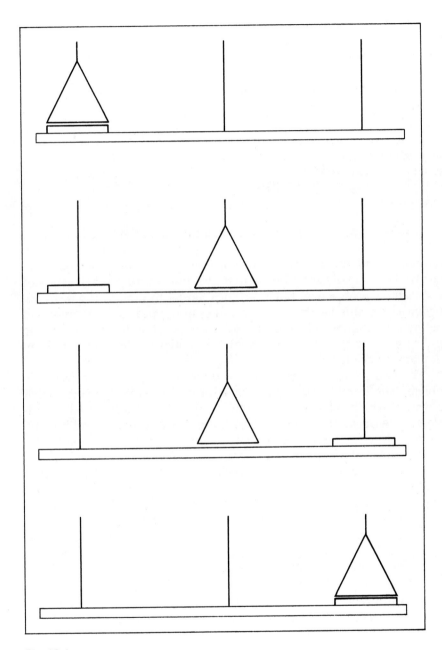

Fig. 10.1
Moving *N* disks.

```
        if N > 0
          then
            begin
              move(N − 1,a,c,b);
              writeln('Move from ',a,'to', b);
              move(N − 1,c,b,a)
            end
      end;
    begin
      read(numdisks);
      move(numdisks,1,3,2)
    end.
```

It is instructive to compare this solution with the solution of Section 9.1. First of all we note that the programs are entirely different in appearance, and it is not at all obvious that their output is almost identical. We could easily modify the iterative program to print the state of the system at each move, but it is much harder to modify the recursive program to do this because the state does not appear to be represented at all by the program. The iterative solution describes the motion of the top disk explicitly but it is very hard to visualize the motion of the top disk from the recursive program.

The two solutions correspond to different ways of perceiving the problem. The iterative program is in a sense natural in that it describes the way in which we would move the disks of a physical model. Nevertheless it is considerably longer than the recursive program and it maintains an elaborate data structure that we now see to be unnecessary.

The efficiency of the two solutions is the same to within a constant scale factor. Each program prints each of the $2^N − 1$ operations required to move a pile of N disks. In practice, the running times of the programs will not be precisely the same but they will not differ greatly. The iterative version makes many accesses to arrays and the recursive version makes many procedure calls. Consequently the execution times will depend on the relative efficiency of array accesses and procedure calls on the machine used to test the two programs.

We can draw several conclusions from these examples. First, we can often use recursion to express solutions in a concise and clear manner. Second, in some circumstances recursive algorithms are needlessly inefficient. Obviously, if we are able to replace a recursive algorithm with exponential time complexity by a nonrecursive algorithm with linear time complexity, we should do so. Finally, in many situations recursive solutions are no less efficient than nonrecursive solutions and in most such cases the recursive algorithm is simpler to design and easier to understand than the nonrecursive algorithm.

10.2 RECURSIVE DATA STRUCTURES

We saw in Chapter 8 that there is a correspondence between control structures and data structures. We can extend this correspondence by demonstrating the close relationship between recursive algorithms and recursive data structures. In this section we consider lists and trees, and some simple algorithms for manipulating them.

We can define a list recursively: a list is either empty or it consists of a head followed by a list. Applying this definition to the list A B we obtain:

1) A B is a list consisting of a head A and a list B;

2) B is a list consisting of a head B and a list Λ;

3) Λ is an empty list.

We have given the name Λ to the empty list for the purpose of this explanation. Although we do not normally need a symbol for the empty list, provided that we understand that lists are implicitly terminated by the empty list, empty lists play an important role in the implementation of list algorithms.

The recursive definition of a tree is similar to the recursive definition of a list: a *tree* is either empty or it consists of a *root* and some other trees. There are many ways of representing trees, and we have already encountered a number of tree diagrams in this book. It is often convenient to represent trees in a linear manner, and the tree of Fig. 10.2 can be written in this way:

$$(A \ (B \ (C \ D)) \ (E))$$

This tree has root A and subtrees $(B \ (C \ D))$ and (E).

The remainder of this section consists of two examples. The first example demonstrates the recursive processing of lists and the second demonstrates the recursive processing of trees.

Ackermann's Function Revisited

As an example of recursive list processing, we develop a program that evaluates Ackermann's function symbolically. The output of the program resembles the evaluation of $A(2, 1)$ shown in (10.1.1). We can see

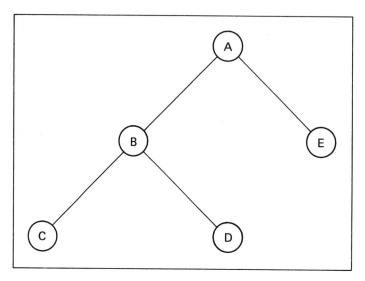

Figure 10.2
The tree (A (B (C D)) (E)).

from the definition of Ackermann's function that if we start with integer values of its arguments m and n, the first argument is always an integer but the second argument may be a recursive invocation of the function. Accordingly we can represent an invocation by a list. Each component of the list contains an integer and a pointer to the next component. The last component of the list has a null pointer and its integer is the value of the second argument; the other components of the list contain values of the first argument. Some simple examples of this data structure are shown in Fig. 10.3.

We define the list in Pascal using a pointer type and a record type, as follows:

```
type
  pointer = ↑ cell;
  cell = record
            head : integer;
            tail : pointer
         end;
```

The recursive nature of this definition would be more apparent if we wrote it this way:

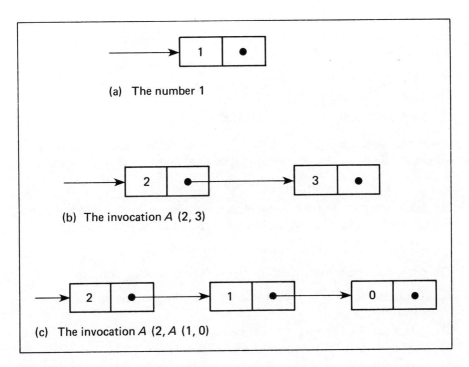

(a)   The number 1

(b)   The invocation A (2, 3)

(c)   The invocation A (2, A (1, 0)

Fig. 10.3
Representation of invocations of Ackermann's function.

```
type
    cell = record
              head : integer;
              tail : cell
           end;
```

We are not allowed to do this in Pascal. The pointer that must be introduced to make the definition acceptable in Pascal should be regarded as
a visible manifestation of the implementation, not as an intrinsic component of a recursive data structure.

In the Pascal program, a value of type *pointer* denotes a list. If the
list is empty, this value is **nil**. Thus the reserved word **nil** corresponds to
the name Λ that we gave to the empty list.

The heart of the program is a procedure *transform* that accepts a
list and makes one transformation to it according to the definition of
Ackermann's function. This procedure is called repeatedly until it re-

turns a single number that is the value of the function with the given arguments. There are three transformation rules corresponding to the three clauses of the definition.

1) $A(0, n)$ becomes $n + 1$
2) $A(m, 0)$ becomes $A(m - 1, 1)$
3) $A(m, n)$ becomes $A(m - 1, A(m, n - 1))$

We must be careful to apply these rules in the correct sequence. It is legitimate algebraically, for example, to use the first rule to replace

$$A(0, A(1, 1)) \quad \text{by} \quad 1 + A(1, 1)$$

but the representation we have chosen compels us to replace the rightmost invocation first. Thus we must use the third rule in this case.

$$A(0, A(1, 1)) \quad \text{is transformed to} \quad A(0, A(0, A(1, 0)))$$

The procedure *transform* must recognize the following situations.

1) If the list has no tail, it represents a number and no transformation is possible.
2) If the tail of the list is an invocation of the function, *transform* must be applied recursively to that invocation.
3) If the tail of the list is a number, the list represents an invocation of the form $A(m, n)$ and we can apply one of the three preceding rules.

In the version of *transform* that follows, we have used a function *cons* that accepts an integer and a pointer, constructs the corresponding list, and returns a pointer to it.

```
procedure transform (var list : pointer);
  begin
    with list↑ do
      if tail ≠ nil
        then
          if tail↑.tail ≠ nil
            then transform(tail)
          else if head = 0 { Apply rule 1 }
            then list := cons(tail↑.head + 1,nil)
          else if tail↑.head = 0 { Apply rule 2 }
            then list := cons(head − 1,cons(1,nil))
          else { Apply rule 3 }
            list := cons(head − 1,cons(head,cons(tail↑.head
                                          − 1,nil)))
```

```
  end;
```

This procedure is not as mysterious as it may seem to be at first. Remember that *head* is an integer and *tail* is a pointer and that the second argument of *cons* is a pointer. *Transform* returns a list and consequently, when we apply rule 1, we return the list *cons(tail↑.head* + 1, **nil**) rather than the integer *tail↑.head* + 1.

```
  function cons (hd : integer; tl : pointer): pointer;
    var
      p : pointer;
    begin
      new(p);
      p↑.head := hd;
      p↑.tail := tl;
      cons := p
    end;
```

Next we need a procedure to display the current list so that we can see the intermediate steps. The procedure *display* takes a list as its argument. If the tail of the list is null, *display* merely reports the value of its head. If the tail is not null, *display* prints an invocation of Ackermann's function, calling itself recursively to display the second argument.

```
  procedure display (list : pointer);
    begin
      with list↑ do
        if tail = nil
          then write(head)
          else
            begin
              write('A(',head,',');
              display(tail);
              write(')')
            end
    end;
```

The complete program is easily assembled from these components.

```
  program Ackermann (input,output);
    type
      pointer = ↑ cell;
      cell = record
               head : integer;
               tail : pointer
```

```
        end;
var
  m,n : integer;
  list : pointer;
function cons (hd : integer; tl : pointer) : pointer;
  { See text }
procedure display (list :pointer);
  { See text }
procedure transform (var list : pointer);
  { See text }
begin { Ackermann }
  read(m,n);
  list := cons(m,cons(n,nil));
  write('      ');
  display(list);
  writeln;
  repeat
    transform(list);
    write('= ');
    display(list);
    writeln
  until list↑.tail = nil
end;
```

When this program is executed with $m = 1$ and $n = 1$ it produces this output:

$$
\begin{aligned}
& A(1, 1) \\
= {} & A(0, A(1, 0)) \\
= {} & A(0, A(0, 1)) \\
= {} & A(0, 2) \\
= {} & 3
\end{aligned}
$$

The relationship between the printed strings and the internal lists is shown in Fig. 10.4. At each stage, *transform* operates on the last but one list component.

Code Generation

The next example demonstrates a method that is used by compilers to generate machine code. Code generation algorithms are complex; consequently we restrict our attention to simple expressions and we do not

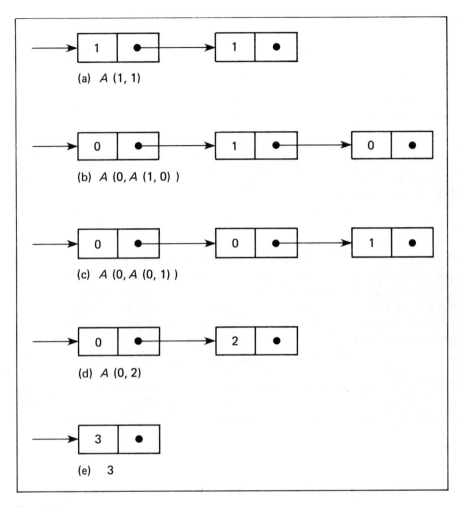

(a) *A* (1, 1)

(b) *A* (0, *A* (1, 0))

(c) *A* (0, *A* (0, 1))

(d) *A* (0, 2)

(e)   3

Fig. 10.4
Evaluation of *A* (1, 1).

attempt to produce optimal code. The program reads expressions containing operands, operators, and parentheses. An operand is a single
letter and an operator is either + or *. Parentheses are used to control
the order of evaluation. The code generated for the expression

$$A * B + C$$

is

$$LOAD\ R0,A$$
$$MUL\ R0,B$$
$$ADD\ R0,C$$

If we want to do the addition first, we add parentheses, obtaining the expression

$$A * (B + C)$$

for which the generated code is

$$LOAD\ R0,B$$
$$ADD\ R0,C$$
$$MUL\ R0,A$$

We assume that the instruction *LOAD* moves the value of an operand into a register; *ADD* adds the value of an operand to a register; and *MUL* multiplies the contents of a register by the value of the operand. The value of the entire expression is to be left in the register $R0$. The code for the two preceding examples required only one register, but we cannot generate code for some expressions without using additional registers. Consider this expression:

$$(A + B) * (C + D)$$

The code generated for this expression must evaluate $A + B$, evaluate $C + D$, and then multiply the two results. It is clear that this cannot be done with a single register, and something like the following code is required.

$$LOAD\ R0,A$$
$$ADD\ R0,B$$
$$LOAD\ R1,C$$
$$ADD\ R1,D$$
$$MUL\ R0,R1$$

We divide the problem into two subproblems. First we construct a tree that represents the expression and then we generate code from the tree. Both parts of the solution use recursive methods to process the tree. The program has the following form.

> Construct a tree from the given expression;
> generate code during a traversal of the tree.

There are three rules for constructing expressions and we use them to guide us in writing the functions that analyze expressions. The rules are:

1) An expression is the sum of one or more terms.
2) A term is the product of one or more factors.
3) A factor is either a one-letter identifier or an expression enclosed in parentheses.

These rules constitute a grammar with the following productions:

$$
\begin{aligned}
\text{expression} &= \text{term} \mid \text{term "+" expression} \\
\text{term} &= \text{factor} \mid \text{factor "*" term} \\
\text{factor} &= \text{letter} \mid \text{"(" expression ")"}
\end{aligned}
$$

Observe that these productions are recursive: an expression contains terms; a term contains factors; and a factor may contain an expression. This recursion is mirrored in the functions that we develop to analyze expressions.

We cannot proceed further without a data structure. The most appropriate data structure for this problem is a binary tree, and we make the following definitions:

```
type
    tagtype = (identifier,operator);
    link = ↑ node;
    node = record
                case tag : tagtype of
                    identifier : (idname : char);
                    operator (opcode : char;
                                left, right : link)
            end;
```

A node representing an identifier contains only the name of the identifier and a node representing an operator contains the code for the operator (+ or *) and pointers to its operands.

The functions *expression*, *term*, and *factor* analyze expressions, terms, and factors respectively. Each returns a pointer to the root of a tree representing the part of the expression that it has analyzed. Fig. 10.5 shows some simple trees; in these trees nodes of type *identifier* are drawn as squares and nodes of type *operator* are drawn as circles. In the following implementation, the global variable *ch* of type *char* contains the character that is currently being analyzed. When *expression* is called, *ch* already contains the first character of the expression. When *expression* returns, *ch* contains the character following the expression.

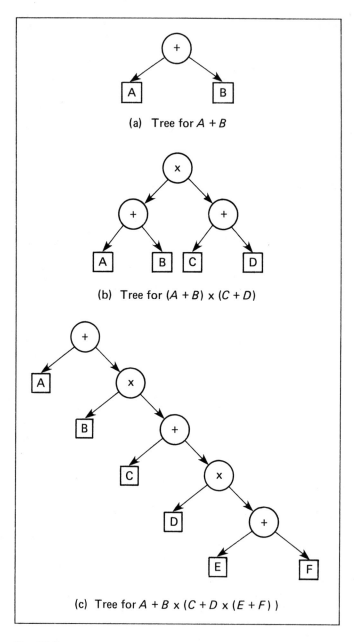

(a) Tree for $A + B$

(b) Tree for $(A + B) \times (C + D)$

(c) Tree for $A + B \times (C + D \times (E + F))$

Fig. 10.5
Expressions and
their trees.

```
function expression : link;
  var expr : link;
  function term : link;
    var tm : link;
    function factor : link;
      begin
        if ch = '('
          then
            begin
              read(ch);
              factor := expression
            end
          else factor := newid(ch);
        read(ch)
      end;
    begin { term }
      tm := factor;
      while ch = '*' do
        begin
          read(ch);
          tm := newop('*',tm,factor)
        end;
      term := tm
    end;
  begin { expression }
    expr := term;
    while ch = '+' do
      begin
        read(ch);
        expr := newop('+',expr,term)
      end;
    expression := expr
  end;
```

The functions *newid* and *newop* construct trees and return pointers to them. Here are their definitions:

```
function newid (iden : char) : link;
  var ptr : link;
  begin
    new(ptr);
    ptr↑.tag := identifier;
    ptr↑.idname := iden;
```

```
      newid := ptr
   end;

   function newop (op : char; lptr, rptr : link) : link;
      var ptr : link;
      begin
        new(ptr);
        ptr↑.tag := operator;
        ptr↑.opcode := op;
        ptr↑.left := lptr;
        ptr↑.right := rptr;
        newop := ptr
      end;
```

We can now develop the code generator. We specify the procedure *code* as follows: the call *code(E, n)* generates code that evaluates the expression *E*, leaving the value of *E* in the register *Rn*. There are three cases to consider.

1. *E* is an operand *id*. In this case the code generated is

$$LOAD\ Rn,id$$

2. The root of *E* is an operator *op*; one of the operands is an identifier *id*; and the other operand is a subexpression *S*. In this case we call *code(S, n)* to generate code that leaves the value of *S* in *Rn*, and then generate either *ADD Rn, id* or *MUL Rn, id* according to the value of *op*.

3. The root of *E* is an operator *op*, and both of the operands are expressions. This is the case in which we need more than one register. Suppose that the left subexpression is S_L and the right subexpression is S_R. We call *code(S_L, n)* and then *code(S_R, n+1)*. When the code generated by these calls is executed, we will have the value of S_L in *Rn* and the value of S_R in *R(n+1)*. Thus we generate either *ADD Rn, R(n+1)* or *MUL Rn, R(n+1)*, according to the value of *op*.

The following procedure embodies these rules. The generated code is written to the output file in symbolic form. Some compilers generate code in this way and then call an assembler to generate the machine code; other compilers generate machine code directly. Note the way in which the case control structure mirrors the use of case in the definition of *node*. Recursion allows us to process the tree one level at a time and consequently to express complex ideas in simple code.

```
procedure code (expr : link; reg : integer);
  begin
    with expr↑ do
      case tag of
        identifier :
          writeln('LOAD R',reg,',',idname);
        operator :
          if right↑.tag = identifier
            then
              begin
                code(left,reg);
                writeop(opcode);
                writeln('R',reg,',',right↑.idname)
              end
          else if left↑.tag = identifier
            then
              begin
                code(right,reg);
                writeop(opcode);
                writeln('R',reg,',',left↑.idname)
              end
          else
            begin
              code(left,reg);
              code(right,reg + 1);
              writeop(opcode);
              writeln('R',reg,',R',reg + 1)
            end
      end
  end;
```

This procedure uses the procedure *writeop* to write the operation codes
for addition and multiplication. Here it is:

```
procedure writeop (op : char);
  begin
    case op of
      '+' : write('ADD   ');
      '*' : write('MUL   ')
    end
  end;
```

It is not necessary to give the complete code generation program because its components have all appeared in this explanation. The following is a skeleton program to which the flesh is easily added.

```
program codegenerator (input, output);
  type
    tag = (identifier, operqtor);
    link = ↑ node;
    node = record
              case tag : tagtype of
                identifier : (idname : char);
                operator : (opcode : char;
                            left, right : link)
          end;
  var
    ch : char;
  function expression : link;
    function newid (iden : char) : link;
      { Body of newid }
    function newop (op : char; lptr, rptr : link) : link;
      { Body of newop }
    function term : link;
      function factor : link;
        { Body of factor }
      { Body of term }
    { Body of expression }
  procedure code (expr : link; reg : integer);
    procedure writeop (op : char);
      { Body of writeop }
    { Body of code }
  begin { codegenerator }
    read(ch);
    code(expression,0)
  end.
```

The code generated for the expressions of Fig. 10.5 follows. Note that the program uses registers economically, especially in the final example.

1. $A + B$

    LOAD R0, A
    ADD   R0, B

2. $(A + B) * (C + D)$

$$LOAD \quad R0, A$$
$$ADD \quad R0, B$$
$$LOAD \quad R1, C$$
$$ADD \quad R1, D$$
$$MUL \quad R0, R1$$

3. $A + B * (C + D * (E + F))$

$$LOAD \quad R0, E$$
$$ADD \quad R0, F$$
$$MUL \quad R0, D$$
$$ADD \quad R0, C$$
$$MUL \quad R0, B$$
$$ADD \quad R0, A$$

A complete code generator must correctly process other operators, such as $-$ and $/$ (which are not commutative) and expressions containing more than one operand type. It is evident that we have only solved a small part of the general problem of code generation. Nevertheless the problem we have solved is by no means a simple one, and it is certainly harder to solve without using recursion.

These examples demonstrate the affinity of recursive procedures and recursive data structures. Recursion is a powerful notation that enables us to express the solutions of a variety of problems in a simple and elegant manner. As we have seen, a powerful notation has two advantages over a weaker notation. First, it enables us to write down the solutions of simple problems succinctly. The second advantage, which is more important in the long term, is that a powerful notation enables us to solve problems that were previously insoluble. Recursion does this by increasing the complexity of the programming tasks we can handle without becoming confused by detail. The introduction of recursion into programming languages was an event comparable to the introduction of calculus into applied mathematics.

10.3 BACKTRACKING

We have discussed a number of problems for which the solution is constructed as a series of steps. *Jugs*, *Students and Professors*, and *Tower of Hanoi* are examples of this genre. In Chapter 9 we saw that a problem of this kind can sometimes be solved by constructing its state-action graph and finding the shortest paths from the initial state to the goal state. The shortest paths technique has two disadvantages. First, it is not a method that we often use ourselves. The shortest paths algorithm finds all first steps, and then all second steps, and so on. We tend to consider a *sequence* of steps, and if the sequence does not lead to a goal state, we abandon it and try another sequence. The second disadvantage of the shortest paths algorithm is that it requires a large amount of storage space; to achieve efficient execution we must store large sets of nodes that have been visited.

A backtracking algorithm attempts to find a path from the initial state to the goal state by moving through the state space until it either finds a goal or cannot go any further, and then it backs up and finds alternative paths if necessary. Fig. 10.6 shows a graph in which the nodes have been labeled according to the order in which they would be visited by a backtracking algorithm. The initial node is labeled * and the first path visits the nodes labeled 1, 2, ... , 6. Note that the algorithm must be able to recognize that node 4 has been visited so that it does not spend the rest of its life visiting nodes 4, 5, and 6 over and over again. When it has reached node 6 the algorithm backs up to the last node at which there was a choice of paths and follows another path. In this case, it first backs up to node 3 and visits nodes 7 and 8, and then it backs up to the initial node and visits nodes 9 and 10.

Two further features are usually associated with backtracking algorithms. The first is that when the goal state is reached, the search is abandoned. If node 8 in Fig. 10.6 is the goal state, nodes 9 and 10 would not be visited. The second feature is that in most problems for which backtracking is applicable, the solution required is the entire path. Thus the output that we would require from a backtracking search of Fig. 10.6 with node 8 as the goal state would be 1, 2, 3, 7, 8. Note that this is not the shortest path: backtracking, unlike shortest paths, does not necessarily find the shortest path.

The backtracking algorithm can be expressed naturally by a recursive procedure. This is not surprising because we have already seen that recursion can be used for list and tree traversal. The algorithm is quite subtle, however, and it should be studied carefully.

```
procedure explore (node; var reached)
  if node = goal
    then reached := true
  else if node has already been visited
    then reached := false
  else
    repeat
      choose nextnode
      step := step + 1
```

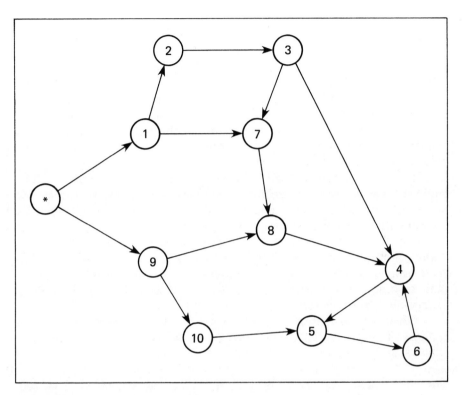

Fig. 10.6
A directed graph labeled by a backtracking algorithm.

$$route\,[step] := nextnode$$
$$explore(nextnode, reached)$$
if not *reached*
   then $step := step - 1$
until *reached* or no more nodes to visit

We initiate a backtracking search by calling

$$explore(initial, reached)$$

Each time *explore* is entered it does one of three things. If the parameter *node* is the goal node, *explore* returns with *reached* set to true. If
the parameter *node* is a node that has already been visited, it cannot be
on the path to the goal and *explore* returns with *reached* set to false.
The third possibility is that the node is not the goal node and it has not

been visited before. In this case *explore* tries each of the paths leading from this node. The next node on the path is called *nextnode* and it is recorded in the array *route*. *Explore* is called recursively to explore all the paths that lead from this node. If it returns with *reached* set to false, *nextnode* is not on a path to the goal and the algorithm backtracks. In this example backtracking involves only decrementing *step*. In general, backtracking involves undoing all of the actions performed in choosing and recording the next step. If the recursive invocation of *explore* returns with *reached* set to true, *nextnode* is on the path to the goal and this level terminates successfully.

The array *route* and the counter *step* are global variables. They could be passed as variable parameters to *explore* but this does not make the algorithm easier to understand. We record a trial move by incrementing *step* and storing the nodes to which we are moving in *route*. If the recursive call to *explore* returns with *reached* false, this node is not on the path to the goal and we remove it from *route* by decrementing *step*. When *explore* terminates, either *reached* is true and the path to the goal is described by *route* [1], *route* [2], ..., *route* [*step*], or *reached* is false and *step* is zero.

When this algorithm is used to search the graph of Fig. 10.6, it follows the path 1, 2, ..., 6. At this point, *step* is 6 and *route* contains:

$$1 \quad 2 \quad 3 \quad 4 \quad 5 \quad 6$$

The next call to *explore* visits node 4, which has already been visited. *Reached* is set to *false* and the algorithm backtracks to nodes 5 and 4, where there are no alternative paths, and then to node 3. It visits node 7 and then node 8, which is the goal node. When it terminates, *reached* is true, *step* is 5, and *route* contains

$$1 \quad 2 \quad 3 \quad 7 \quad 8$$

The backtracking algorithm is suitable in many situations in which searching is required. We conclude this section by developing a Pascal maze-running program. We assume that the maze is represented by an array of 0s representing paths and 1s representing walls. Fig. 10.7 shows a simple maze represented in this fashion. There is a wall surrounding the maze, which simplifies the program, and the initial and goal nodes are at (2, 2) in the top left corner and at (12, 12) in the lower right corner respectively.

From any cell in a maze of this kind, there are four possible steps. Diagonal moves are not allowed. We represent these moves by an array *next* whose components are 1, 0, −1, and 0. If we are at the cell (x, y), the cells we can move to are

$(x + next[i], y + next[5-i])$ for $i = 1, 2, 3,$ and $4.$

We indicate that a cell of the maze has been visited by writing 1 in it. This means that the maze is altered by the program and cannot be used again. It would be tidier to use a separate array to record the visited cells but the additional space required does not seem to be warranted by the application.

1	1	1	1	1	1	1	1	1	1	1	1	1
1	0	1	0	0	0	0	0	0	0	0	0	1
1	0	1	0	1	0	1	1	1	1	1	0	1
1	0	1	0	1	0	1	0	0	0	1	0	1
1	0	1	1	1	0	1	0	1	1	1	0	1
1	0	0	0	0	0	1	0	0	0	0	0	1
1	0	1	0	1	1	1	1	1	1	1	0	1
1	0	1	0	1	0	1	0	0	0	0	0	1
1	0	1	0	1	0	1	0	1	1	1	1	1
1	0	1	0	1	0	1	0	1	0	0	0	1
1	0	1	1	1	0	1	0	1	0	1	1	1
1	0	0	0	0	0	1	0	0	0	0	0	1
1	1	1	1	1	1	1	1	1	1	1	1	1

Fig. 10.7
A binary maze.

```
program Mazerunner (input, output);
   const
      maxsize = 20; { Largest maze has maxsize * maxsize cells }
      maxlen = 100; { Longest path has maxlen steps }
   type
```

```
      ordinate = 1..maxsize;
      pathindex = 0..maxlen;
var
      xpos, ypos, xgoal, ygoal, xstart, ystart, size : ordinate;
      s, step : pathindex;
      reached : boolean;
      next : array [1..4] of −1..1;
      maze : array [ordinate,ordinate] of 0..1;
      route : array [pathindex] of record
                                        xord, yord : ordinate
                                    end;

procedure explore (xpos, ypos : ordinate;
                        var reached : boolean);
   var
      dir : 0..4;
      xnext, ynext : ordinate;
   begin
      if (xpos = xgoal) and (ypos = ygoal)
         then reached := true
      else if maze[xpos,ypos] ≠ 0
         then reached := false
      else
         begin
            maze[xpos,ypos] := 1; { Mark visited cell }
            dir := 0;
            repeat
               dir := dir + 1; { Choose direction }
               xnext := xpos + next[dir];
               ynext := ypos + next[5 − dir];
               step := step + 1;
               route[step].xord := xnext; { Record this move }
               route[step].yord := ynext;
               explore(xnext,ynext,reached);
               if not reached
                  then step := step − 1 { Backtrack }
            until reached or (dir = 4)
         end
   end; { explore }

begin { Mazerunner }
```

```
{ Read maze data and print them }
read(size,xstart,ystart,xgoal,ygoal);
write('Initial node is (',xstart,',',ystart,')');
writeln('    Goal node is (',xgoal,',',ygoal,')');
writeln;
writeln('Maze');
for ypos := 1 to size do
  begin
    writeln;
    for xpos := 1 to size do
      begin
        read(maze[xpos,ypos]);
        write(maze[xpos,ypos]:3)
      end
  end;
writeln; writeln;
{ Initialize next position vector }
next[1] := 0;
next[2] := 1;
next[3] := 0;
next[4] := -1;
{ Explore the maze }
step := 0;
explore(xstart,ystart,reached);
if reached
  then
    for s := 1 to step do
      with route[s] do
        writeln('(',xord,',',yord,')')
  else writeln('No path')
end. { Mazerunner }
```

In the code generation and maze running programs we use recursion to simplify the design of a graph-traversing algorithm. In traversal problems, we often have to record the steps we have made in order to retrace them or report them when the traversal is complete. Recursion helps us to do this by recording the values of parameters and local variables of partially completed calls of the same procedure or group of procedures. We can always eliminate recursion if we want to by introducing an explicit stack on which to store these values, but in doing so we lose the notational advantage of recursion.

Although the two preceding programs both traverse graphs, there are important conceptual differences between them. Code generation is typical of problems in which the graph has relatively few nodes and must be traversed completely. A simple recursive solution is often adequate for problems of this kind. Maze running, on the other hand, belongs to a large family of problems in which the graph is much larger and need not be completely traversed. In general, we are seeking only the paths that lead from the initial node to a goal node. In many cases the graph is so large that it cannot be traversed completely.

The problem of playing chess falls into this category. All possible games of chess can be represented by paths in a state-action graph in which each edge represents a legal move. This graph contains about 10^{120} nodes and consequently it cannot be traversed by any algorithm in a reasonable amount of time. The problem of writing a chess-playing program is to devise a way of exploring small parts of this graph, containing only a few million nodes, without missing any useful moves.

SUMMARY

Recursive solutions are appropriate for many problems. The recursive solution may be implemented by a recursive procedure or it may merely provide the insight necessary for the development of a nonrecursive program. Recursion is most helpful when it is used to manage the storage of variables of partially executed procedures. If there are no such variables, it is generally a straightforward exercise to construct a nonrecursive algorithm.

Recursive programs are reputed to be inefficient. Three separate issues are involved and it is important that they are not confused. First, there are computers which execute procedure calls slowly. This will certainly affect the performance of recursive programs, which rely heavily on procedure calls. But this is a defect of the implementation of recursion, not of recursion itself. Moreover, the time spent in executing procedure calls in a recursive program must be balanced against the time spent accessing arrays in an equivalent nonrecursive program. The second issue is that a recursive algorithm may have exponential time complexity whereas an equivalent nonrecursive algorithm has linear time complexity. This is true, for example, of the two algorithms for computing Fibonacci numbers discussed in Section 10.1. Obviously recursion should not be used in these cases. The final issue is that there are problems that are intrinsically hard to solve, and a recursive solution is no worse than a nonrecursive solution. For example, $2^N - 1$ steps are required to move a pile of N disks in *Tower of Hanoi* and consequently any program that prints these steps must perform more than $2^N - 1$ operations. Similarly, Ackermann's function is inherently hard to evaluate and there is no fast way of evaluating it.

Recursion is most useful when it is used to solve difficult problems such as code generation and problems requiring backtracking. It has the advantages of a powerful notation over a weak notation regardless of whether or not we actually use recursion in the implementation.

FURTHER READING

Hennie, in his book *Introduction to Computability*, provides some background for Ackermann's function and explains its theoretical importance. LISP is a more suitable programming language than Pascal for symbolic evaluation of the kind used in program *Ackermann* of Section 10.2. LISP was developed by John McArthy in the late 1950s and it is one of the oldest programming languages in widespread use. *LISP*, by Winston and Horn, is a good recent text.

Hayes prefers the nonrecursive version of *Tower of Hanoi* to the recursive version and he gives reasons for his preference in his paper, "A Note on the Towers of Hanoi Problem."

Parsing and code generation are treated in depth by Aho and Ullman in *Principles of Compiler Design*. They explain why nonrecursive parsing is felt by many people to be preferable to recursive parsing, and they describe the construction of nonrecursive parsers.

Reingold, Nievergelt, and Deo describe backtracking algorithms and ways of improving their performance in *Combinatorial Algorithms*.

Godel, Escher, Bach: An Eternal Golden Braid, by Hofstadter, contains an interesting discussion of the more curious aspects of recursion.

Bird has described techniques for systematically introducing and removing recursion, and also for tabulation. These are described in his papers "Notes on Recursion Elimination," "Improving Programs by the Introduction of Recursion," and "Tabulation Techniques for Recursive Programs."

The programs *calculator*, *concordance*, and *crossreference* in *Programming in Pascal* by Grogono provide further examples of the development of recursive programs. Other examples of the development of recursive Pascal programs may be found in the books *Data Structures Using Pascal* by Tenenbaum and Augenstein and *Fundamental Structures of Computer Science* by Wulf, Shaw, Hilfinger, and Flon.

EXERCISES

10.1 Give nonrecursive definitions of the following functions:

  a) $s(0) = 1$
  $s(n) = s(s(n - 1) - 1) + 1$ for $n \geq 1$

  b) $f(0) = 0$
  $f(n) = f(n - 1) + 2n - 1$ for $n \geq 1$

  c) $a(0) = 0$
  $a(1) = 1$
  $a(n) = 5a(n - 1) - 6a(n - 2)$ for $n \geq 2$
  [*Hint*: try $a(n) = r^n$.]

10.2 Write recursive versions of the bisection algorithm (Section 7.5) and the binary search algorithm (Section 9.4).

10.3 Design a recursive algorithm that plots a straight line using the following principle: plot the midpoint of the given line and then plot the two parts of the given line created by dividing it at the midpoint.

10.4 The programs *Ackermann* and *codegenerator* of this chapter use the Pascal standard procedure *new* to create new nodes but they do not return used nodes to free storage. Alter them so that *dispose* is called to recover used nodes. Note that this problem does not arise in languages, such as LISP and Algol-68, in which garbage collection is performed automatically.

10.5 The problem of paying an amount of money in bills and coins is solved easily by recursion if we assume that unlimited supplies of bills and coins of every denomination are available. If the supply of cash is limited, however, a backtracking algorithm is required. For example, you can pay 40¢ exactly if you have a quarter and four dimes, but the recursive algorithm would pay a quarter and then a dime and then it would get stuck because there are no nickels available. (Quarters, dimes, and nickels are worth 25¢, 10¢, and 5¢ respectively.) Write a backtracking procedure that solves the following problem: given an amount to be paid and a finite quantity of money, either show how the amount can be paid or report that it cannot be paid exactly.

10.6 Could another backtracking algorithm label Fig. 10.6 differently?

10.7 Write a backtracking program that places N queens on an $N \times N$ chessboard in such a way that no queen is attacking any other queen, if such a position exists.

10.8 The function $G(n)$ is defined by the following recursive definitions:

$$G(n) = G(G(n + 11)) \quad \text{for } 0 \le n \le 100$$
$$G(n) = n - 10 \quad \text{for } n > 100$$

What is the value of $G(0)$? [*Hint*: this function is called the 91 function.]

BIBLIOGRAPHY

Adams, J. L. *Conceptual Blockbusting*: *A Pleasurable Guide to Better Problem Solving*. San Francisco: San Francisco Book Co., 1976.

Aho, A. V., J. E. Hopcroft, and J. D. Ullman. *The Design and Analysis of Computer Algorithms*. Reading, Mass.: Addison-Wesley, 1974.

Aho, A. V. and J. D. Ullman. *Principles of Compiler Design*. Reading, Mass.: Addison-Wesley, 1977.

Alagic, S. and M. A. Arbib. *The Design of Well-Structured and Correct Programs*. New York: Springer-Verlag, 1978.

Baase, S. *Computer Algorithms*: *Introduction to Design and Analysis*. Reading, Mass.: Addison-Wesley, 1978.

Bachman, C. W. The programmer as navigator. *Comm. ACM*, **16**:11 (Nov. 1973), 653–658.

Barstow, D. R. *Knowledge-Based Program Construction*. Amsterdam: Elsevier North Holland, 1979.

Bird, R. S. Notes on recursion elimination. *Comm. ACM*, **20**:6 (June 1977), 434–439.

Bird, R. S. Improving programs by the introduction of recursion. *Comm. ACM*, **20**:11 (Nov. 1977), 856–863.

Bird, R. S. Tabulation techniques for recursive programs. *ACM Computing Surveys*, **12**:4 (Dec. 1980), 403–418.

Bjørner, D., ed. *Abstract Software Specifications*. Lecture Notes in Computer Science #86. New York: Springer-Verlag, 1980.

Bresenham, J. E.   Algorithm for the computer control of a digital plotter. *IBM Syst J*, 4:1 (1965), 25–30.

Bronowski, J.   *The Ascent of Man*. Boston: Little, Brown, 1973.

Cohen, I. B.   Newton's discovery of gravity. *Scientific American*, **244**:3 (March 1981), 166–179.

Dahl, O. J., E. W. Dijkstra, and C. A. R. Hoare.   *Structured Programming*. New York: Academic Press, 1972.

Dahlquist, G., and A. Björck.   *Numerical Methods*. Trans. Ned Anderson. Englewood Cliffs, N.J.: Prentice-Hall, 1974.

Dijkstra, E. W.   *A Discipline of Programming*. Englewood Cliffs, N.J.: Prentice-Hall, 1976.

Ekstrom, P., and D. Wineland.   The isolated electron. *Scientific American*, **243**:2 (August 1980), 104–121.

Floyd, R. W.   Assigning Meanings to Programs. *Proc. Amer. Math. Soc. Symp. in Applied Mathematics*, **19** (1967), 19–31.

Gardner, M.   *Mathematical Puzzles of Sam Loyd*. New York: Dover, 1959.

Gardner, M.   *Mathematical Puzzles and Diversions*. London: Bell, 1961.

Gardner, M.   *More Mathematical Puzzles and Diversions*. London: Bell, 1963.

Gardner, M.   *Mathematical Magic Show*. New York: Vintage Books, 1965.

Gardner, M.   *Mathematical Carnival*. New York: Knopf, 1975.

Gardner, M.   *Aha! Insight*. San Francisco: Scientific American-Freeman, 1978.

Geschke, C. M., J. H. Morris, and E. H. Satterthwaite.   Early experience with Mesa. *Comm. ACM*, **20**:8 (Aug. 1977), 540–553.

Grogono, P.   *Programming in Pascal*. Reading, Mass.: Addison-Wesley, 1978.

Hayes, P. J.   A note on the towers of Hanoi problem. *Comput. J.*, **20**:3 (1977), 282–285.

Hennie, F.   *Introduction to Computability*. Reading, Mass.: Addison-Wesley, 1977.

Hoare, C. A. R.   An axiomatic basis for computer programming. *CACM*, **12**:10 (Oct. 1969), 576–580 and 583.

Hofstadter, D. R. *Godel, Escher, Bach: An Eternal Golden Braid.* New York: Basic Books, 1979.

Johnson, L. W., and R. D. Riess. *Numerical Analysis.* Reading, Mass.: Addison-Wesley, 1977.

Kent, E. W. *The Brains of Men and Machines.* New York: BYTE/McGraw-Hill, 1981.

Kernighan, B. W., and P. J. Plauger. *Software Tools.* Reading, Mass.: Addison-Wesley, 1976.

Kernighan, B. W., and P. J. Plauger. *Software Tools in Pascal.* Reading, Mass.: Addison-Wesley, 1981.

Knuth, D. E. *The Art of Computer Programming, Vol. II: Seminumerical Algorithms.* Reading, Mass.: Addison-Wesley, 1969.

Knuth, D. E. Ancient Babylonian algorithms. *CACM,* 15:7 (July 1972), 671-677.

Knuth, D. E. *The Art of Computer Programming, Vol. I: Fundamental Algorithms.* Reading, Mass.: Addison-Wesley, 1973.

Knuth, D. E. *The Art of Computer Programming, Vol. III: Sorting and Searching.* Reading, Mass.: Addison-Wesley, 1973.

Knuth, D. E. Reciprocal of Inakibit-Anu incorrectly rendered. *CACM,* 19:2 (Feb. 1976), 108.

Knuth, D. E. Big omicron and big omega and big theta. *SIGACT News,* 8:2 (1976), 18-24.

Koestler, A. *The Sleepwalkers.* London: Hutchinson, 1959.

Koestler, A. *The Act of Creation.* London: Hutchinson, 1964.

Ledgard, H. F. The case for structured programming. *BIT,* 13 (1973), 45-57.

Liskov, B., A. Snyder, R. Atkinson, and C. Schaffert. Abstraction mechanisms in CLU. *COMM. ACM,* 20:8 (Aug. 1977), 564-576.

Marcotty, M., H. F. Ledgard, and G. V. Bochmann. A sampler of formal definitions. *ACM Computing Surveys,* 8:2 (June 1976).

Miller, G. A. The magical number seven, plus or minus two. *Psychological Review,* 63, pp. 81-97.

Minsky, M. A framework for representing human knowledge. P. H. Winston (ed.) In *The Psychology of Computer Vision.* New York: McGraw-Hill, 1975.

Morris, J. H. Types are not sets. *Proc. First POPL Conf.,* 1973, 120-124.

Newell, A., and H. A. Simon. *Human Problem Solving.* Englewood

Cliffs, N.J.: Prentice-Hall, 1972.

Newman, W. F., and R. F. Sproull. *Principles of Interactive Computer Graphics*. New York: McGraw-Hill, 1979.

Nievergelt, J., F. C. Farrar, and E. M. Reingold. *Computer Approaches to Mathematical Problems*. Englewood Cliffs, N.J: Prentice-Hall, 1974.

Polya, G. *How to Solve It*. Princeton, N.J: Princeton Univ. Press, 1973.

Reingold, E. M., J. Nievergelt, and N. Deo. *Combinatorial Algorithms*. Englewood Cliffs, N.J.: Prentice-Hall, 1977.

Standish, T. A. *Data Structure Techniques*. Reading, Mass.: Addison-Wesley, 1980.

Stoll, R. R. *Sets, Logic, and Axiomatic Theories*. San Francisco: W. H. Freeman, 1974.

Tarjan, R. On the efficiency of a good but not linear set merging algorithm. *JACM*, 22:2 (April 1975), 215-225.

Tenenbaum, A. M., and M. J. Augenstein. *Data Structures Using Pascal*. Englewood Cliffs, N.J.: Prentice-Hall, 1981.

Weizenbaum, J. *Computer Power and Human Reason*. San Francisco: W. H. Freeman, 1976.

Welsh, J., and M. McKeag. *Structured System Programming*. Englewood Cliffs, N.J.: Prentice-Hall, 1980.

Wichmann, B. A., and A. H. J. Sale. The Pascal validation suite. *Pascal News*, 16 (Oct. 1979), 10-154.

Wickelgren, W. *How to Solve Problems: Elements of a Theory of Problems and Problem Solving*. San Francisco: W. H. Freeman, 1974.

Winston, P. H., and B. K. P. Horn. *LISP*. Reading, Mass.: Addison-Wesley, 1981.

Wirth, N. Program development by stepwise refinement. *CACM*, 14:4 (April 1971), 221-227.

Wirth, N. The programming language Pascal. *Acta Informatica*, 1 (1971), 35-63.

Wirth, N. On the composition of well-structured programs. *ACM Computing Surveys*, 6:4 (Dec. 1974), 247-259.

Wirth, N. Modula. *Software: Practice and Experience*, 7 (1977), 3-84.

Wulf, W. A., M. Shaw, P. N. Hilfinger, and L. Flon. *Fundamental Structures of Computer Science*. Reading, Mass.: Addison-Wesley, 1981.

Zelkowitz, M. V., A. C. Shaw, and J. D. Gannon. *Principles of Software Engineering and Design*. Englewood Cliffs, N.J.: Prentice-Hall, 1979.

INDEX